CONTENTS

Glossary

Make your own glossary of key terms:

Term	Definition	Picture/Example
Linear		
Gradient		
Intercept		
Discrete data		
Continuous data		
Variable		
Constant		
Coefficient		
Origin		
Asymptote		

ISBN: 9780170419376

Straight lines

Co-ordinates revision

Remember: Co-ordinates are in alphabetical order, (x, y).

Write down the co-ordinates of the lettered points shown at right. The first one is done for you.

a	(3,4)	**b**	(,)
c	(,)	**d**	(,)
e	(,)	**f**	(,)
g	(,)	**h**	(,)
i	(,)	**j**	(,)
k	(,)	**l**	(,)
m	(,)	**n**	(,)
o	(,)	**p**	(,)

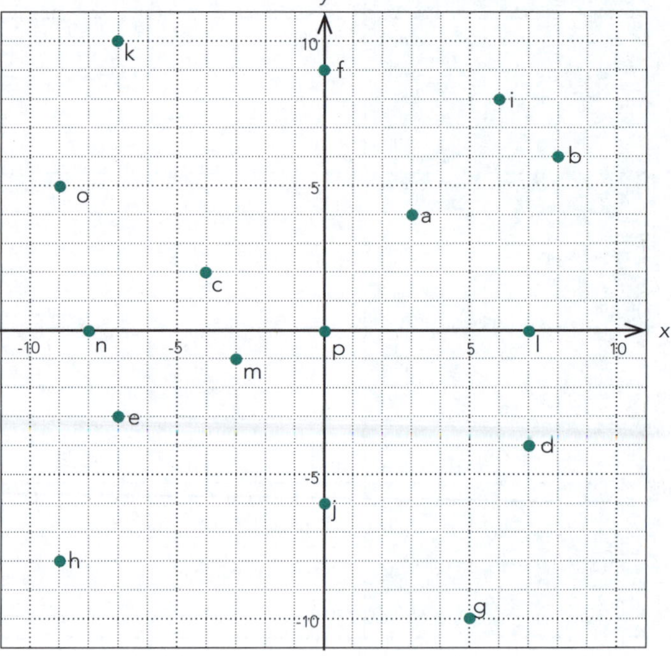

Plot and label the following co-ordinate points on the grid.

a	(7 , 5)	**b**	(-3, 4)
c	(-2, 9)	**d**	(1, -6)
e	(7, -3)	**f**	(-4, -8)
g	(-9, -7)	**h**	(6, -9)
i	(2, 8)	**j**	(-9, 8)
k	(4, 0)	**l**	(-8, -3)
m	(2, -10)	**n**	(-5, 2)
o	(0, -8)	**p**	(-9, 0)

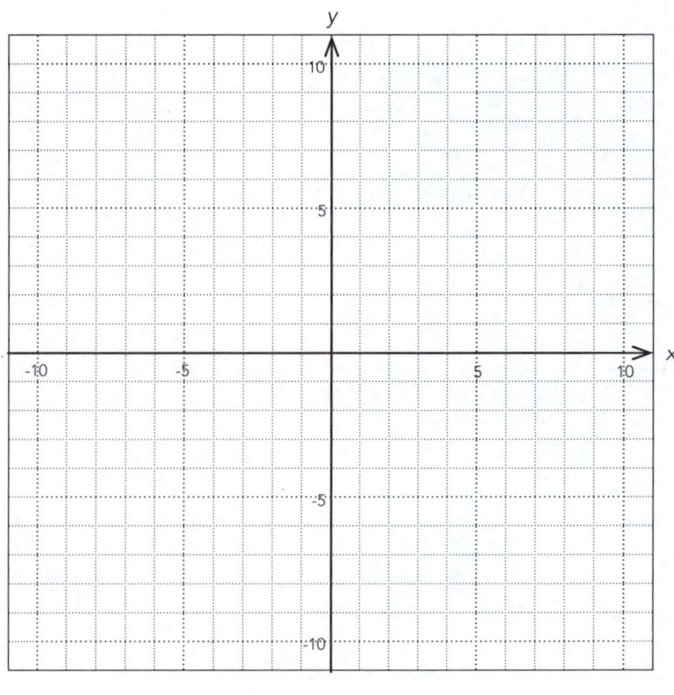

 ISBN: 9780170419376

Linear patterns with discrete data

- Discrete data is data that can be counted, e.g. 'number of …', prices of items that can be bought with only $5 notes, heights that are measured to the nearest centimetre.
- You need to be able to continue a pattern, plot these on a graph, find a rule and use it.

Example:
Alex makes patterns with buttons as shown.

Pattern 1 Pattern 2 Pattern 3

a Complete the table.

Pattern # (n)	# of buttons (B)
1	5
2	7
3	9
4	**11**
5	**13**
6	**15**

+2 +2 +2 +2 +2

Look for the pattern: in this case, **+2**.

b Plot the points on the graph.

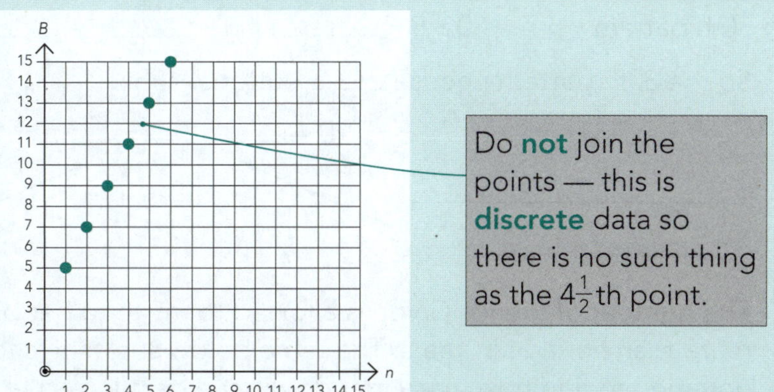

c Give the equation for the number of buttons (B) in any pattern (n).

Use the format $B =$ **+2** $n +$ **+3** So the equation is $\mathbf{B = 2n + 3}$

Insert the **+2** from the table. Insert the # of buttons for pattern number 0.

d Use your equation to find how many buttons would be in his 20th pattern.

20th pattern ⟶ $n = 20 \therefore B = 2 \times 20 + 3 = 43$. So the 20th pattern would have 43 buttons.

e Explain how the equation relates to the pattern.

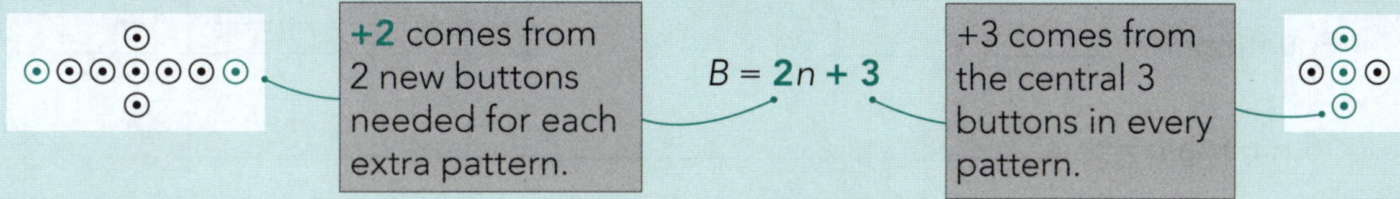

f Which pattern would have 87 buttons?

$87 = 2n + 3$ **(− 3)**
$84 = 2n$ **(÷ 2)**
$\therefore$ $n = 42$. So pattern 42 has 87 buttons.

For each of the following, complete the table, plot the values on the graph, find and use the equation, and explain how the equation relates to the pattern.

1 Bridget makes the following pattern with buttons.
How many buttons are needed for the 30th pattern?

Pattern 1 Pattern 2 Pattern 3

Pattern # (n)	# of buttons (B)
1	5
2	9
3	13
4	
5	
6	

Equation: $B =$ ______$n +$ ______

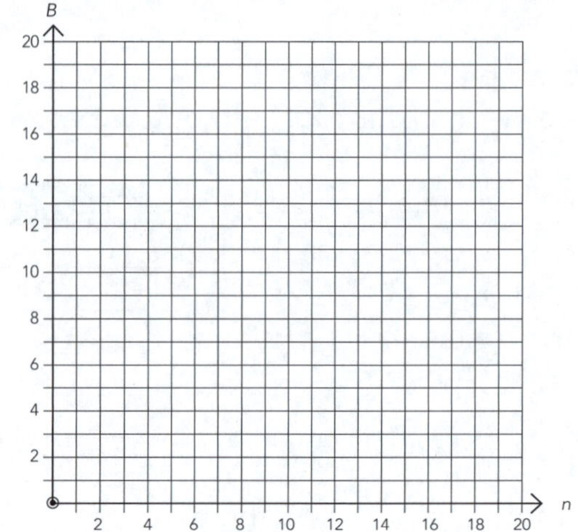

30th pattern $\Rightarrow n = 30 \therefore B =$ ______ x 30 + ______ = ______.

So the 30th pattern needs ______ buttons.

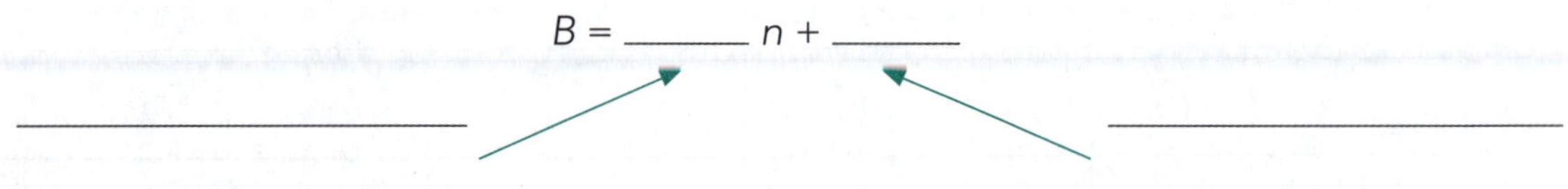

$B =$ ______ $n +$ ______

______________________ ______________________

______________________ ______________________

2 The number of friends Chloe is allowed to invite to her birthday parties is three more than her age in years. The table below shows this for her early years. Use your equation to find how many friends will she be allowed to invite to her 18th birthday.

Age # (n)	# of friends (F)
1	4
2	5
3	6
4	
5	
6	

Equation: $F =$ ______$n +$ ______

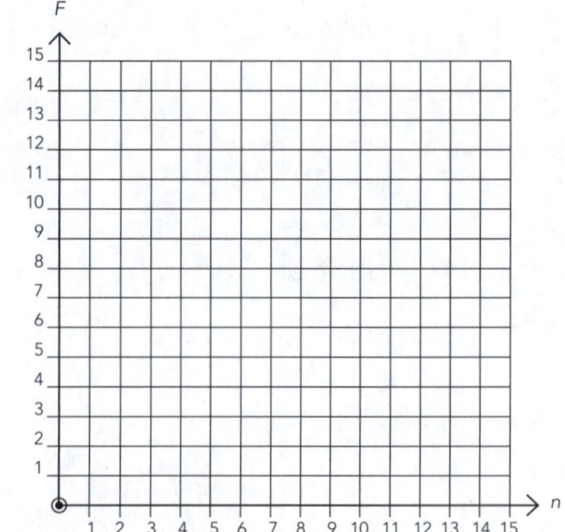

18th pattern $\Rightarrow$ ____

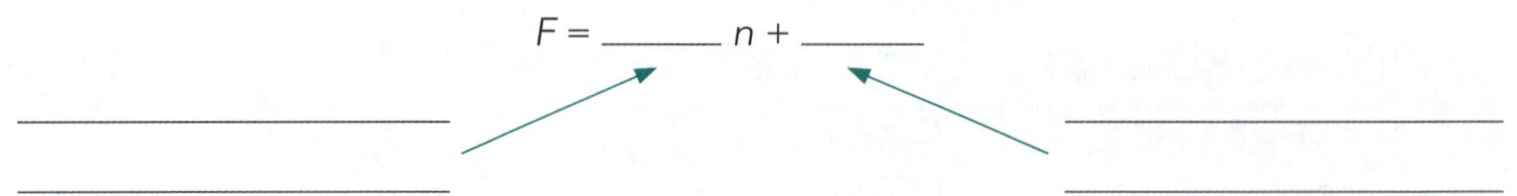

$F =$ ______ $n +$ ______

______________________ ______________________

______________________ ______________________

ISBN: 9780170419376

3 Nick makes the following pattern with matches. How many matches are needed for the 25th pattern?

Pattern 1 Pattern 2 Pattern 3

Pattern # (n)	# of matches (M)
1	4
2	7
3	10
4	
5	
6	

Equation: $M =$ ______ $n +$ ______

25th pattern ⇒ ______________________________

$M =$ ______ $n +$ ______

______________________ ______________________

______________________ ______________________

4 Tahu's dad will give Tahu $50 if he passes NCEA Level 1, plus $5 for each Excellence credit he earns. The table below shows how much Tahu will get for his first few Excellence credits, provided he passes Level 1. Use your equation to find how much Tahu will get if he passes NCEA Level 1 and he earns 20 Excellence credits.

# of Excellence credits (n)	$ earned (D)
1	55
2	60
3	65
4	
5	
6	

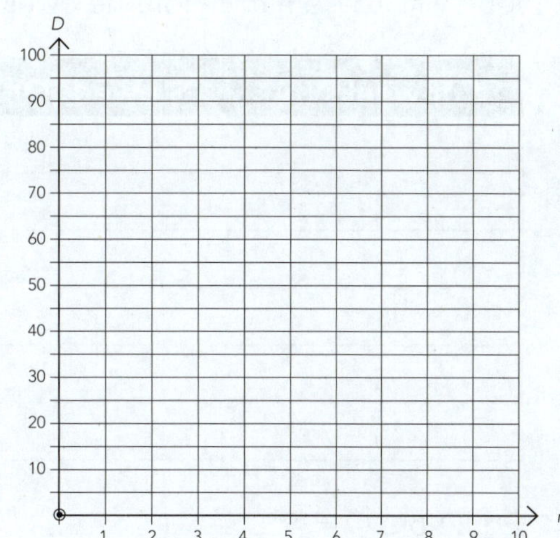

Equation: $D =$ ______________________

20 Excellence credits ⇒ ______________________________

$D =$ ______________________

______________________ ______________________

______________________ ______________________

5 Anna is planning a wedding breakfast at which guests will be seated at small tables arranged to form larger tables as shown. How many guests can she seat if she makes a large table from 10 smaller tables? Use your graph to work out how many tables she will need for 50 guests.

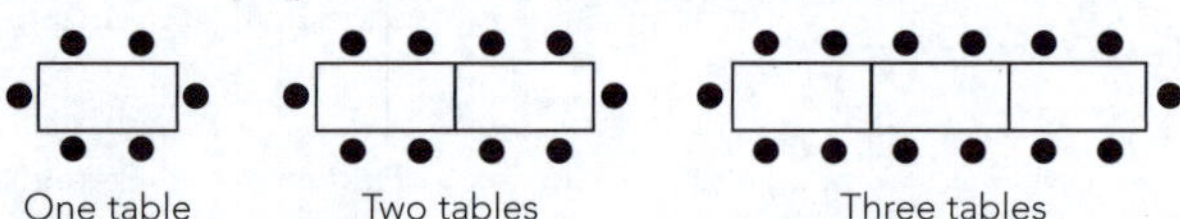

# of tables (n)	# of guests (G)
1	
2	
3	
4	
5	
6	

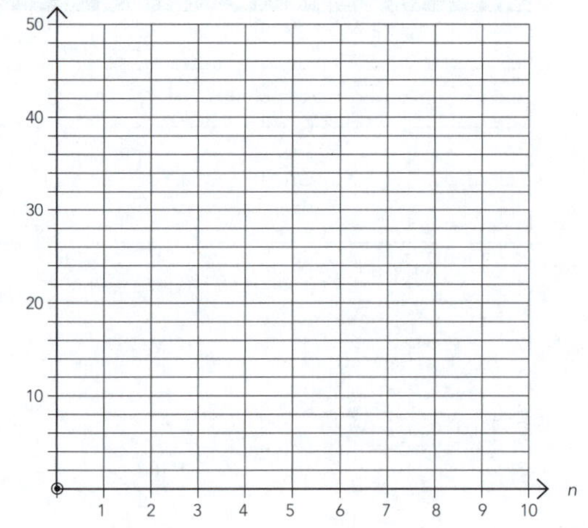

Equation: G = ____________________

10 smaller tables ⇒ ____________________

50 guests ⇒ ____________________

G = ____________________

____________________ ____________________

____________________ ____________________

6 Matt has borrowed $500 from his mum to buy a phone. He is paying her back at $20 per week. Use your equation to calculate how much he owes after 12 weeks. How long will it take him before he owes her $40?

# of weeks (n)	$ owed (O)
1	
2	
3	
4	
5	
6	

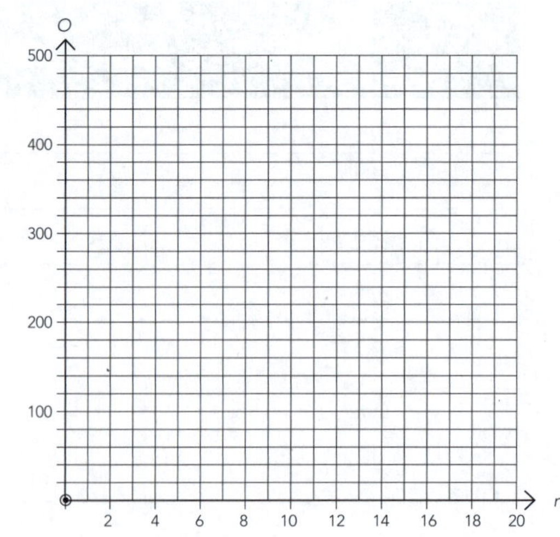

Equation: O = ______n + ______

12 weeks after starting ⇒ ____________________

He owes $40 ⇒ ____________________

O = ____________________

____________________ ____________________

____________________ ____________________

 ISBN: 9780170419376

The gradient of a line

The gradient is the steepness, or slope, of a line.

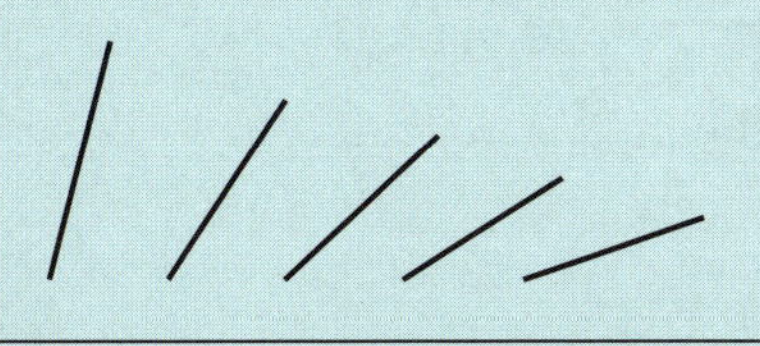

These lines all have positive gradients.

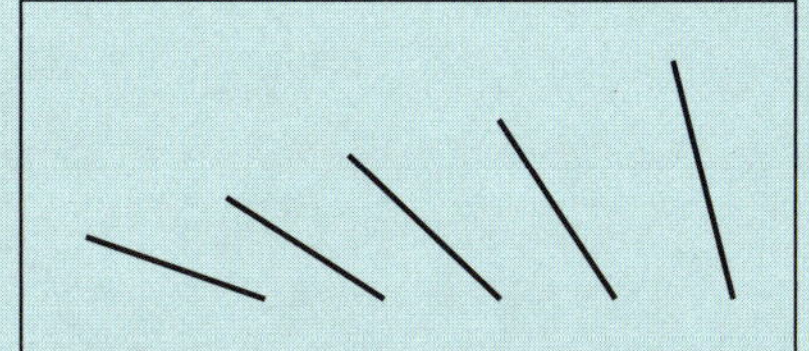

These lines all have negative gradients.

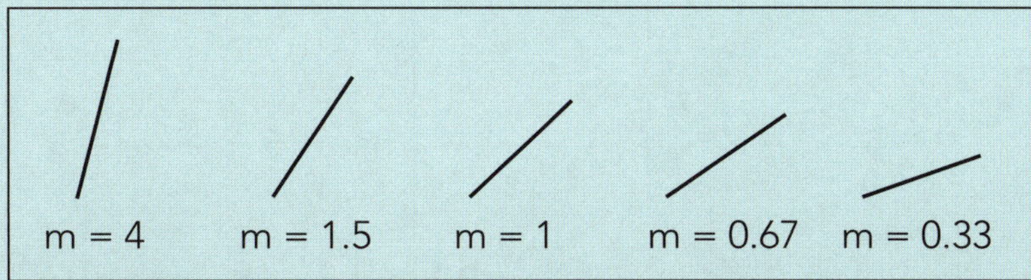

The steeper the line, the bigger the gradient.

The gradient is calculated using the formula $m = \frac{\text{change in } y}{\text{change in } x}$ or $\frac{\text{rise}}{\text{run}}$.

The easiest way to do this is to draw a right-angled triangle on the line.

$$m = \frac{\text{rise}}{\text{run}}$$

$$= \frac{5}{6}$$

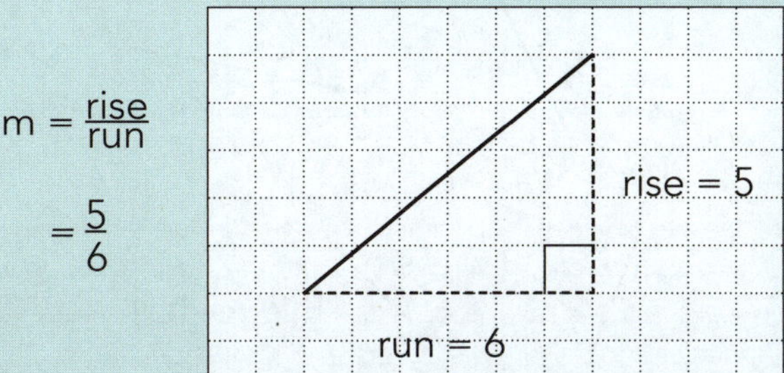

This time the gradient is *negative*.

$$m = -\frac{\text{rise}}{\text{run}}$$

$$= -\frac{3}{7}$$

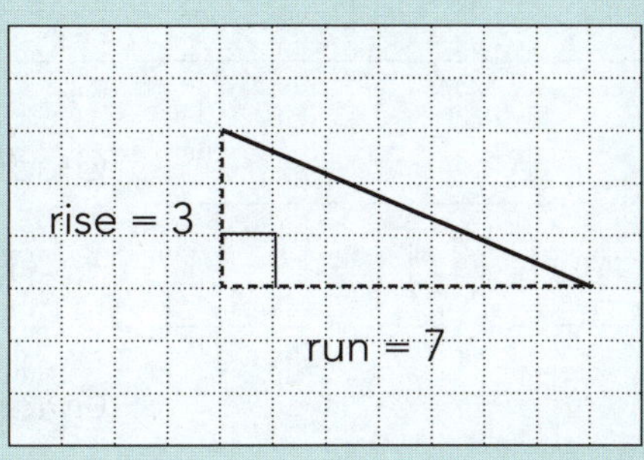

$$m = \frac{rise}{run} = \frac{0}{7} = 0$$

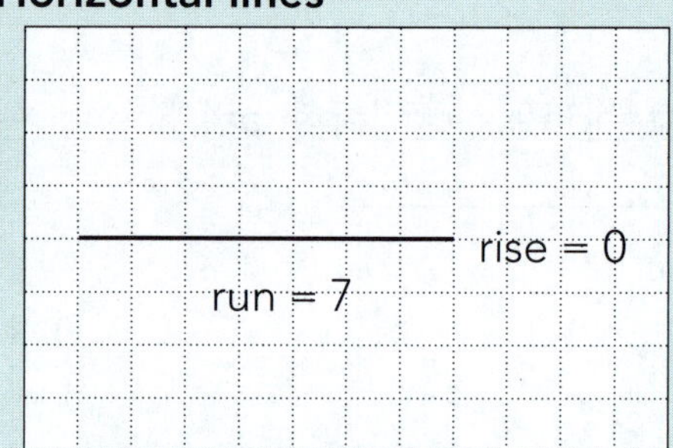

$$m = \frac{rise}{run} = \frac{5}{0} = \text{undefined}$$

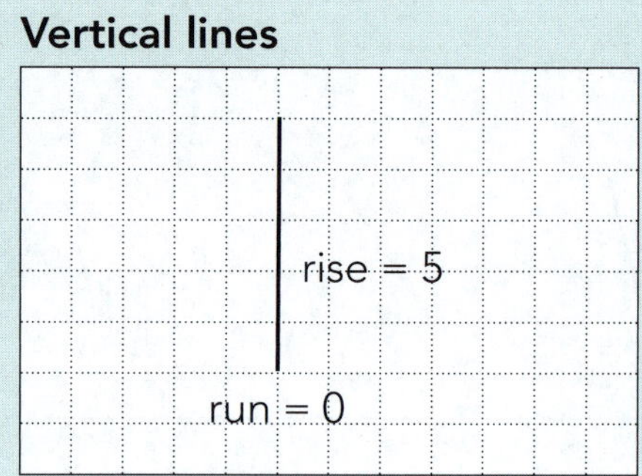

1 Calculate the gradients of these lines.

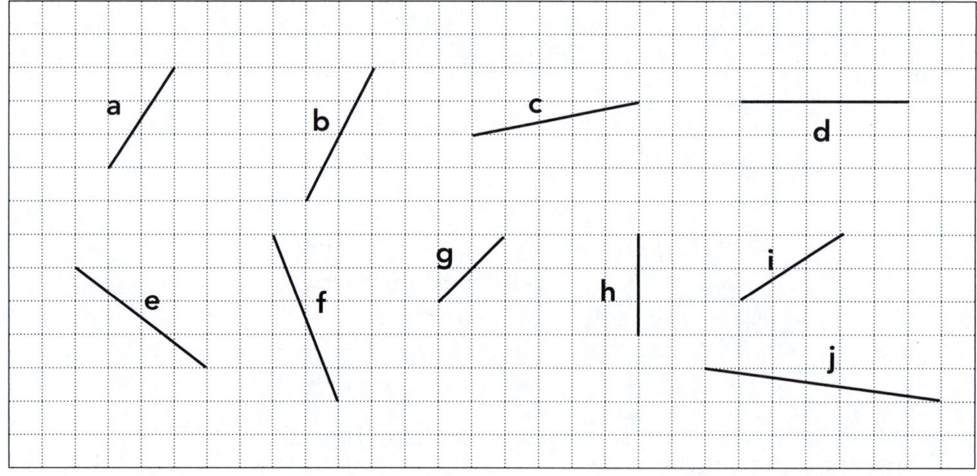

Gradient a = $\frac{rise}{run}$ ____________ Gradient b = ____________

Gradient c = ____________ Gradient d = ____________

Gradient e = ____________ Gradient f = ____________

Gradient g = ____________ Gradient h = ____________

Gradient i = ____________ Gradient j = ____________

ISBN: 9780170419376

2 Draw line segments to show these gradients.

a $m = \frac{1}{2}$

b $m = 2$

c $m = \frac{2}{5}$

d $m = -\frac{3}{2}$

e $m = \frac{3}{7}$

f $m = -\frac{3}{4}$

g $m = -5$

h $m = -1\frac{1}{2}$

i $m = 0$

j $m = 3$

ISBN: 9780170419376

Drawing straight lines — continuous data

- Continuous data is unrounded measured data.
- It is shown as a line on a graph.

1 Plotting points using the equation

There are several ways of plotting graphs, but this method will work with *any* type of graph — lines and curves.

Example:
Plot the line given by the equation $y = 3x - 5$.

Step 1: Create a table for values of x and y.

x	3x – 5	y	Point
0	3(0) – 5	-5	(0, -5)
1	3(1) – 5	-2	(1, -2)
2	3(2) – 5	1	(2, 1)
3	3(3) – 5	4	(3, 4)
4	3(4) – 5	7	(4, 7)

Step 2: Plot the points on a graph.

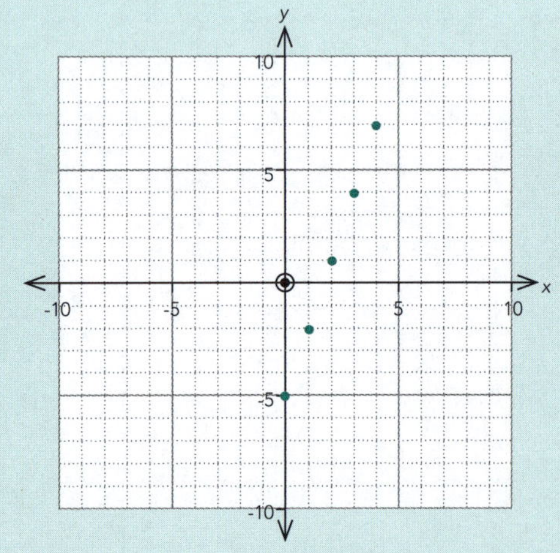

Step 3: Join the points with a **ruled** line.

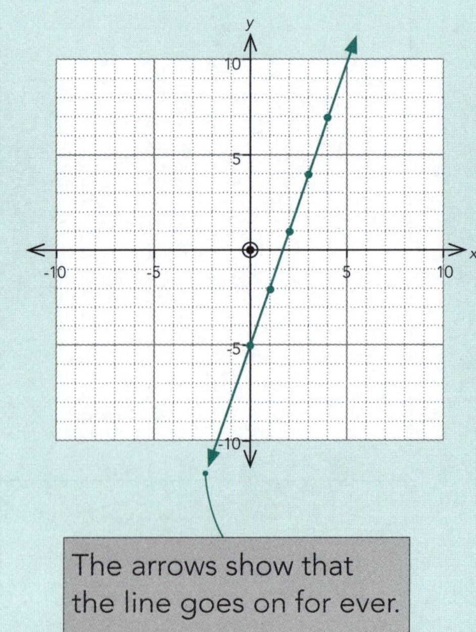

ISBN: 9780170419376

Complete the tables and draw the graph for each of the following.

1 $y = 2x + 1$

x	2x + 1	y	Point
0	2(0) + 1	1	(0, 1)
1			
2			
3			
4			

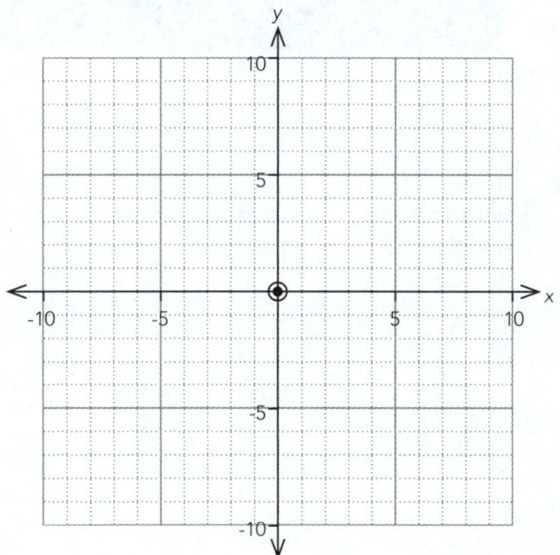

2 $y = 3x + 2$

x	3x + 2	y	Point
0			
1			
2			
3			
4			

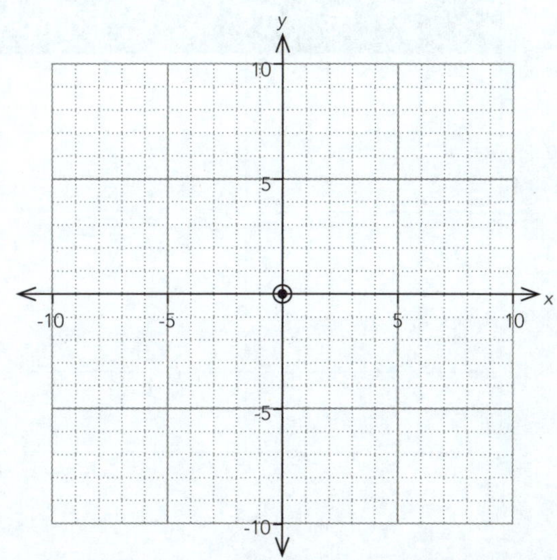

3 $y = 4x - 3$

x	4x – 3	y	Point
0			
1			
2			
3			
4			

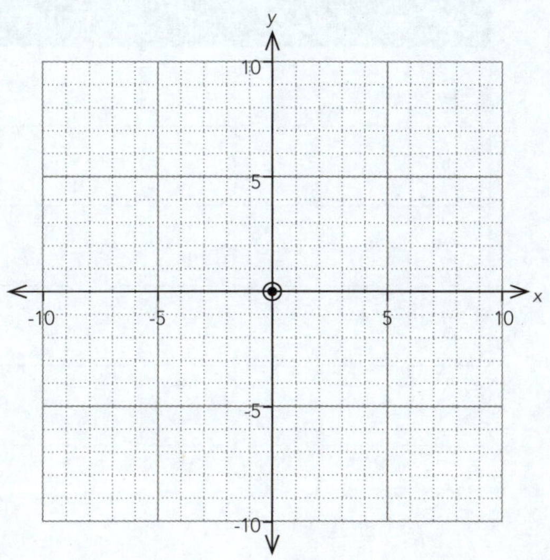

ISBN: 9780170419376

4 $y = -2x + 1$

x	-2x + 1	y	Point
0			
1			
2			
3			
4			

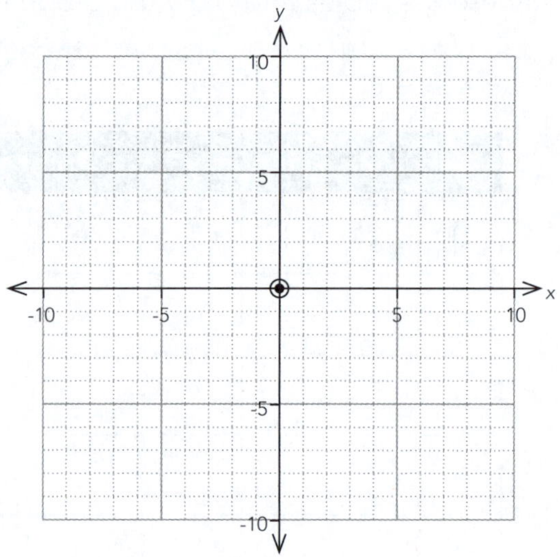

5 $y = 5$

x	5	y	Point
0			
1			
2			
3			
4			

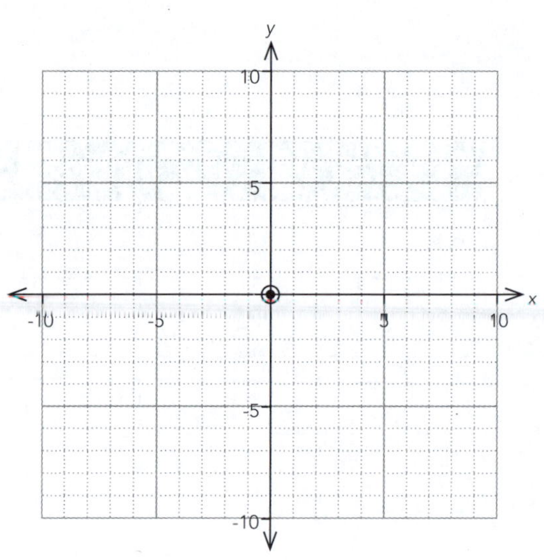

6 $y = -x$

x	-x	y	Point
0			
1			
2			
3			
4			

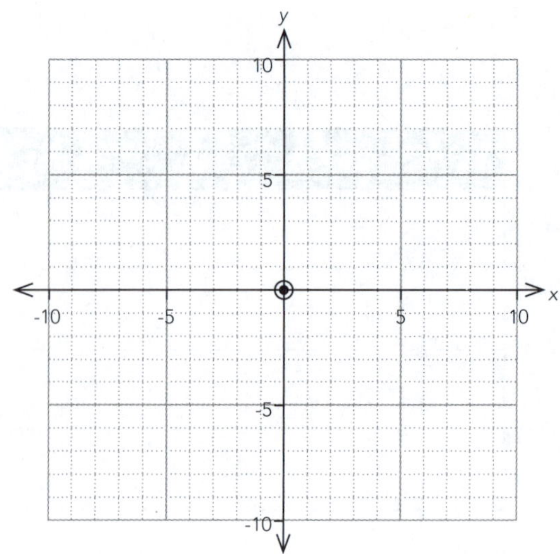

ISBN: 9780170419376

2 Using the *y*-intercept and the gradient

If you are given the equation of a graph, you can convert it into the form $y = mx + c$ before drawing the graph.

m = gradient = $\frac{\text{rise}}{\text{run}}$ — $y = mx + c$ — c = *y*-intercept

Examples:

1 Draw the graph of $y = -\frac{1}{2}x + 4$.

Step 1: Plot the *y*-intercept; in this case the *y*-intercept = **4**.

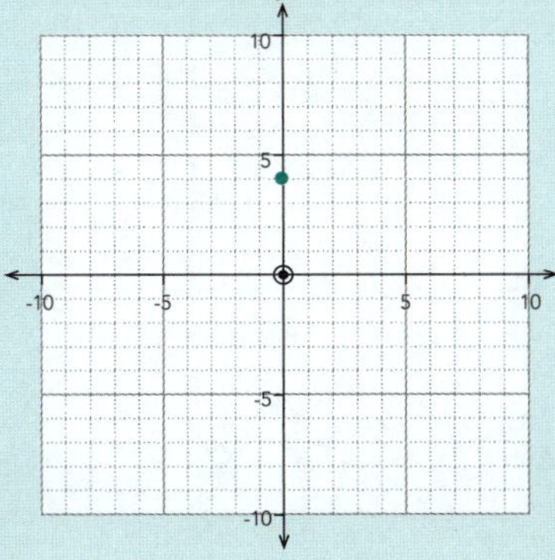

Step 2: From the intercept, plot at least three points along the gradient, in this case $\frac{-1}{2}$.

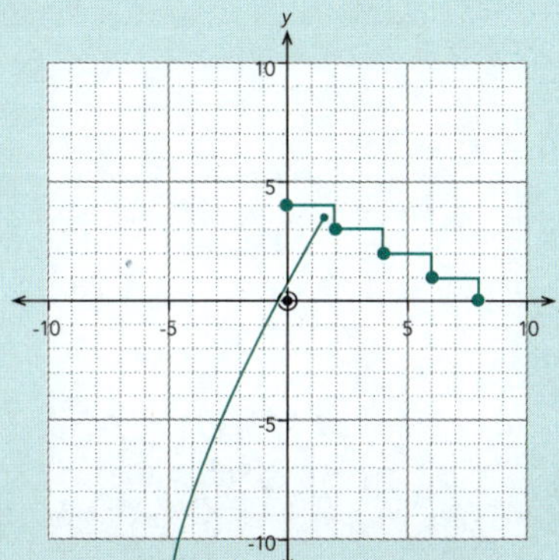

For each point, go across 2 and down 1.

Step 3: Join the points.

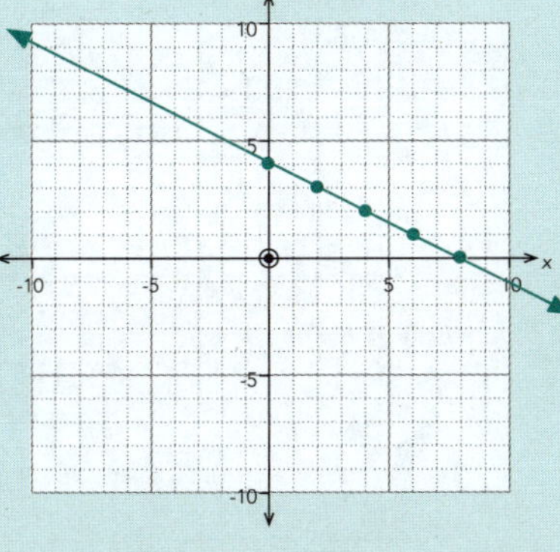

2 Draw the graph of $y = 50x + 300$.

Step 1: Plot the *y*- intercept; in this case the *y*-intercept = **300**.

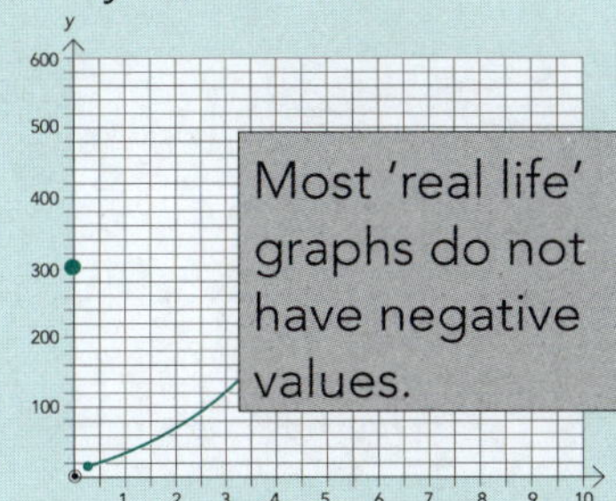

Step 2: From the intercept, plot at least three points along the gradient, in this case **+50**.

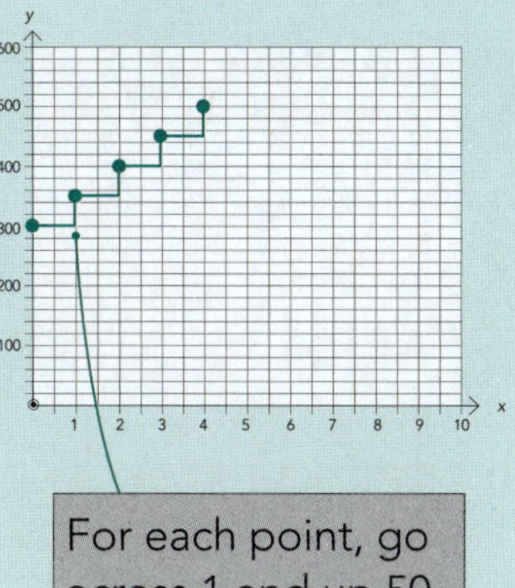

For each point, go across 1 and up 50.

Step 3: Join the points.

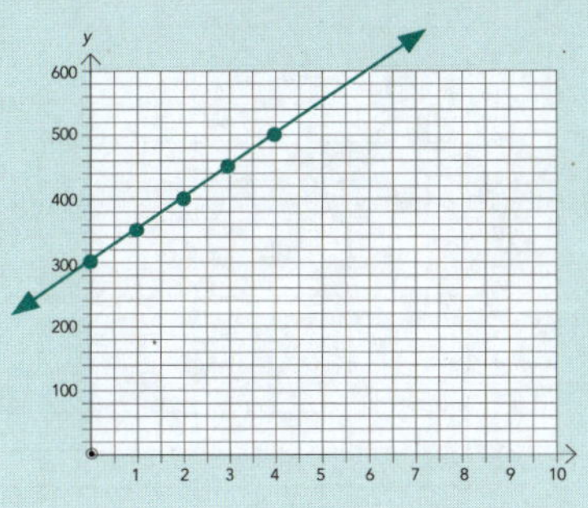

ISBN: 9780170419376

Draw the following lines.

1 $y = 3x + 1$

2 $y = -4x - 2$

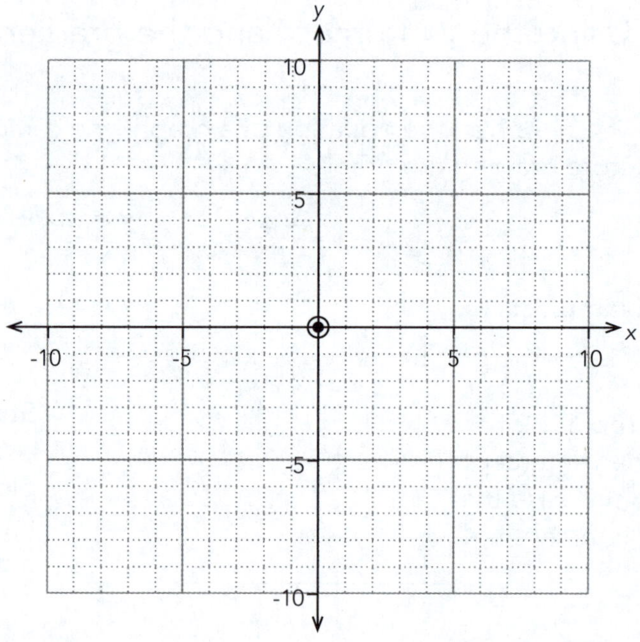

3 $y = 100x + 50$

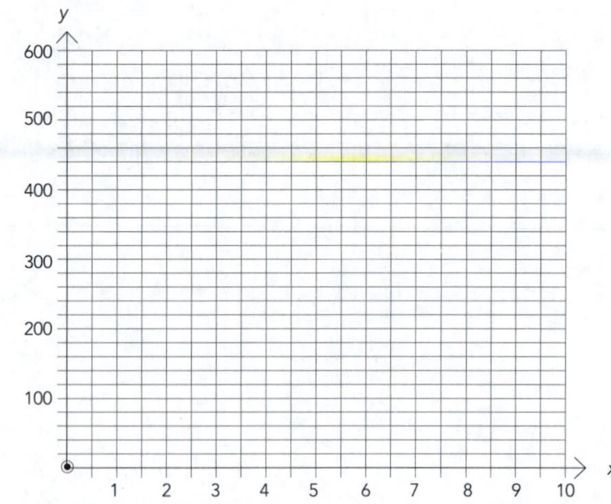

4 $y = -15x + 90$

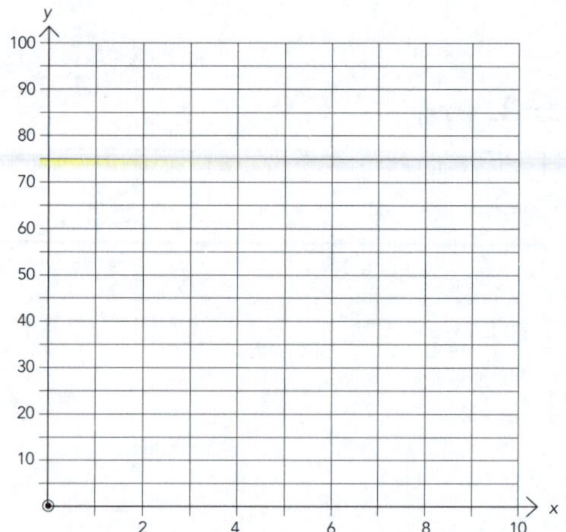

5 $y = -2x + 36$

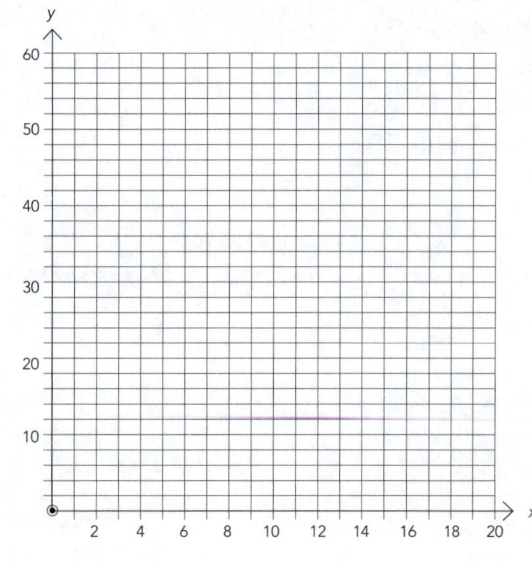

6 $y = -0.2x + 17$

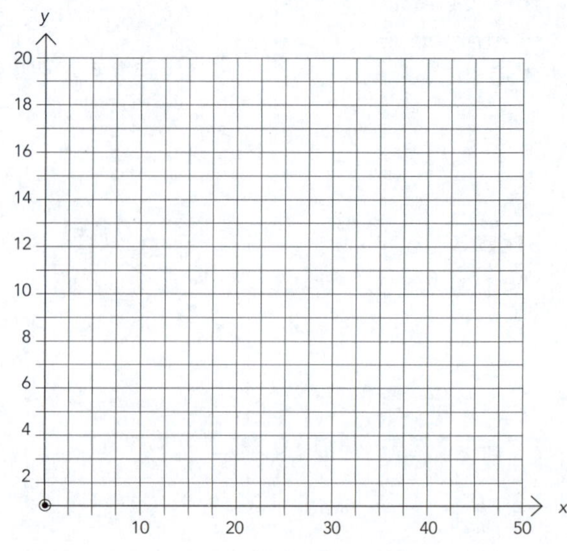

 ISBN: 9780170419376

3 Using the *x*- and *y*-intercepts

- Often you will need to draw the graph of an equation that is not in $y = mx + c$ form.
- If it is in the form $ax + by = c$, it is usually easier to use the intercept-intercept method in order to draw the graph.

Examples:

1 Draw the graph of $4x - 3y = 24$.

Step 1: Make $x = 0$.
Then $4(0) - 3y = 24$
$\therefore\ y = \mathbf{-8}$
Plot the point (0, **-8**).

Step 2: Make $y = 0$.
Then $4x - 3(0) = 24$
$\therefore\ x = \mathbf{6}$
Plot the point (**6**, 0).

Step 3: Join the points.

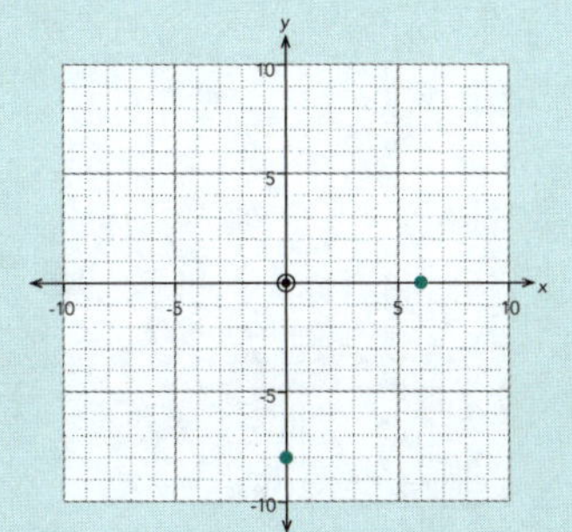

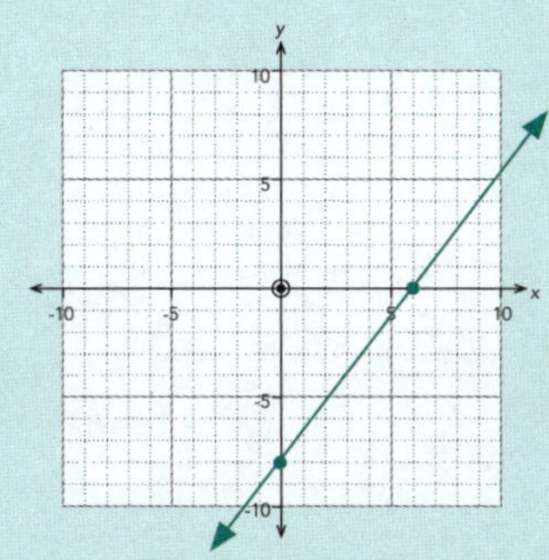

2 Draw the graph of $5x + 4y = 120$.

Step 1: Make $x = 0$.
Then $5(0) + 4y = 120$
$\therefore\ y = \mathbf{30}$
Plot the point (0, **30**).

Step 2: Make $y = 0$.
Then $5x + 4(0) = 120$
$\therefore\ x = \mathbf{24}$
Plot the point (**24**, 0).

Step 3: Join the points.

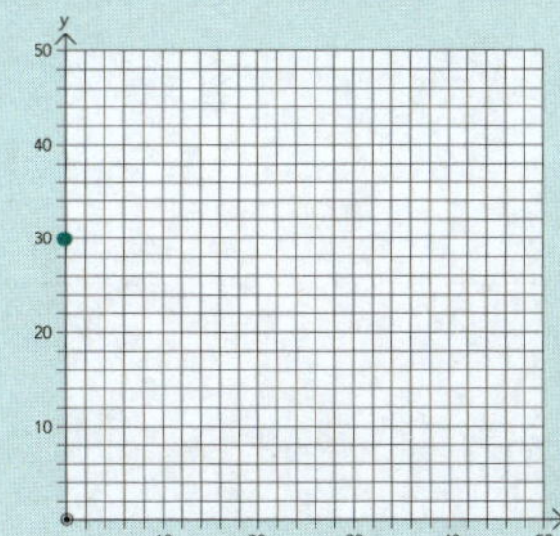

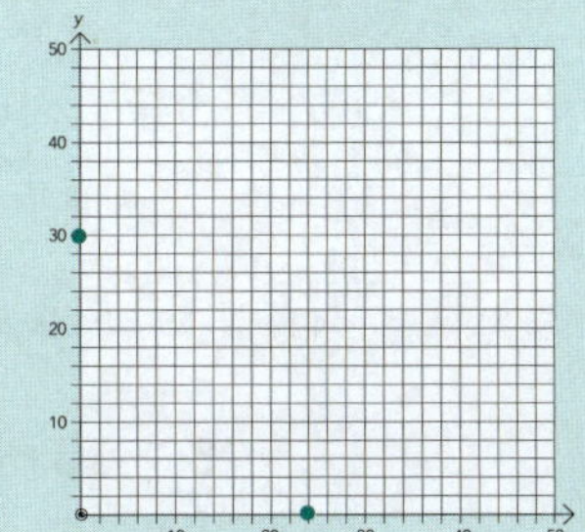

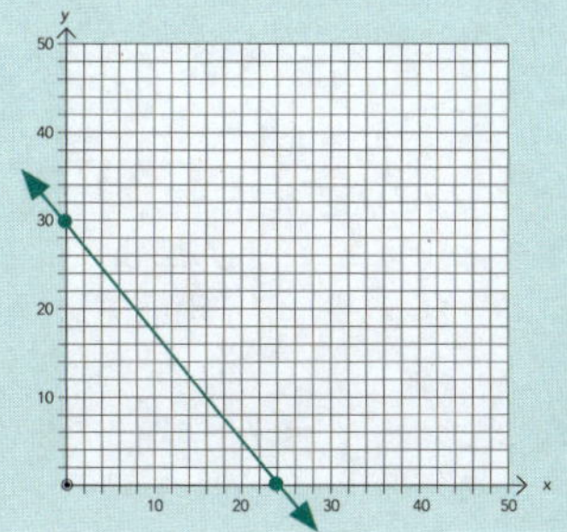

Draw the following lines.

1 $2x - 5y = 20$
$x = 0 \rightarrow y =$ ____ $\quad y = 0 \rightarrow x =$ ____

2 $x + 3y = 6$
$x = 0 \rightarrow y =$ ____ $\quad y = 0 \rightarrow x =$ ____

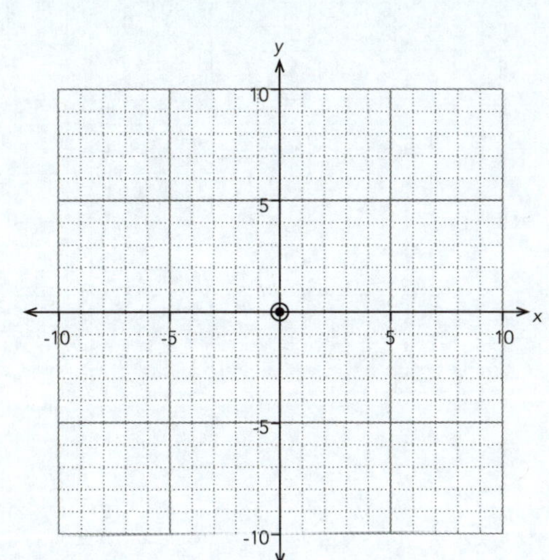

3 $2x + 4y = 100$

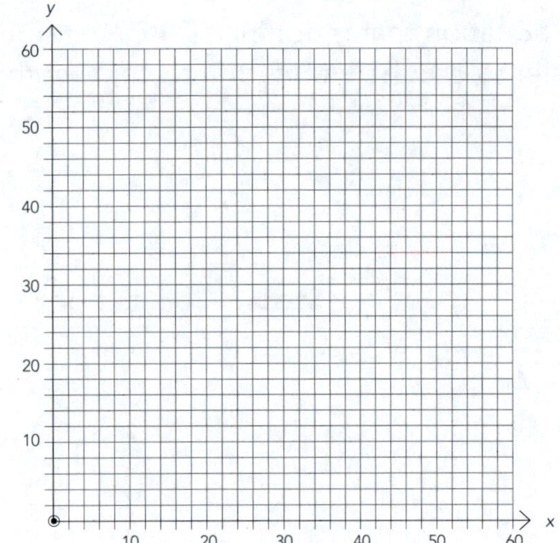

4 $8x + 4y = 200$

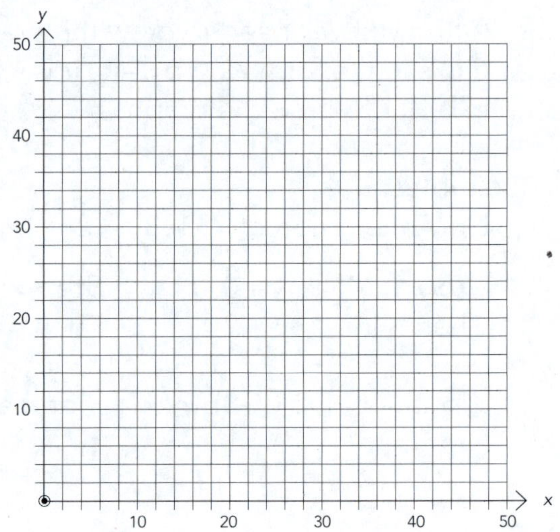

5 $40x + y = 400$

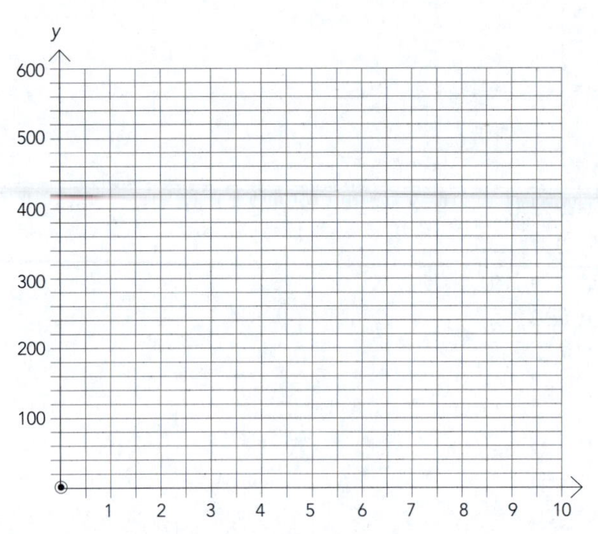

6 $18x + 4y = 360$

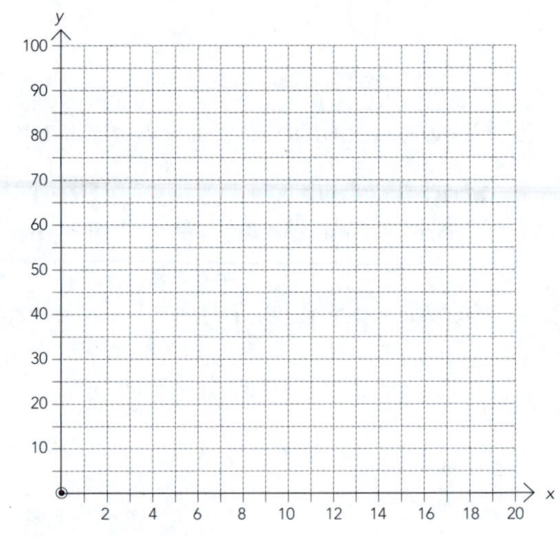

7 $5x + y = 75$

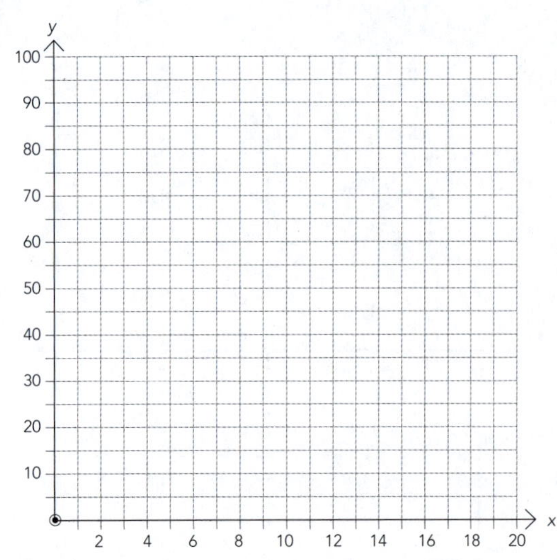

8 $15x + 4y = 120$

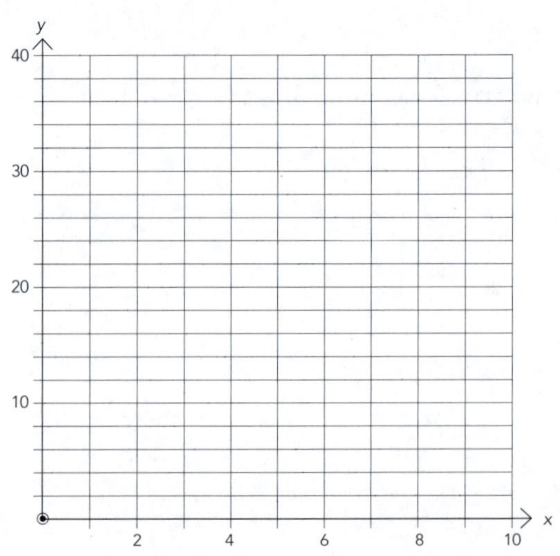

ISBN: 9780170419376

4 Horizontal and vertical lines

Be very careful when drawing these — it's easy to get them the wrong way around.

Examples:

1 Draw the line $x = 3$.

Step 1: Plot at least three points where $x = 3$, e.g. (3, 0), (3, 4), (3, -2).

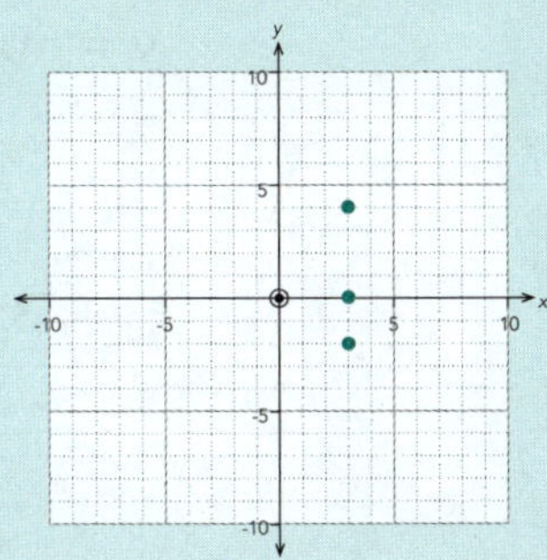

Step 2: Join the points.

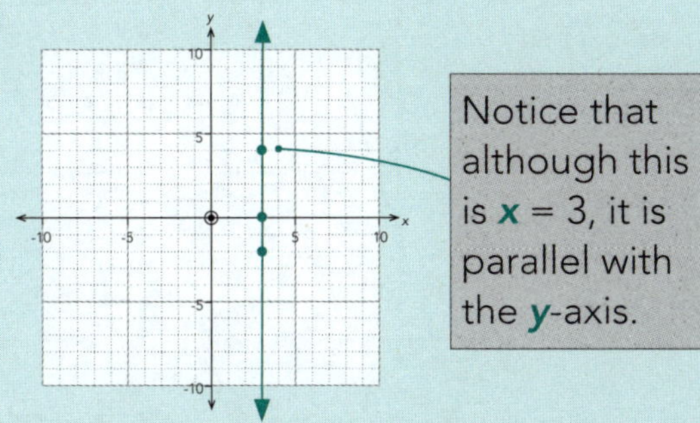

2 Draw the line $y = -5$.

Step 1: Plot at least three points where $y = -5$, e.g. (0, -5), (4, -5), (-2, -5).

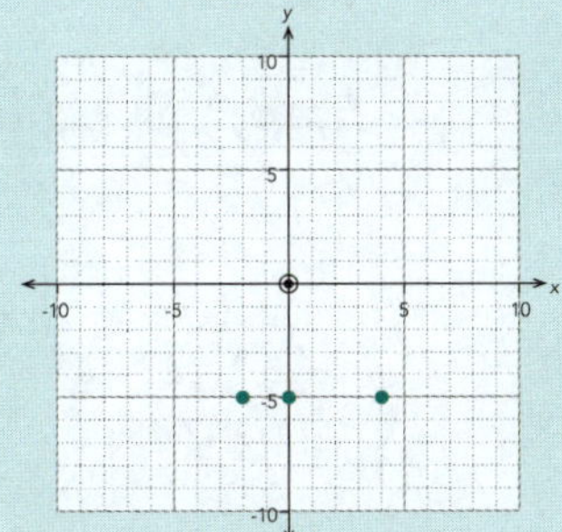

Step 2: Join the points.

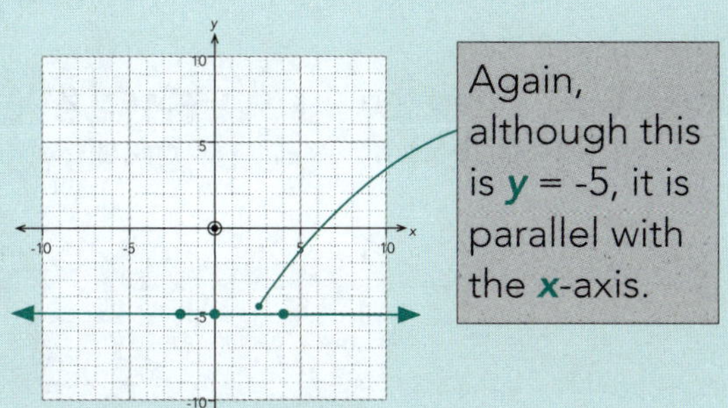

Draw the following lines.

1 $x = 2$ and $y = 7$

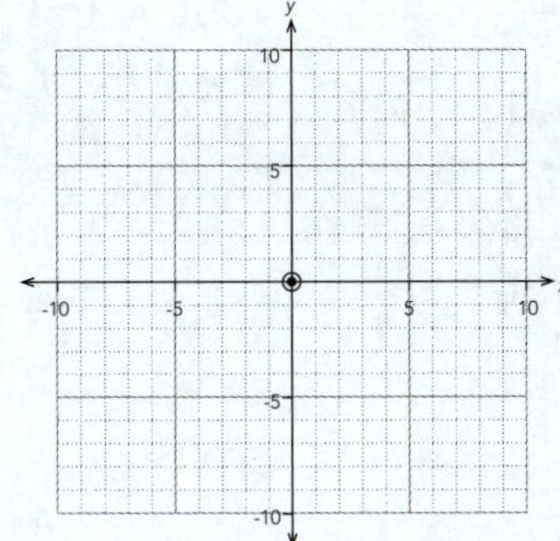

2 $y = 3$ and $x = -4$

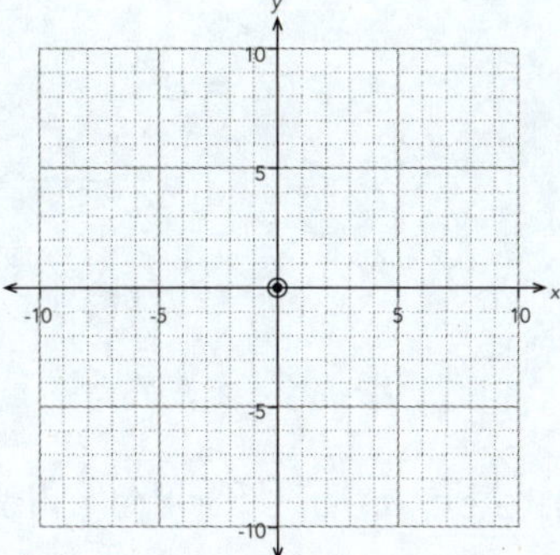

3 $x = 0$ and $y = 9$

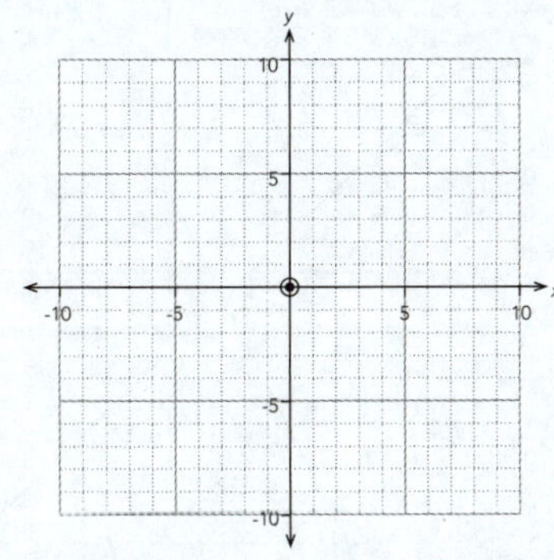

4 $y = 0$ and $x = -6$

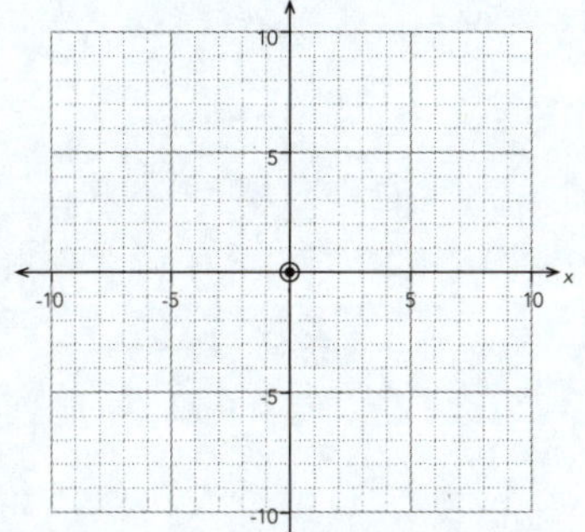

ISBN: 9780170419376

Writing equations from graphs

Use $y = mx + c$ as a template for your equation.
Write equations for the following lines.

Examples:

1 **Step 1**: Find the y-intercept (c).

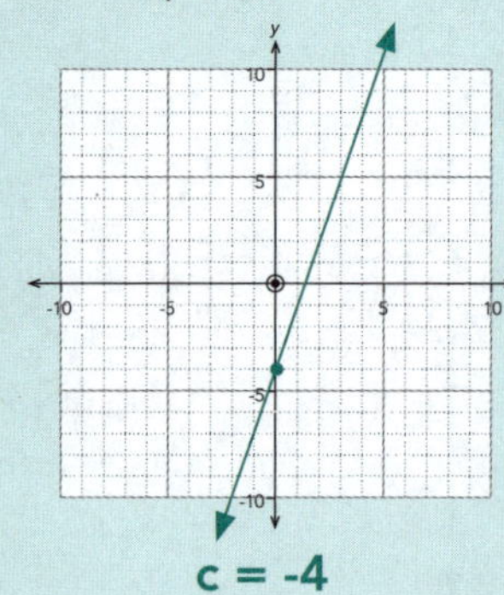

c = -4

Step 2: Work out the gradient (m).

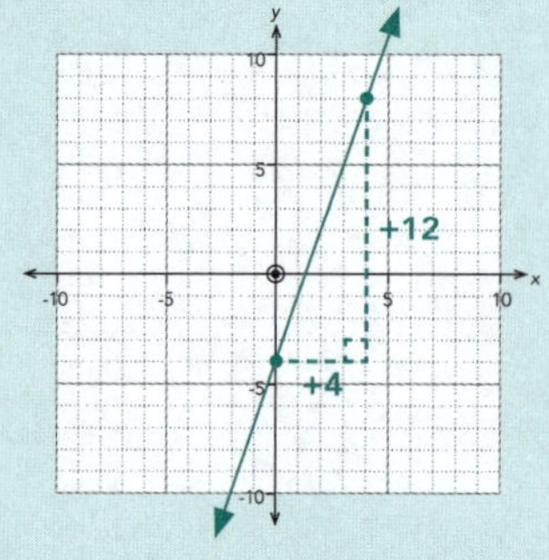

Draw a right-angled triangle between any two points through which the line passes.

$$m = \frac{\text{rise}}{\text{run}} = \frac{+12}{+4} = 3$$

Step 3: Substitute into $y = mx + c$.

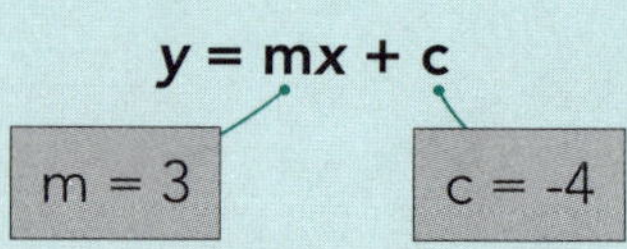

So: $\mathbf{y = 3x - 4}$

2 **Step 1**: Find the y-intercept (c).

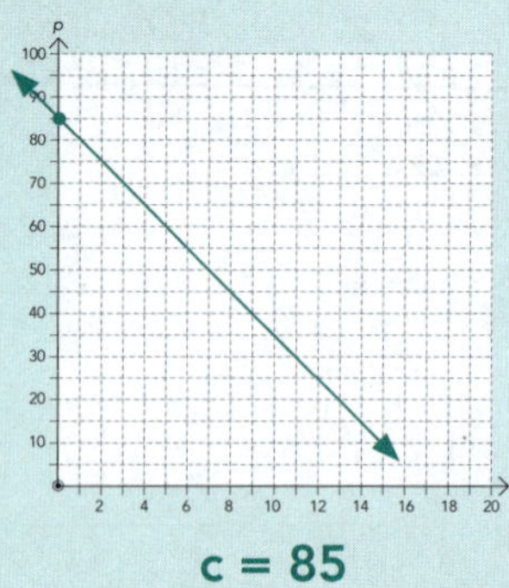

c = 85

Step 2: Work out the gradient (m).

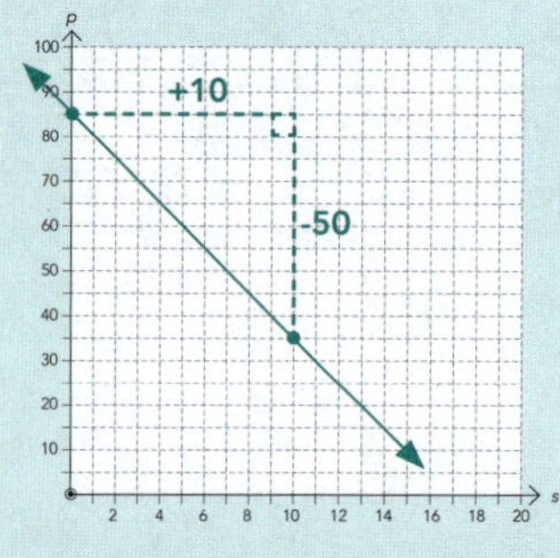

Draw a right-angled triangle between any two points through which the line passes.

$$m = \frac{\text{rise}}{\text{run}} = \frac{-50}{+10} = -5$$

Step 3: Substitute into $y = mx + c$.

y = mx + c

m = -5 c = 85

So: $\mathbf{y = -5x + 85}$

But, in this case, we have P on the y-axis and S on the x-axis. So the equation has to be:

$\mathbf{P = -5S + 85}$

Write equations for the following lines.

1 $y =$ _____x _____

2 $y =$ _____x _____

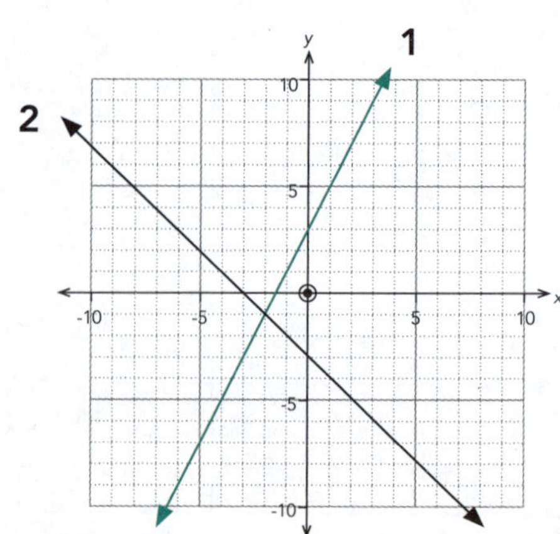

ISBN: 9780170419376

3

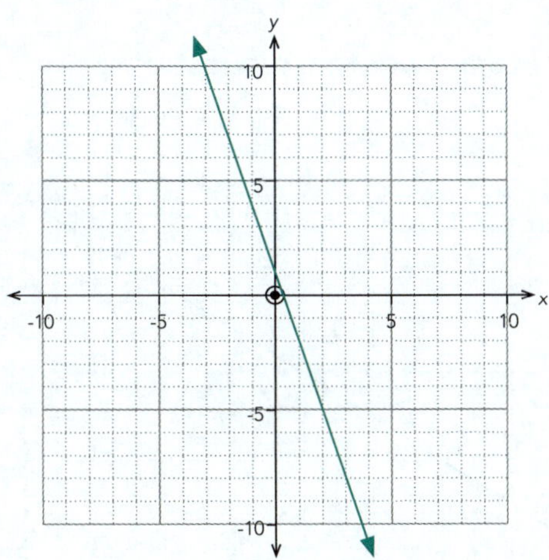

$y =$ ____________________

4

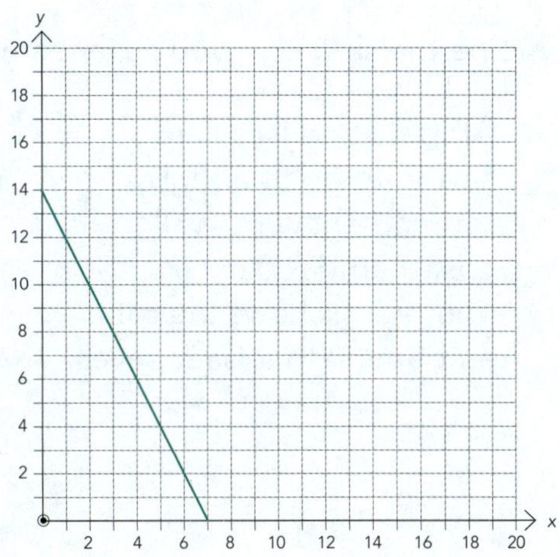

5

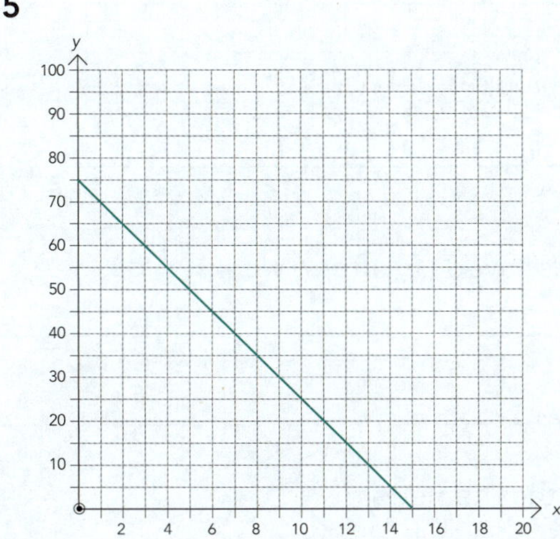

$y =$ ____________________

6

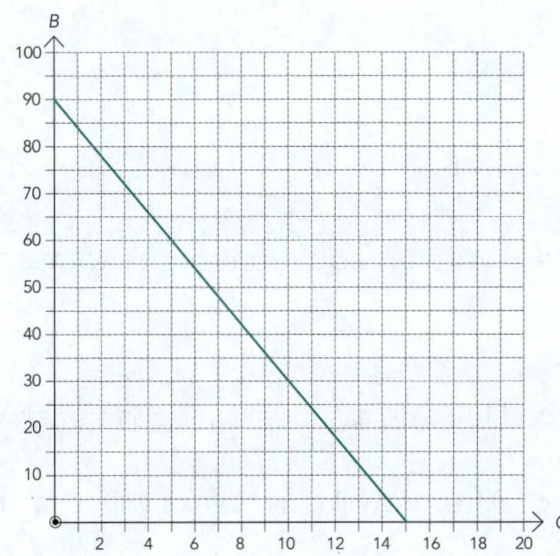

7

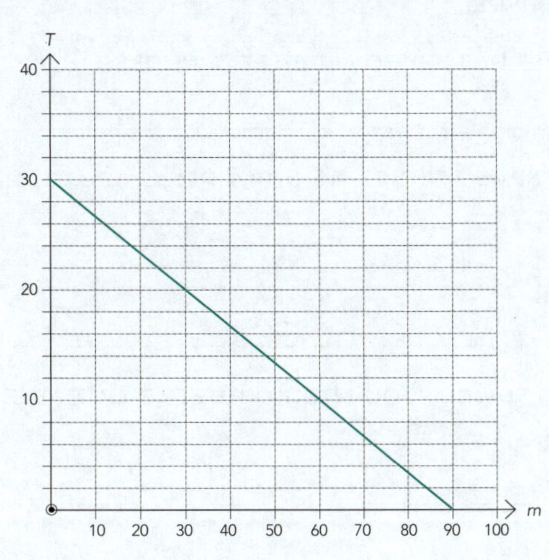

$y =$ ____________________

8

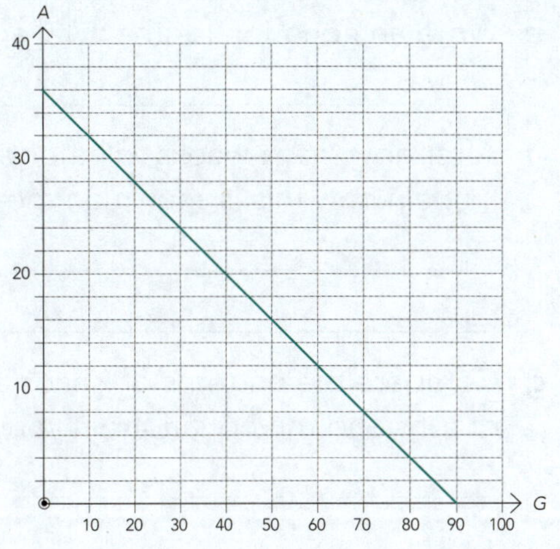

$y =$ ____________________

ISBN: 9780170419376

Applications

Combine the skills that you have learnt so far in order to answer these questions.

1 Arapeta and Isaac are saving to go to a rugby tournament which will cost them \$750 each. The graph shows the total amount (T) that Isaac saves.

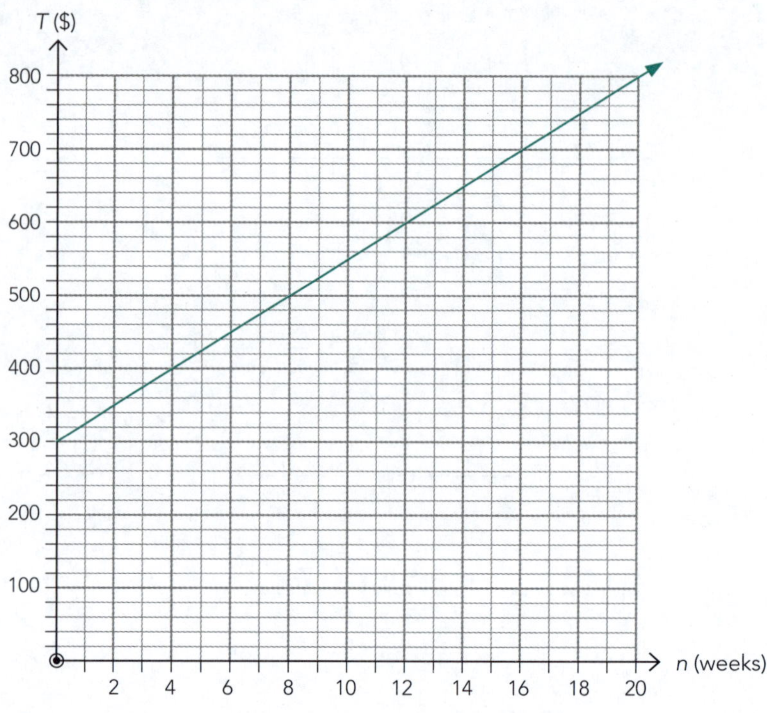

a Write an equation for the total amount Isaac has saved (T) after n weeks.

____

b How much does Isaac save each week? ______________________________

c After how many weeks will Isaac have the \$750 that he needs?

____

d Arapeta started by selling bacon to the staff at his school, and this earned him \$100. He has an after-school job, so he can add \$50 to his savings each week. On the axes above, plot the graph to show how much he saves.

e Write an equation for the total amount Arapeta has saved (T) after n weeks.

____

f After how many weeks will the two boys have saved the same amount? ______________
Explain how this is shown on the graph.

____

____

g Compare the patterns of Isaac's and Arapeta's saving. You should refer to both the graphs and the equations in your comparison.

____

____

____

____

  ISBN: 9780170419376

2 Arapeta and Isaac's teacher needs to hire a van for the rugby tournament. He thinks that they will drive less than 500 km.
The graph shows the total amount (C) in dollars that Vic's Vans will charge.

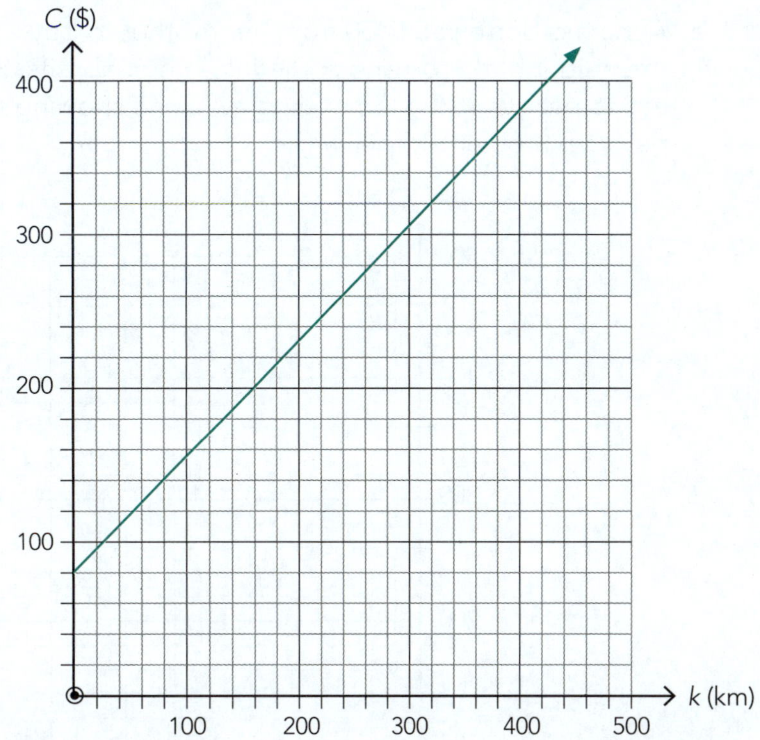

a Write an equation for the cost of hiring a van from Vic's Vans.

____

b How much does it cost for every extra 10 km that they drive?

____

c Rogue Rentals will supply a van for the trip. It will cost them a set fee of $125, plus 60c per kilometre. Draw the graph showing the cost of hiring a van from Rogue Rentals.

d For what mileage will vans from both companies cost the same amount?

____

Explain how this is shown on the graph.

____

____

e Write an equation for the total cost of hiring a van from Rogue Rentals.

____

f Compare the costs of hiring vans from the two companies. You should refer to both the graphs and the equations in your comparison.

____

____

____

____

____

ISBN: 9780170419376

3 a Anna has borrowed $450 from her mother to buy a phone. She gets paid for walking the neighbour's dog and sometimes she babysits. She aims to pay her mother back at $15 per week. On the axes, draw a line showing the amount that Anna owes if she pays her mother $15 per week.

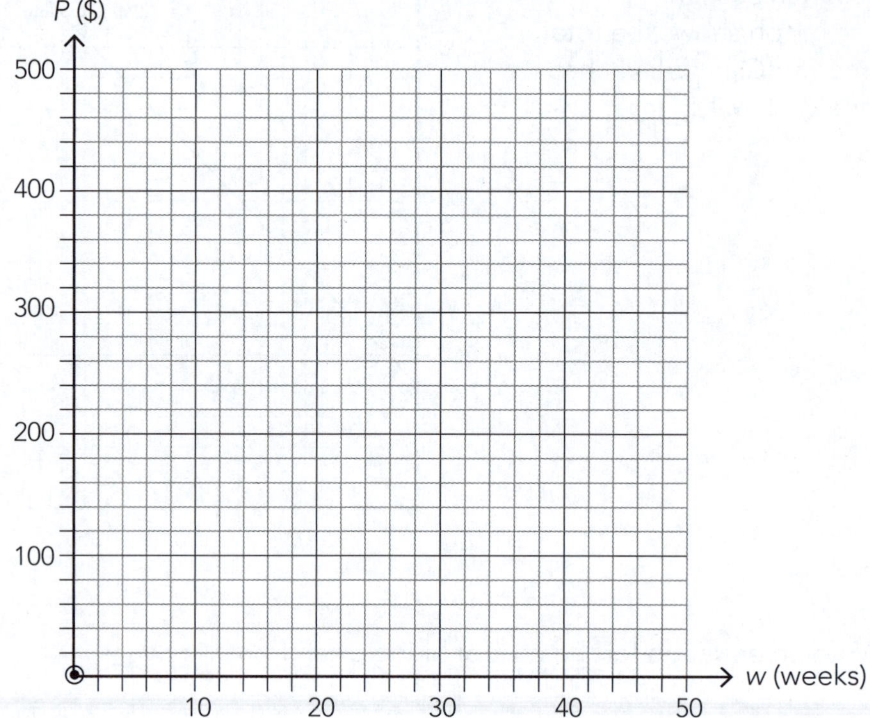

b How much does she owe her mother after paying $15 per week for 12 weeks?

____

c If she continues to repay her mother at $15 per week, after how many weeks will she have paid off her phone? Describe how this is shown on the graph.

____

d Unfortunately, she gets the flu at the end of the 12th week so she can't do any babysitting or dog-walking for two weeks. Consequently, she can't pay her mother again until the 15th week. From then on, she decides to pay her mother only $10 per week. Add to the graph you have drawn to show this new plan for repayment.

e Under her new plan for repayment, after how many weeks in total will she have paid her mother for the phone?

____

f Write an equation for each of the three parts of the graph.

Her initial plan for repayment: ____

____

The period when she had the flu: ____

____

Her new plan for after she recovered from the flu: ____

____

 ISBN: 9780170419376

4 The graph shows Chris's and Hannah's trip to school on Monday morning. The vertical axis shows their distance from school and the horizontal axis is the time since they left their homes. They both left home at the same time.

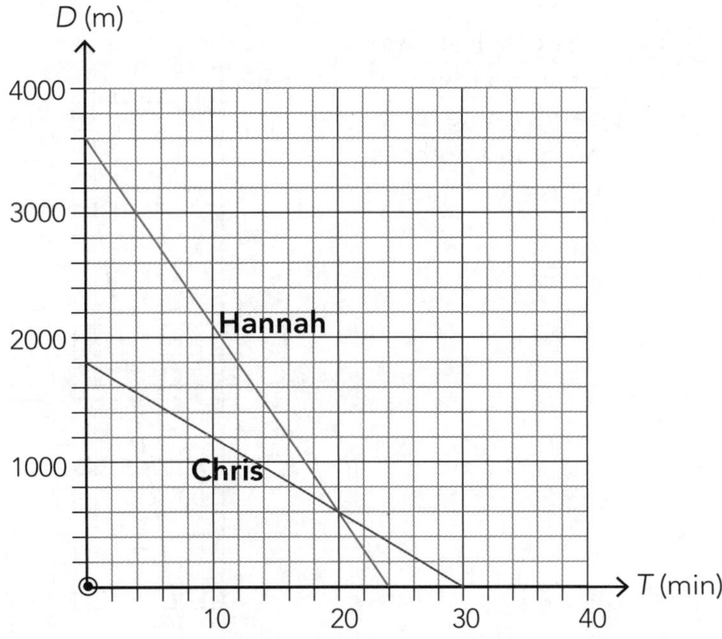

a Write equations for both lines.

Hannah: ______________________________

Chris: ______________________________

b Describe what the graph tells you about each of their journeys.

Hannah: ______________________________

____

Chris: ______________________________

____

c One of them walks to school and the other skateboards. Who does which? Explain your answer.

____

____

d Explain what happened 20 minutes after leaving home.

____

e The graph on the right shows their trips to school on Tuesday. Describe the differences from Monday's graph, and explain how these might have occurred.

____

____

____

____

____

____

____

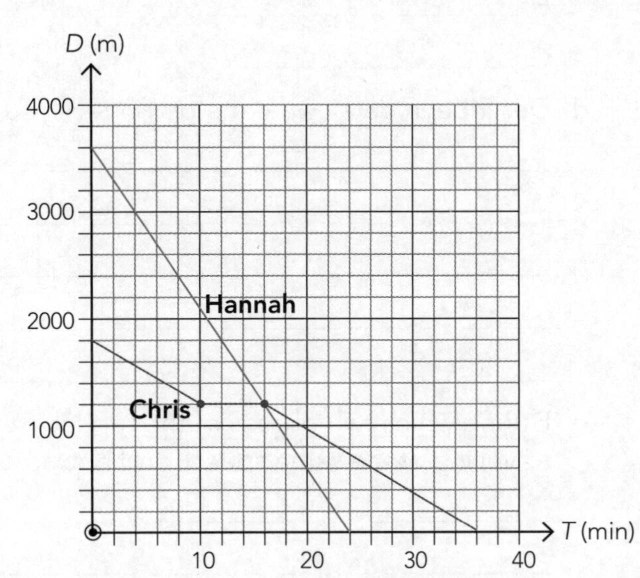

5 The graph shows a car trip from Sam's home to his grandmother's house and back.

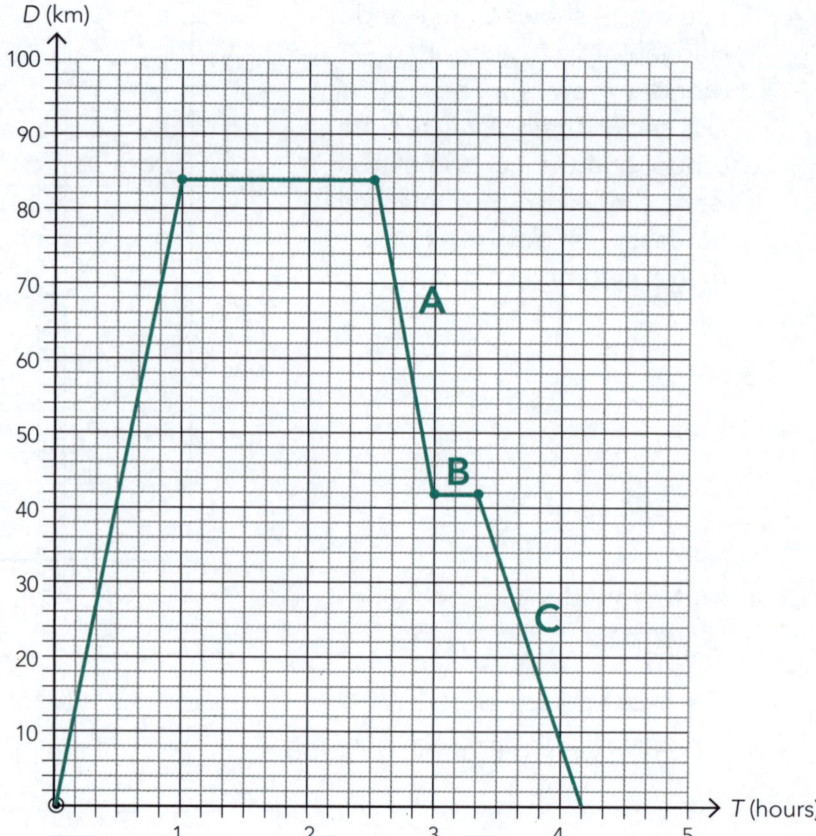

a Write down equations for these sectors of the journey.

$0 \leq T < 1$: ______________________

$1 \leq T < 2.5$: ______________________

b When was the car stationary?

____

c Their trip home has three stages: A, B and C. Write down the gradient of each stage.

A: ______________

B: ______________

C: ______________

d Describe in detail what the graph tells you about the trip home.

____

____

____

____

____

e During which two phases of the trip (apart from when they are stationary) were they travelling at the same speed, and how fast were they travelling?

____

____

 ISBN: 9780170419376

Parabolas

The basic parabola

- The **parabola** is the shape of the graph obtained when any quadratic equation is plotted.
- A **quadratic equation** is an expression in which the highest power of the variable (x) is 2.
- Usually these contain an $\mathbf{x^2}$, but in factorised form quadratic expressions may look like $(x \pm a)(x \pm b)$ or $x(x \pm a)$.
- If you don't know what the graph looks like:
  1 make a table
  2 plot the points
  3 join the points to form a smooth curve.

Example: Draw the graph of $y = x^2$.

x	y
3	9
2	4
1	1
0	0
-1	1
-2	4
-3	9

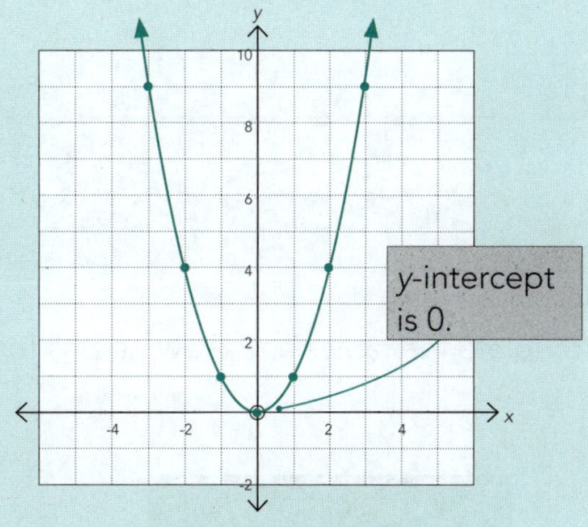

- *All* parabolas are this shape, but they can be shifted, turned upside down and stretched, or any combination of these.

Translated parabolas

1 Vertical translation, $y = x^2 \pm c$

Examples:

1 Draw the graph of $y = x^2$ **+ 1**.

x	y
3	10
2	5
1	2
0	1
-1	2
-2	5
-3	10

Compare this with the graph of $y = x^2$. All the points have moved **up 1**.

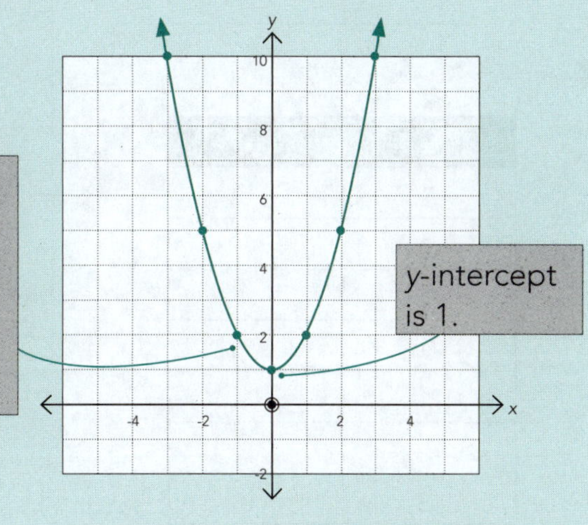

ISBN: 9780170419376

2 Draw the graph of $y = x^2 - 2$.

x	y
3	7
2	2
1	-1
0	-2
-1	-1
-2	2
-3	7

Compare this with the graph of $y = x^2$.
All the points have moved **down 2**.

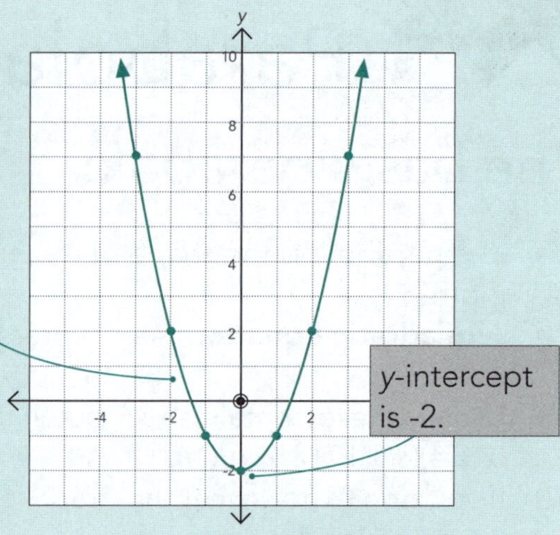

y-intercept is -2.

Remember: Straight lines: Graph of $\mathbf{y = mx + c} \Rightarrow$ the y-intercept is **c**.
Parabolas: Graph of $\mathbf{y = x^2 + c} \Rightarrow$ the y-intercept is **c**.

c is also known as the constant.

For graphs in the form $y = x^2 \pm c$:
c is like an elevator — **it moves the graph up or down by c units.**

Complete the tables and draw graphs for the following equations.

1 $y = x^2 + 3$

x	y
3	
2	
1	
0	
-1	
-2	
-3	

2 $y = x^2 - 1$

x	y
3	
2	
1	
0	
-1	
-2	
-3	

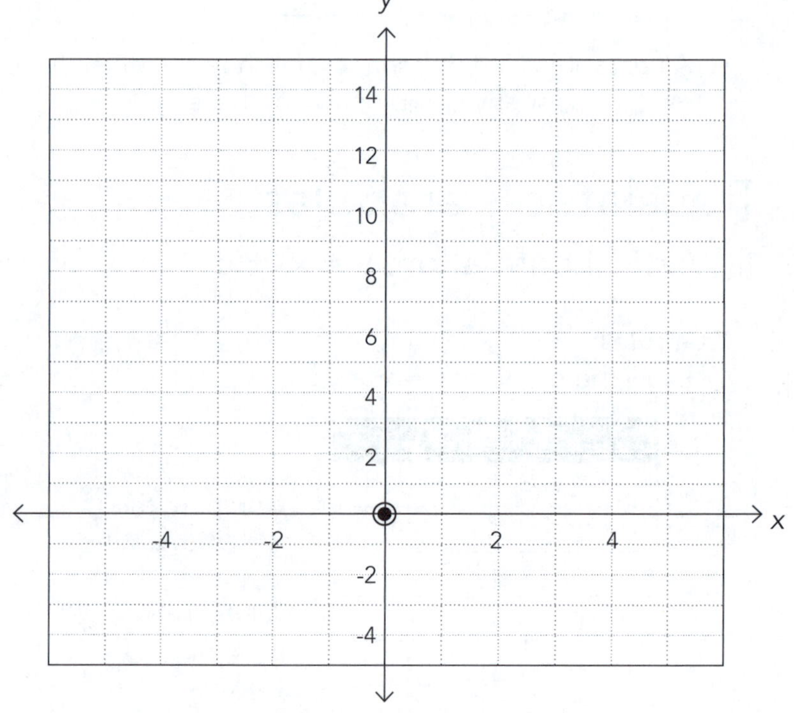

 ISBN: 9780170419376

3 $y = x^2 + 5$

x	y
3	
2	
1	
0	
-1	
-2	
-3	

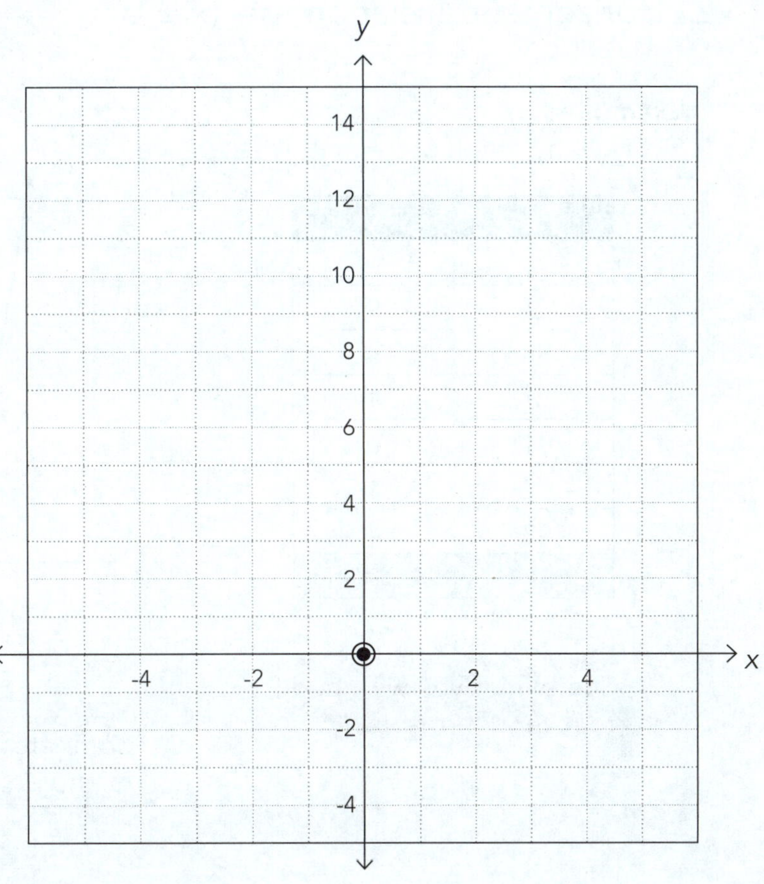

4 $y = x^2 - 4$

x	y
3	
2	
1	
0	
-1	
-2	
-3	

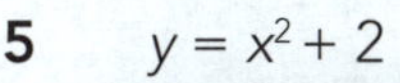

5 $y = x^2 + 2$

x	y
3	
2	
1	
0	
-1	
-2	
-3	

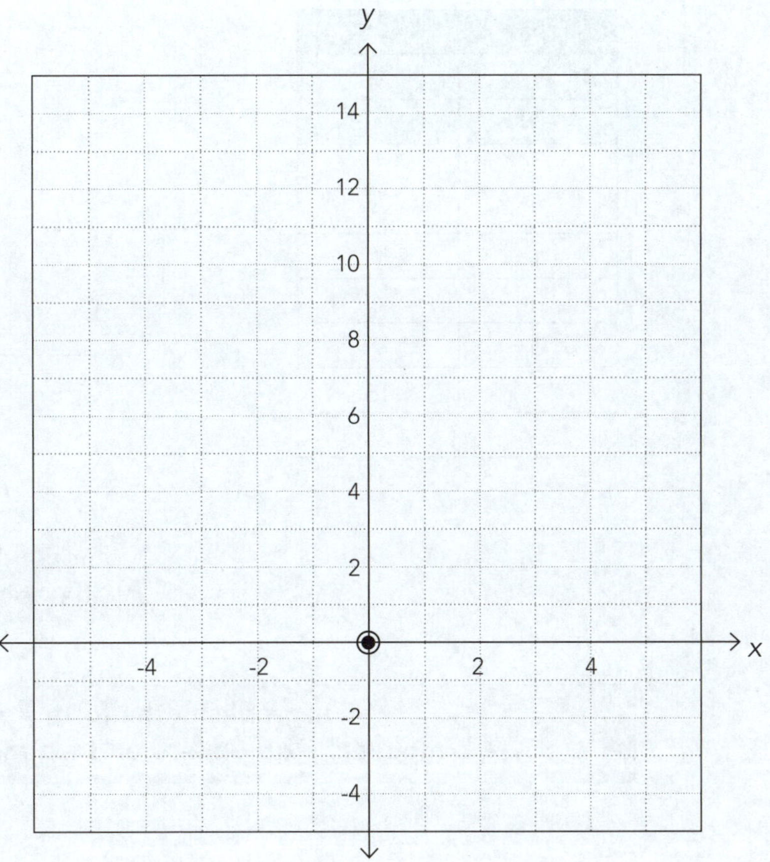

6 $y = x^2 - 5$

x	y
3	
2	
1	
0	
-1	
-2	
-3	

2 Horizontal translation, $y = (x \pm b)^2$

Examples:

1 Draw the graph of $y = (x + 1)^2$.

x	y
3	16
2	9
1	4
0	1
-1	0
-2	1
-3	4
-4	9

Sometimes you will need to extend the table.

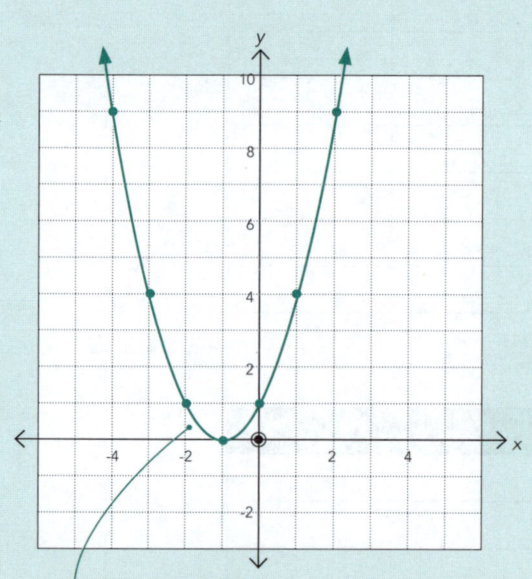

Compare this with the graph of $y = x^2$. All the points have moved **left 1**.

2 Draw the graph of $y = (x - 2)^2$.

x	y
5	9
4	4
3	1
2	0
1	1
0	4
-1	9
-2	16
-3	25

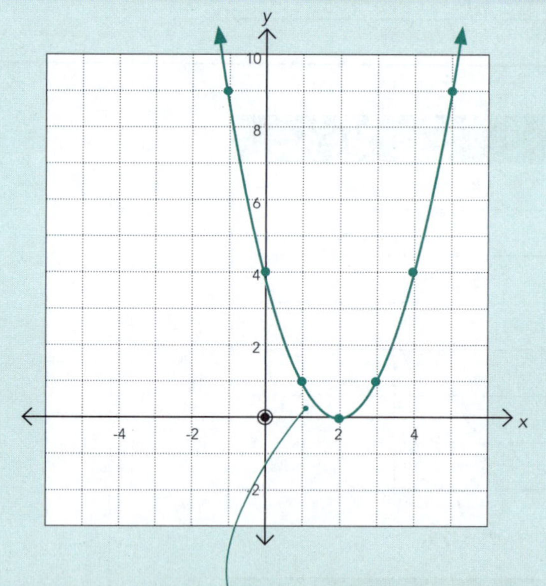

Compare this with the graph of $y = x^2$. All the points have moved **right 2**.

For graphs in the form $y = (x \pm b)^2$:
+ b moves the graph left and **– b moves the graph right.**

 ISBN: 9780170419376

Complete the tables and draw graphs for the following equations.

1 $y = (x + 3)^2$

x	y
1	
0	
-1	
-2	
-3	
-4	
-5	

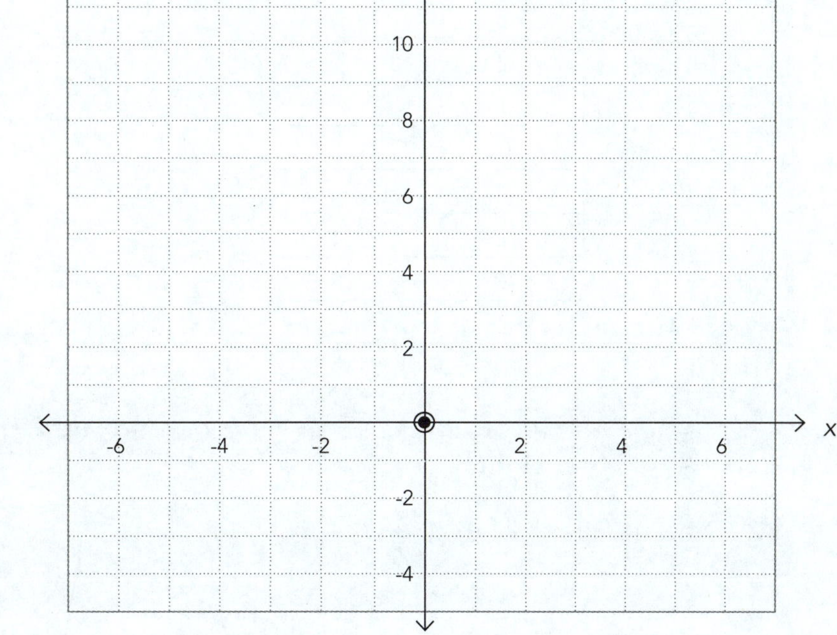

2 $y = (x - 1)^2$

x	y
3	
2	
1	
0	
-1	
-2	
-3	

3 $y = (x + 2)^2$

x	y

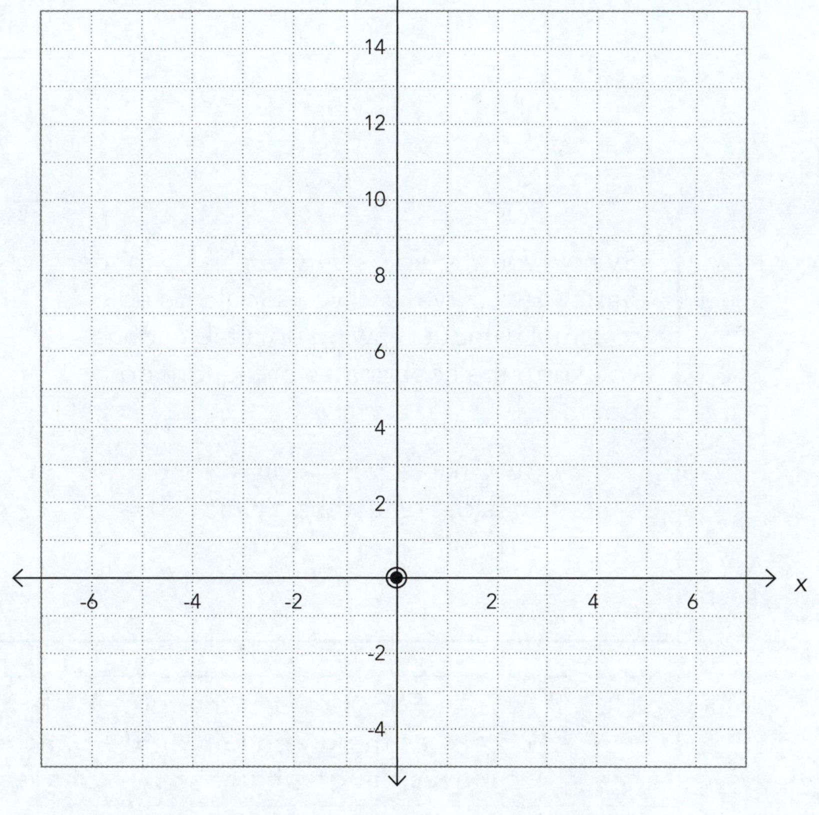

4 $y = (3 - x)^2$

x	y

ISBN: 9780170419376

3 Combinations, $y = (x + b)^2 + c$

The vertex of a parabola is the turning point.

Examples:

1 Draw the graph of $y = (x - 1)^2 + 2$.

x	y
3	6
2	3
1	2
0	3
-1	6
-2	11
-3	18

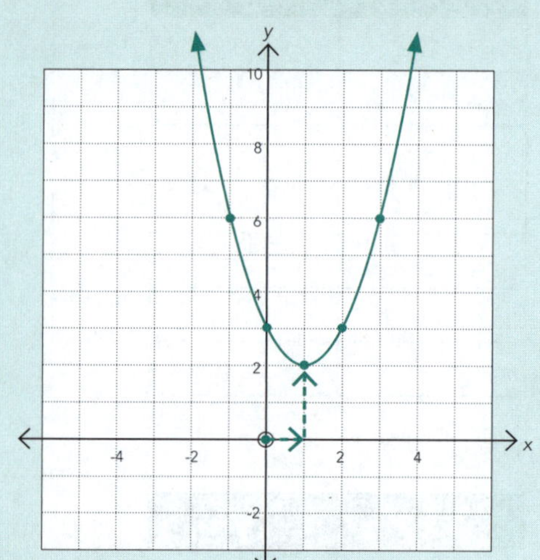

$y = (x - 1)^2 + 2$

$-1 \Rightarrow$ move vertex **right 1**.

$+2 \Rightarrow$ move vertex **up 2**.

2 Draw the graph of $y = (x + 3)^2 - 1$.

$+3 \Rightarrow$ move vertex **left 3**.

$-1 \Rightarrow$ move vertex **down 1**.

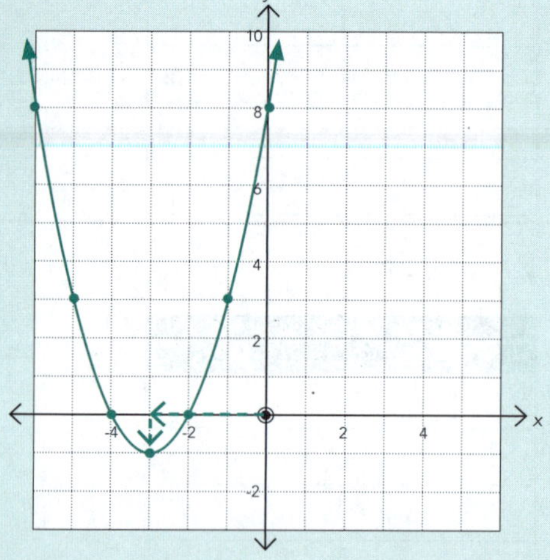

By now you should be very familiar with the basic $y = x^2$ curve, and you should be able to plot it without drawing up a table, once you know the coordinates of the turning point:

Once you have drawn one side, reflect the points in the vertical axis.

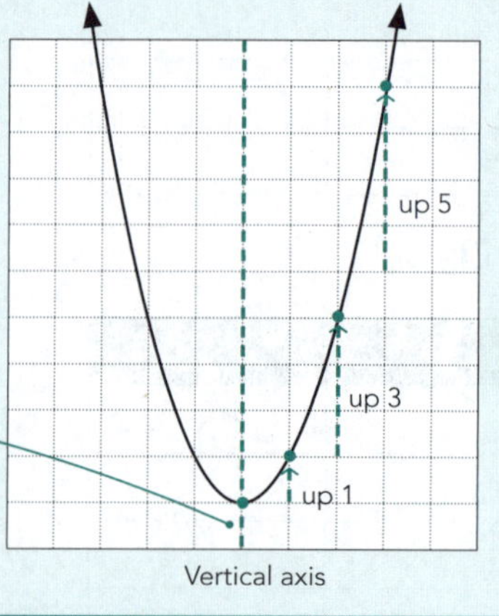

For graphs in the form $y = (x \pm b)^2 \pm c$:

+ b moves the graph left and **– b moves the graph right**

+ c moves the graph up and **– c moves the graph down.**

 ISBN: 9780170419376

Draw graphs for the following equations.

1 $y = (x - 3)^2 + 1$

2 $y = (x - 2)^2 - 4$

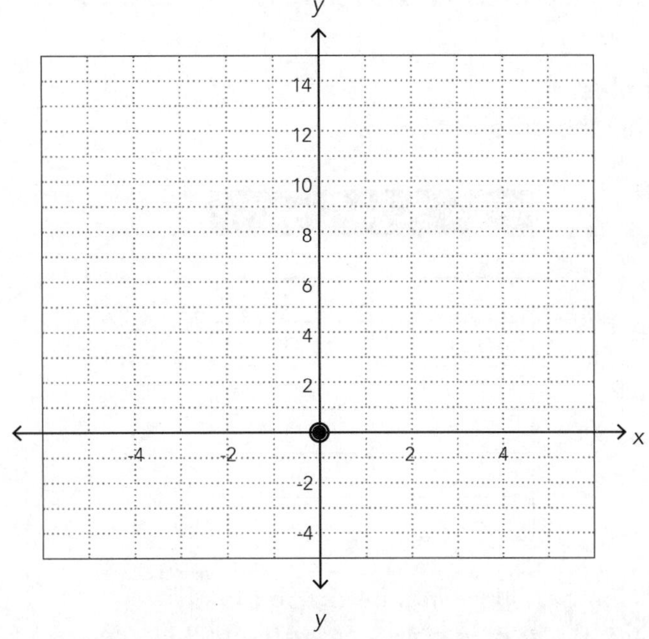

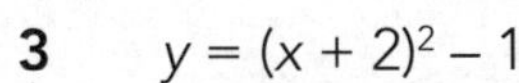

3 $y = (x + 2)^2 - 1$

4 $y = (x - 1)^2 - 5$

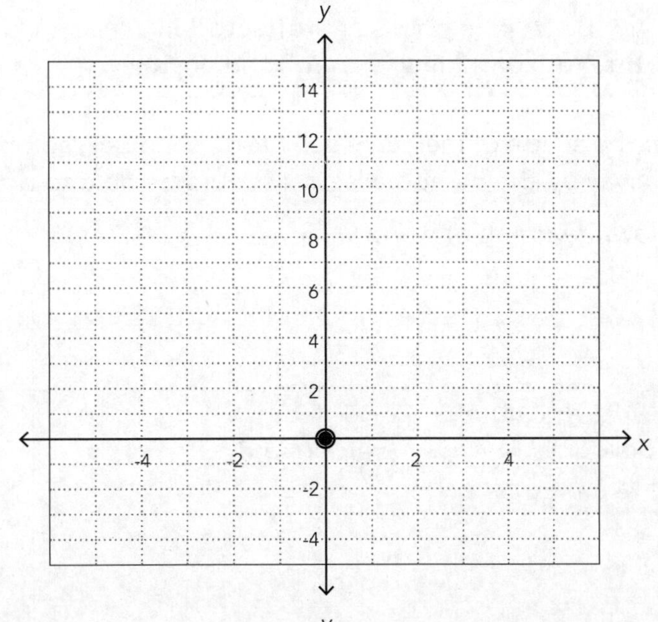

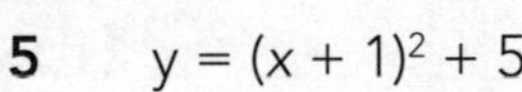

5 $y = (x + 1)^2 + 5$

6 $y = 4 + (x - 2)^2$

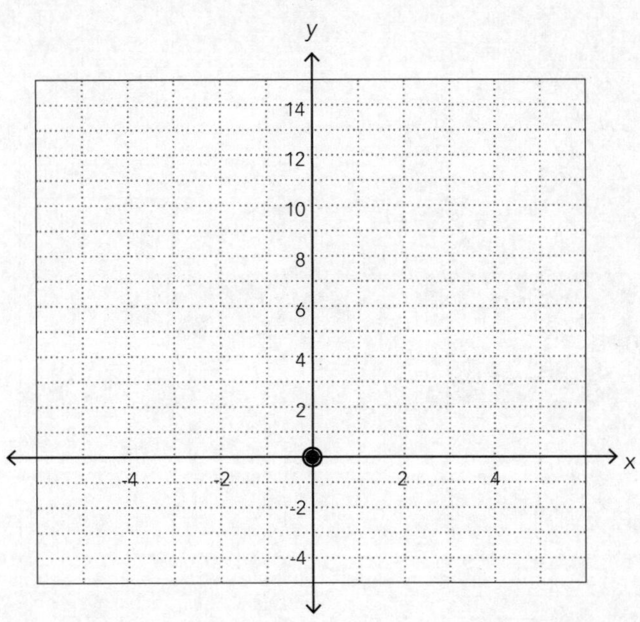

ISBN: 9780170419376

Inverted parabolas, $y = ax^2$......, where a is negative

Examples:

1 Draw the graph of $y = -x^2$.

So, a = -1.

x	y
3	-9
2	-4
1	-1
0	0
-1	-1
-2	-4
-3	-9

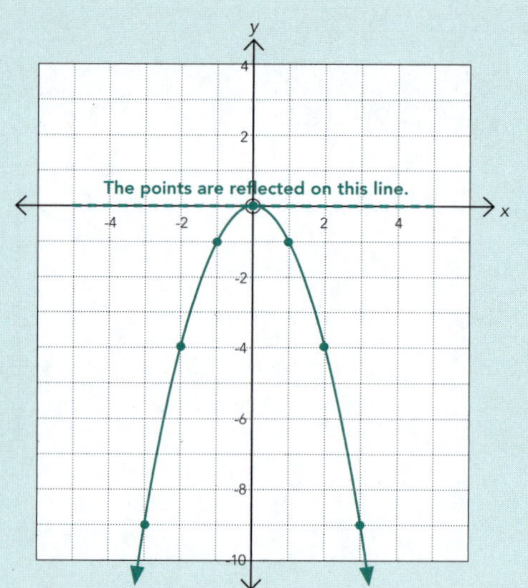

Compare this with the graph of $y = x^2$. All the points are **reflected in the horizontal line through the vertex**.

So far the shape of the curve still hasn't changed, so once you know the vertex and which way up the parabola is, you should be able to draw these without doing a table.

2 Draw the graph of $y = -x^2 + 3$.

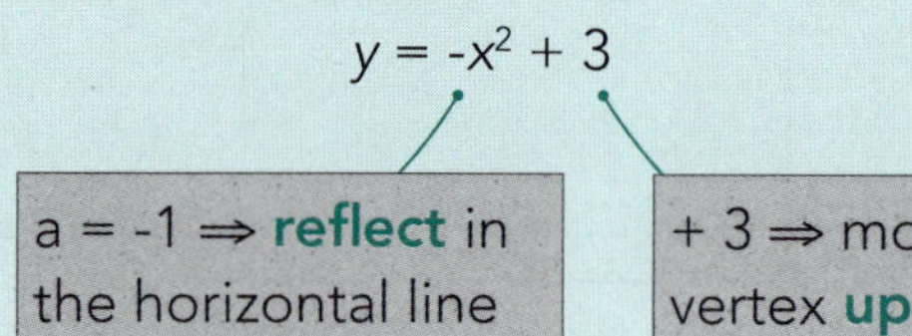

3 Draw the graph of $y = -(x - 2)^2$.

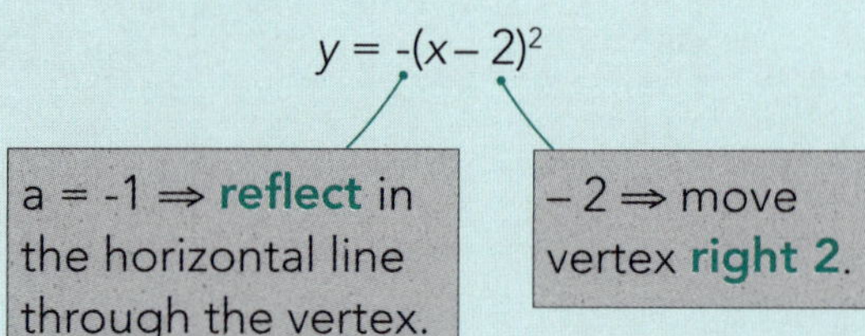

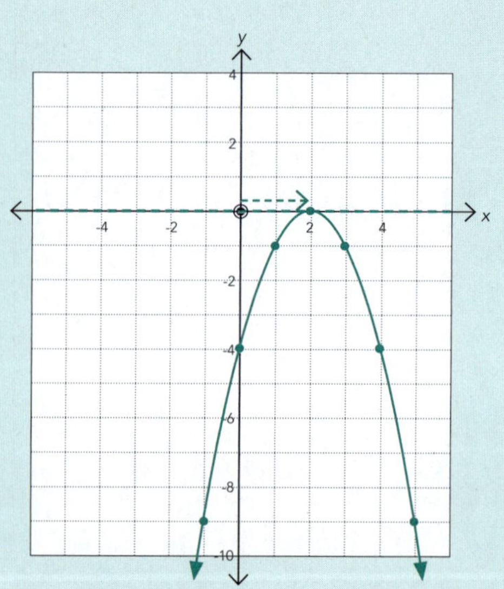

ISBN: 9780170419376

4 Draw the graph of $y = -(x + 2)^2 - 3$.

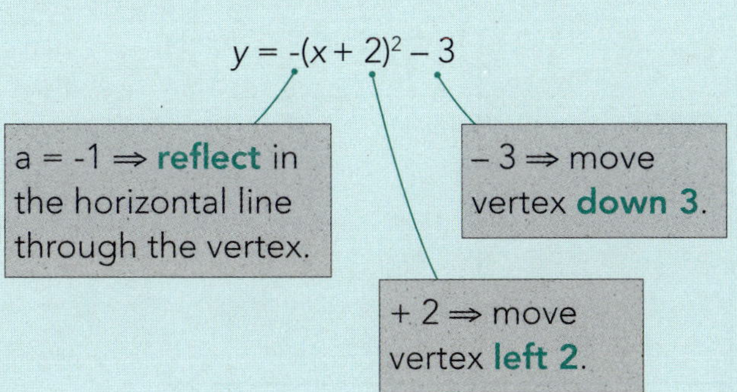

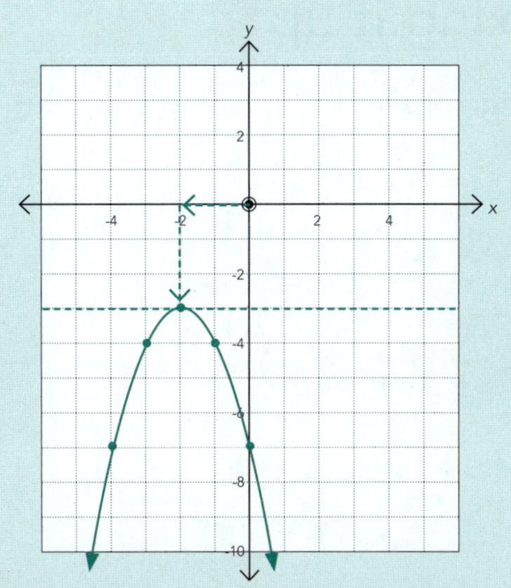

For graphs in the form $y = a(x \pm b)^2 \pm c$:
+ b moves the graph left and – b moves the graph right
+ c moves the graph up and – c moves the graph down
– a reflects the graph in a horizontal line through the vertex.

Draw graphs for the following equations.

1 $y = -(x + 1)^2 - 2$

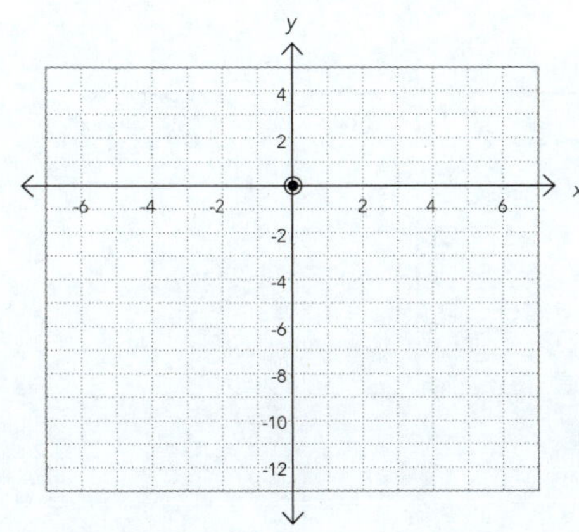

2 $y = -(x - 3)^2 - 1$

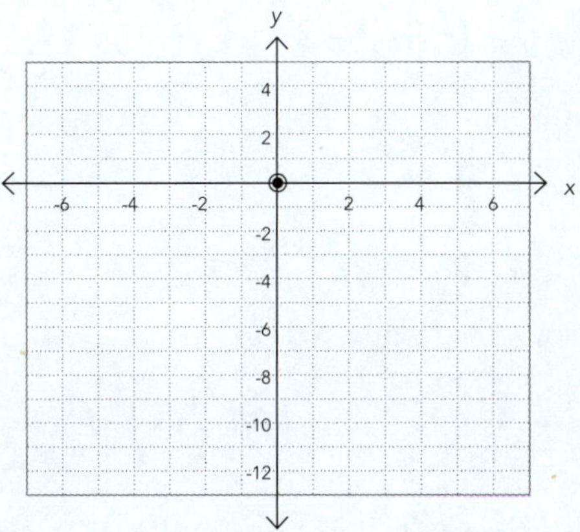

3 $y = -(x + 3)^2 - 3$

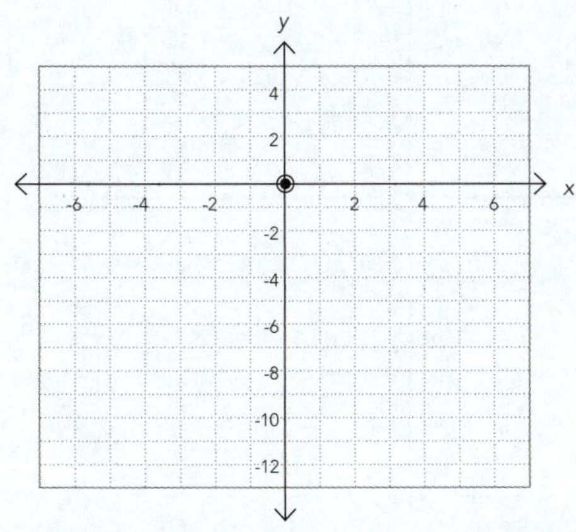

4 $y = 4 - (x - 2)^2$

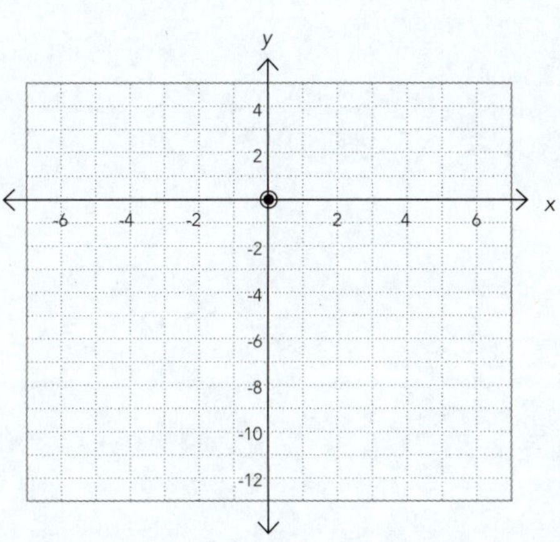

ISBN: 9780170419376

Mixing it up

Draw graphs for the following equations.

1 $y = -(x - 3)^2$

2 $y = 4 - x^2$

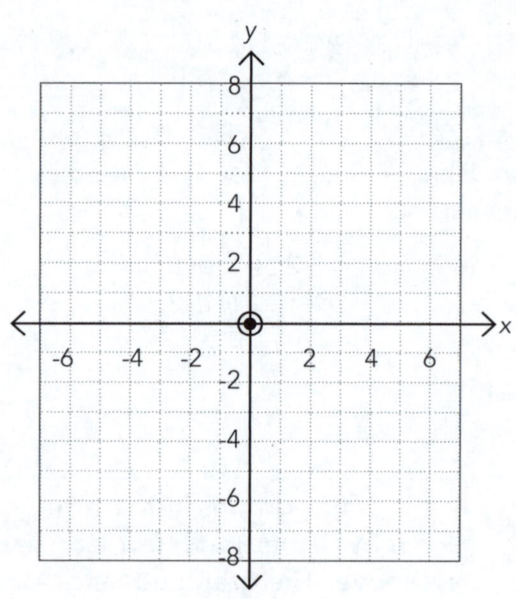

3 $y = -(x + 2)^2 + 1$

4 $y = (x + 4)^2 - 2$

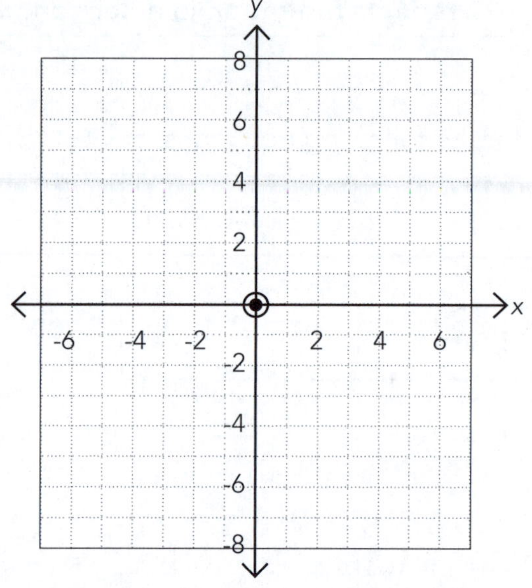

5 $y = 2 - (x + 3)^2$

6 $y = -(x - 2)^2 - 1$

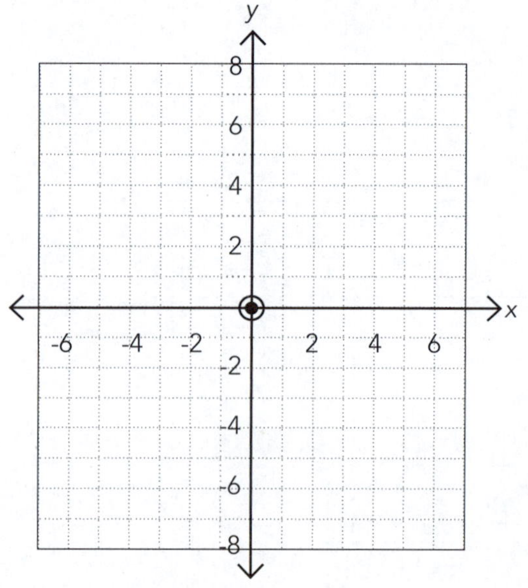

 ISBN: 9780170419376

Stretched parabolas

So far we have plotted graphs with **±1**x^2......, so a = 1. If the x^2 term is multiplied by anything other than **±1**, the shape of the parabola becomes stretched.

Examples:

1 Draw the graph of $y = 2x^2$.

So, a = 2.

x	y
3	18
2	8
1	2
0	0
-1	2
-2	8
-3	18

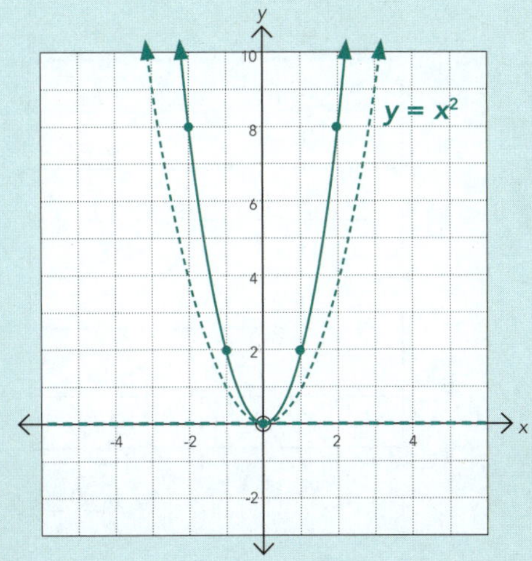

Compare this with the graph of $y = x^2$. All the points are **twice as high as they would have been — the graph has been stretched vertically**.

2 Draw the graph of $y = \frac{1}{2}x^2$.

So, $a = \frac{1}{2}$.

x	y
3	4.5
2	2
1	0.5
0	0
-1	0.5
-2	2
-3	4.5

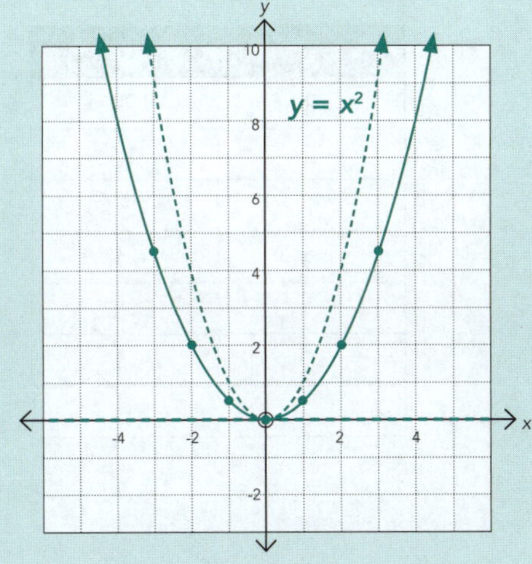

Compare this with the graph of $y = x^2$. All the points are **half the height that they would have been — the graph has been stretched horizontally**.

For graphs in the form $y = a(x \pm b)^2 \pm c$:

+ b moves the graph left and – b moves the graph right

+ c moves the graph up and – c moves the graph down

– a reflects the graph in a horizontal line through the vertex

$a > 1 \Rightarrow$ graph is stretched vertically; $0 < a < 1 \Rightarrow$ graph is stretched horizontally.

Where a ≠ 1, you will need to draw tables and plot the points.

3 Draw the graph of $y = -\frac{1}{4}(x - 3)^2$.

x	y
6	$-2\frac{1}{4}$
5	-1
4	$-\frac{1}{4}$
3	0
2	$-\frac{1}{4}$
1	-1
0	**$-2\frac{1}{4}$**
-1	-4
-2	$-6\frac{1}{4}$
-3	-9

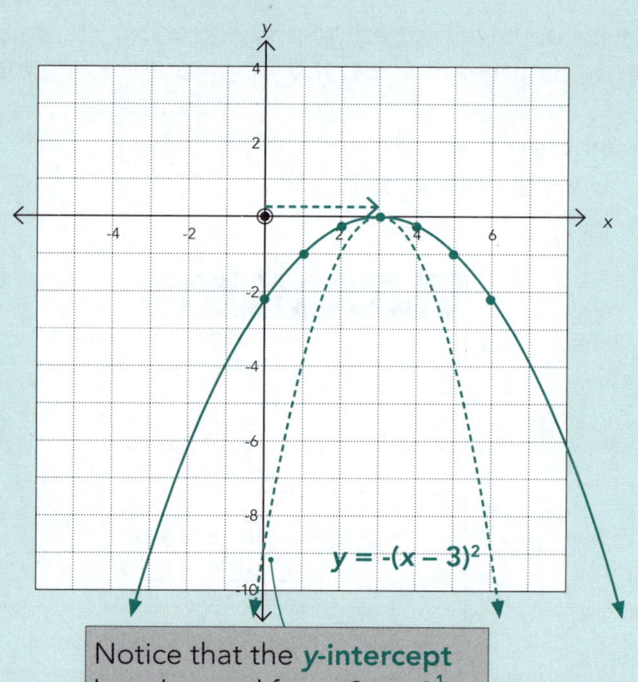

Notice that the **y-intercept** has changed from -9 to **$-2\frac{1}{4}$**.

4 Draw the graph of $y = 2(x + 1)^2 - 3$.

x	y
3	29
2	15
1	5
0	**-1**
-1	-3
-2	-1
-3	5

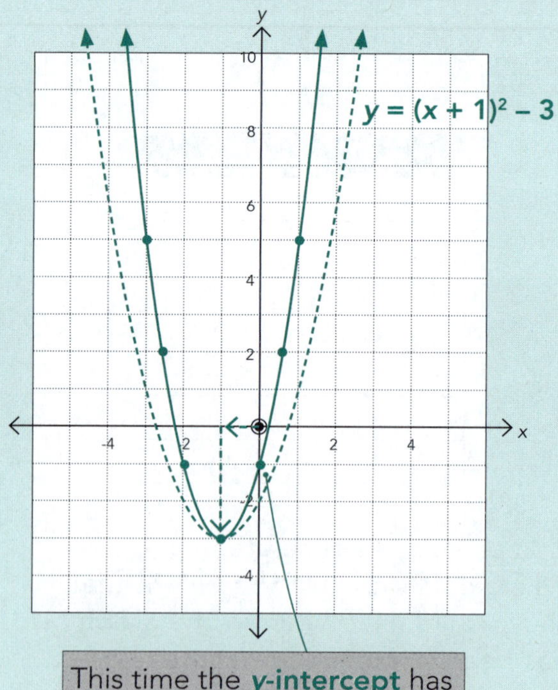

This time the **y-intercept** has changed from **-9** to **-1**.

The y-intercept will be very important when you need to write equations from graphs.

ISBN: 9780170419376

Complete the tables and draw graphs for the following equations.

1 $y = \frac{1}{4}x^2$

x	y
3	
2	
1	
0	
-1	
-2	
-3	

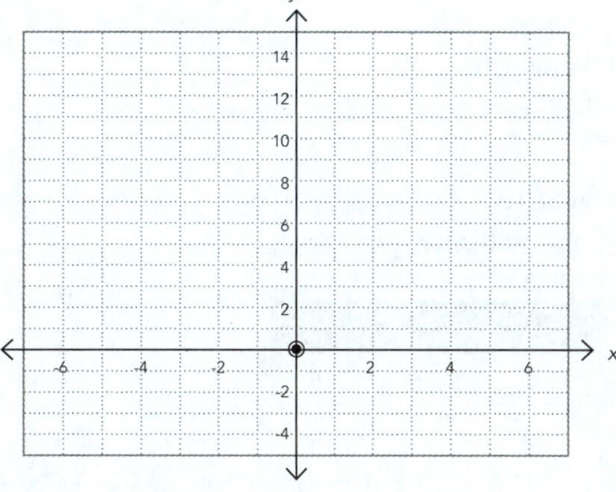

2 $y = -3x^2$

x	y
3	
2	
1	
0	
-1	
-2	
-3	

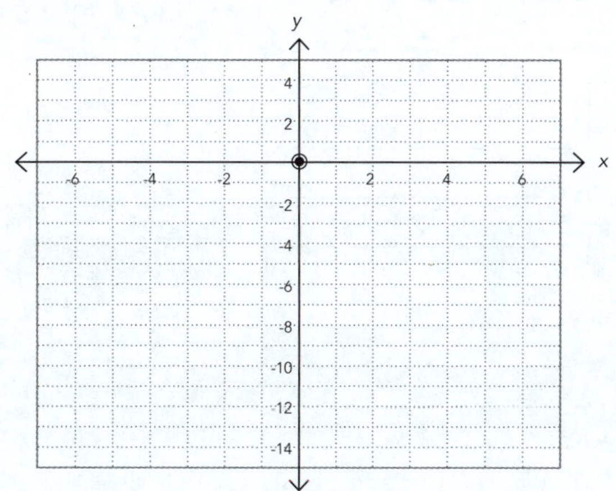

3 $y = -\frac{1}{2}x^2 + 6$

x	y

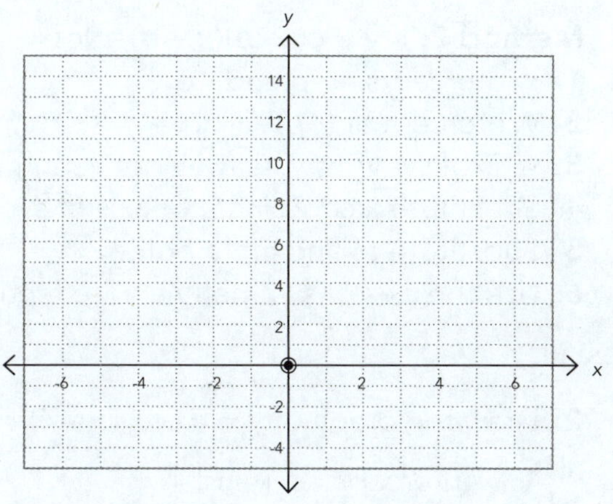

4 $y = 2(x - 3)^2 + 1$

x	y

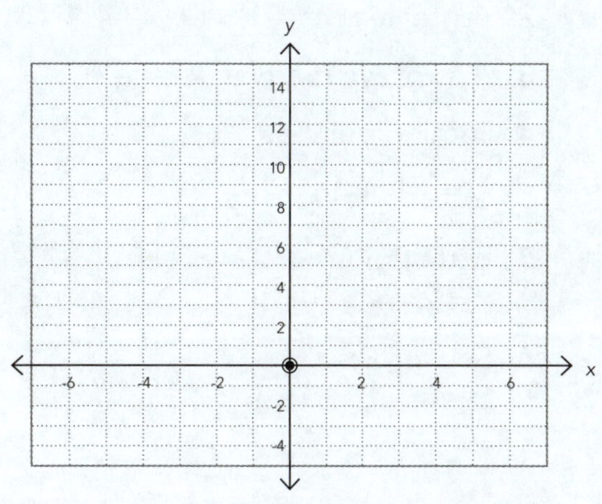

ISBN: 9780170419376

Plotting parabolas with the form $y = a(x \pm p)(x \pm q)$

Examples:

1 Draw the graph of $y = (x + 1)(x - 3)$.

Method 1: Do a table.
This will *always* work.

x	y
4	5 x 1 = 5
3	4 x 0 = 0
2	3 x -1 = -3
1	2 x -2 = -4
0	1 x -3 = -3
-1	0 x -4 = 0
-2	-1 x -5 = 5
-3	-2 x -6 = 12

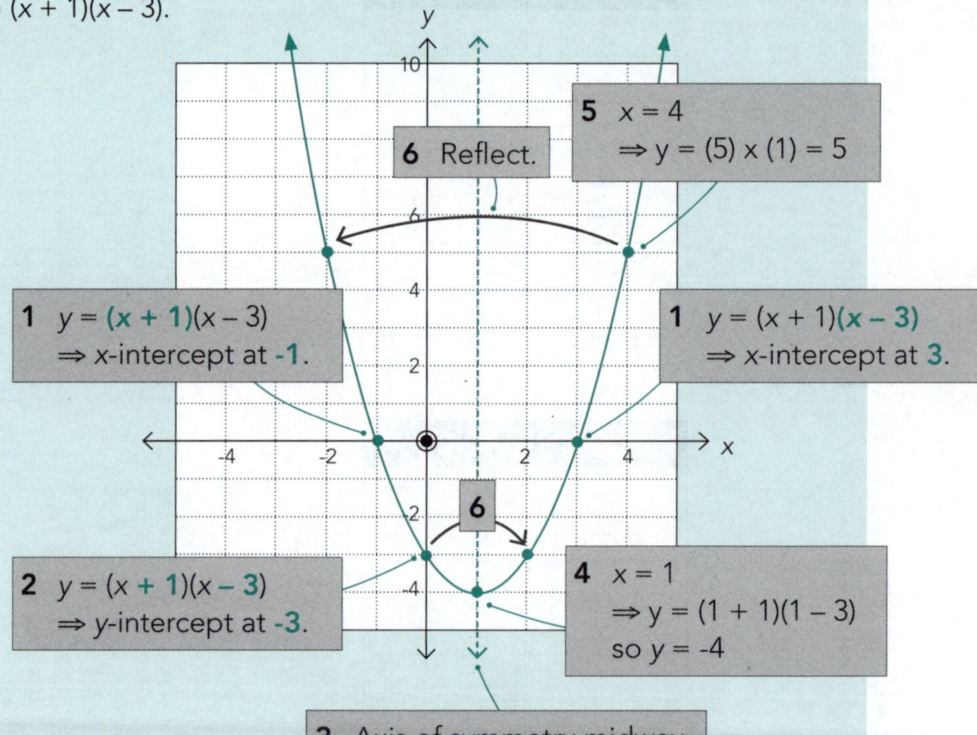

Method 2: If $\mathbf{y = (x + p)(x - q)}$, plot:

1 *x*-intercepts at -p and +q.
2 *y*-intercept at (+p) x (-q).
3 Axis of symmetry halfway between the *x*-intercepts.
4 Substitute *x* coordinate of axis of symmetry into equation to find turning point.
5 Substitute to find extra points.
6 Use the axis of symmetry and reflection to plot missing points.

2 Draw the graph of $y = -(x - 1)(x - 4)$.

1 *x*-intercepts at 1 and 4.

2 *y*-intercept at $-(-1) \times (-4) = -4$.

3 Axis of symmetry at $x = 2\frac{1}{2}$.

4 Turning point at

$y = -(1\frac{1}{2})(-1\frac{1}{2}) = 2\frac{1}{4}$

5 Extra point:
$x = 2 \longrightarrow y = -(1)(-2) = 2$

6 See arrows.

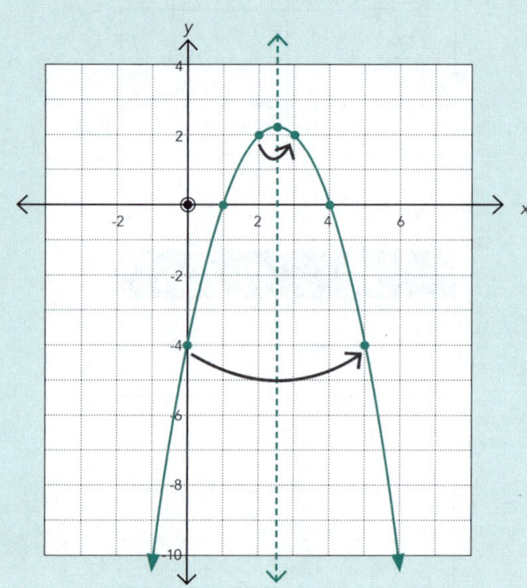

  ISBN: 9780170419376

3 Draw the graph of $y = \frac{1}{2}x(5 - x)$.

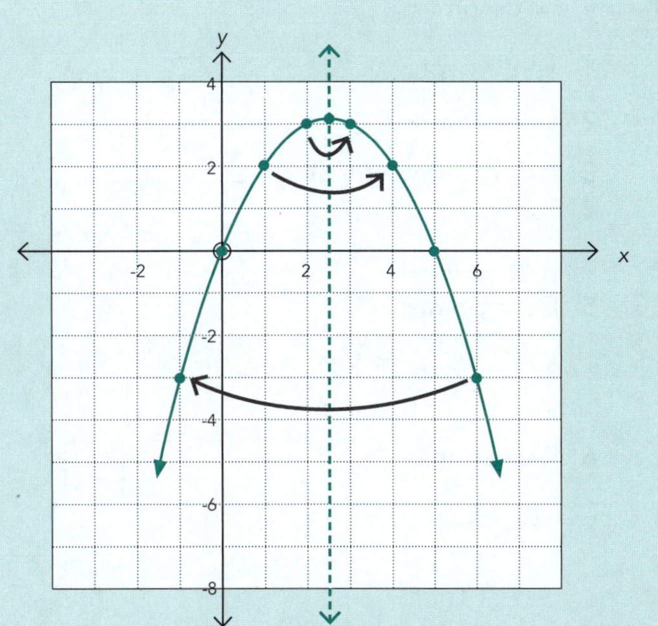

1 x-intercepts at 0 and 5.

2 y-intercept at $\frac{1}{2}(0) \times (5) = 0$.

3 Axis of symmetry at $x = 2\frac{1}{2}$.

4 Turning point at

$y = \frac{1}{2}(2\frac{1}{2})(2\frac{1}{2}) = 3\frac{1}{8}$

5 Extra points:

$x = 1 \Rightarrow y = \frac{1}{2}(1)(4) = 2$

$x = 2 \Rightarrow y = \frac{1}{2}(2)(3) = 3$

$x = 6 \Rightarrow y = \frac{1}{2}(6)(-1) = -3$

6 See arrows.

Draw graphs for the following equations.

1 $y = (x - 2)(x + 4)$

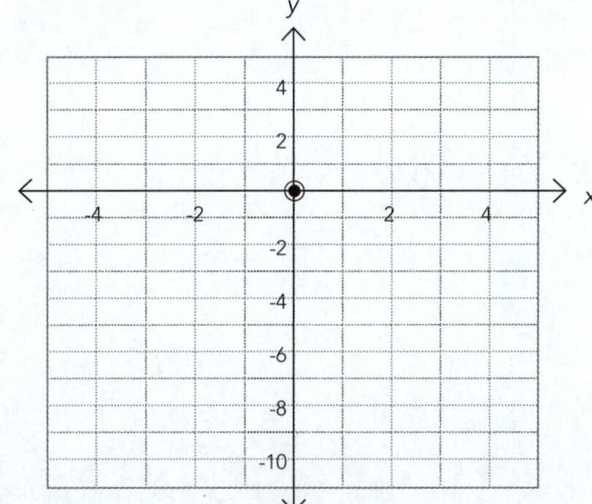

1 x-intercepts: ______________________

2 y-intercept: ______________________

3 Axis of symmetry at x = ____________

4 Turning point at

y = ______________________

5 Extra points:

x = ________ $\Rightarrow y$ =

x = ________ $\Rightarrow y$ =

6 Reflections.

2 $y = -(x + 2)(x - 4)$

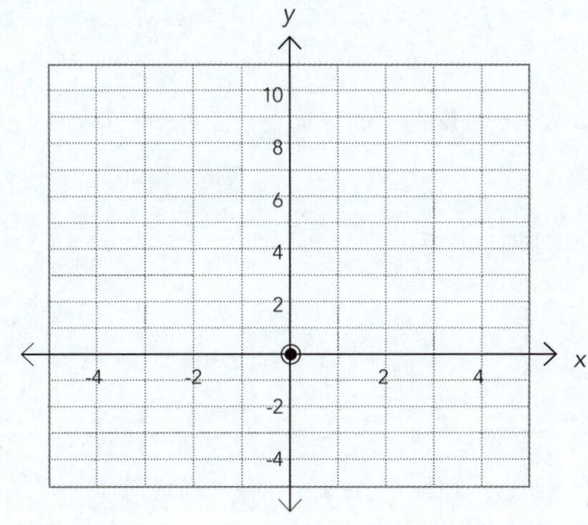

1 x-intercepts: ______________________

2 y-intercept: ______________________

3 Axis of symmetry at x = ____________

4 Turning point at

y = ______________________

5 Extra points:

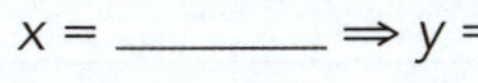

x = ________ $\Rightarrow y$ =

x = ________ $\Rightarrow y$ =

6 Reflections.

ISBN: 9780170419376

3 $y = x(x + 6)$

1 x-intercepts: ______________

2 y-intercept: ______________

3 Axis of symmetry at $x =$ ______________

4 Turning point at

$y =$ ______________

5 Extra points:

$x =$ ________ $\Rightarrow y =$

$x =$ ________ $\Rightarrow y =$

6 Reflections.

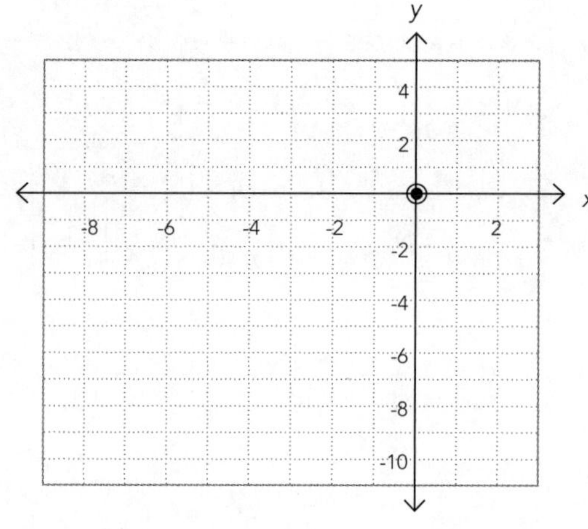

4 $y = -2x(x - 4)$

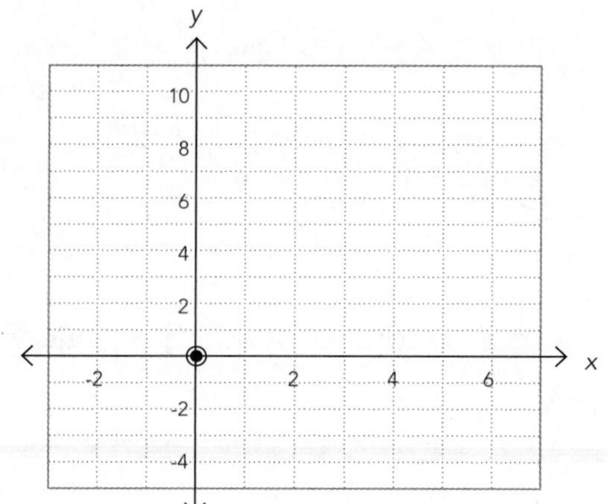

5 $y = \frac{1}{2}(x + 3)(x - 4)$

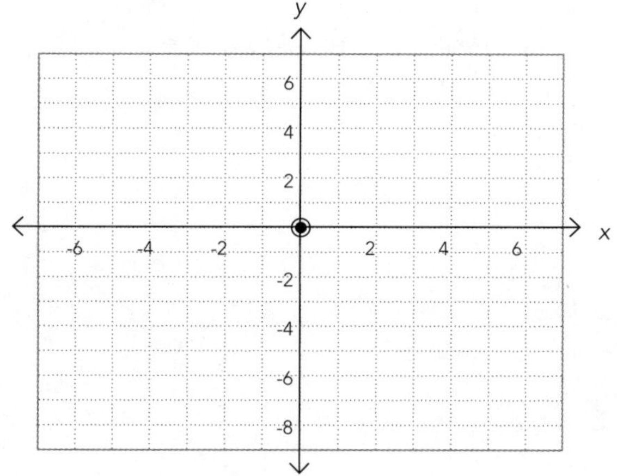

6 $y = (2x - 5)^2$

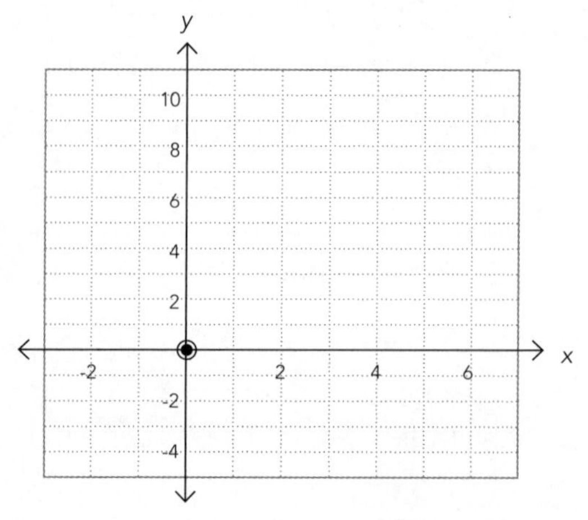

 ISBN: 9780170419376

Writing equations for parabolas

- Start by marking integral points through which the parabola passes.
- It will pass through *either* the x-intercepts 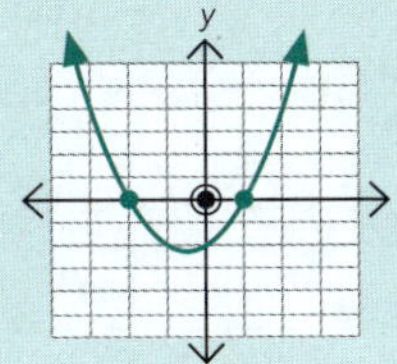 *or* the turning point. 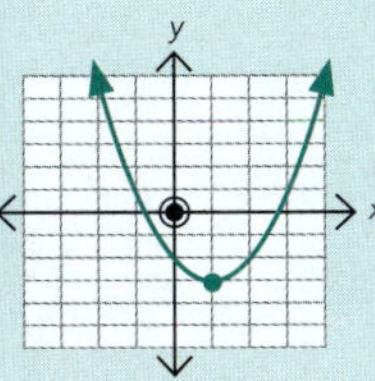

1 The x-intercepts

The equation takes the form $y = a(x \pm p)(x \pm q)$.

Write the equation of the following parabolas.

Examples:

1

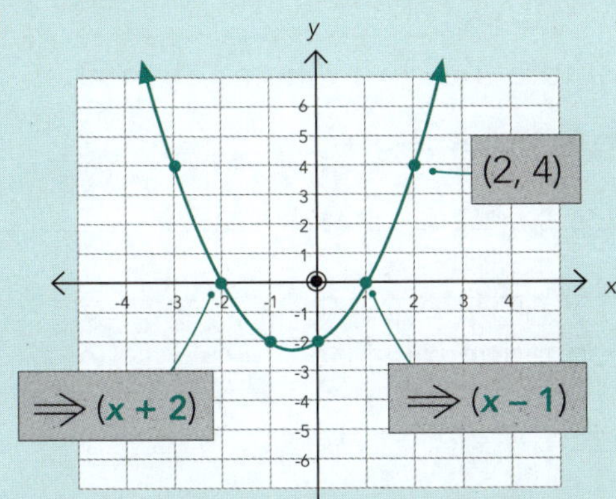

Steps:

1. Mark all the integral points (•).
2. x-intercepts ⇒ equation must be
   $y = a(x - 1)(x + 2)$
3. Substitute the co-ordinates of another integral point, e.g. (2, 4):
   $4 = a(2 - 1)(2 + 2)$
   $4 = 4a$
   $\therefore a = 1$

So the equation must be $y = (x - 1)(x + 2)$.

2

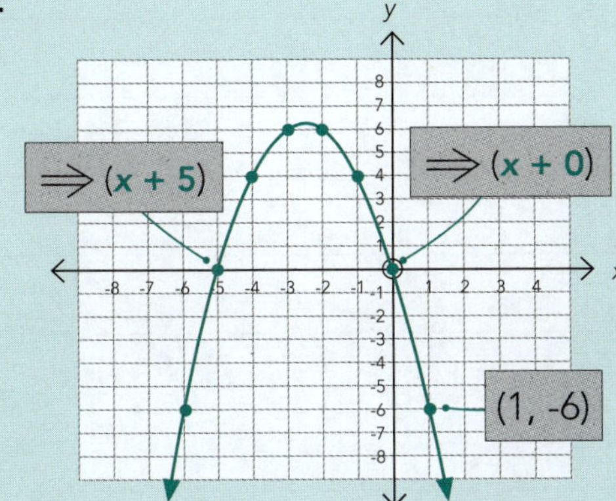

Steps:

1. Mark all the integral points (•).
2. x-intercepts ⇒ equation must be
   $y = a(x + 0)(x + 5) = ax(x + 5)$
3. Substitute the co-ordinates of another integral point, e.g. (1, -6):
   $-6 = a1(1 + 5)$
   $-6 = 6a$
   $\therefore a = -1$

So the equation must be $y = -x(x + 5)$.

3

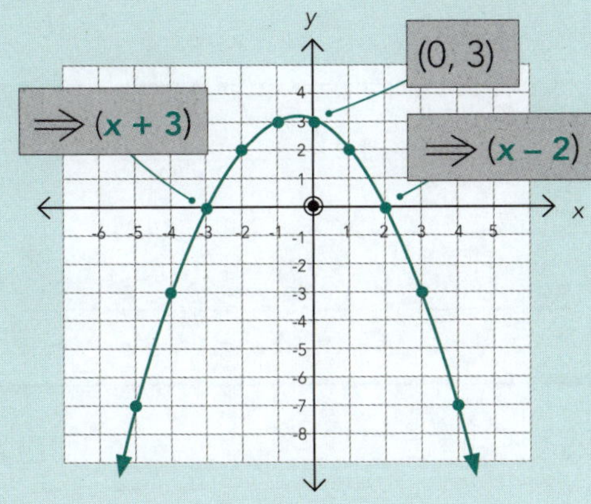

Steps:

1. Mark all the integral points (•).
2. x-intercepts ⇒ equation must be
   $y = a(x - 2)(x + 3)$
3. Substitute the co-ordinates of another integral point, e.g. (0, 3):
   $3 = a(0 - 2)(0 + 3)$
   $3 = -6a$
   $\therefore a = -\frac{1}{2}$

So the equation must be $y = -\frac{1}{2}(x - 2)(x + 3)$.

ISBN: 9780170419376

Write equations for the following parabolas.

1

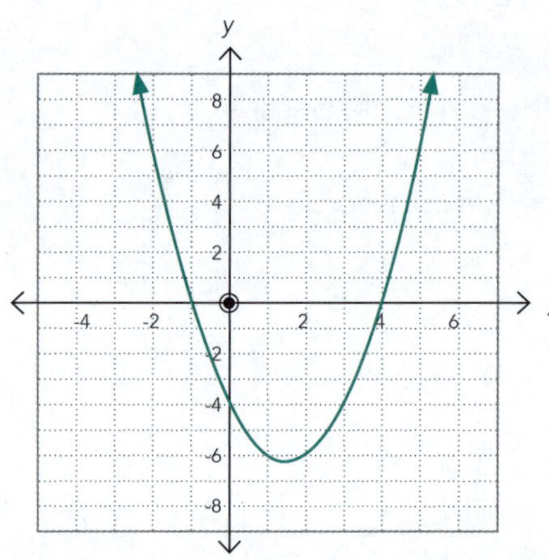

1 Mark all the integral points (•).
2 *x*-intercepts ⇒ equation must be

$y = a(x\_\_\_\_\_\_)(x\_\_\_\_\_\_)$

3 Substitute the co-ordinates of another integral point, e.g. (____, ____):

____

____

So the equation must be

y **=** __________________________

2

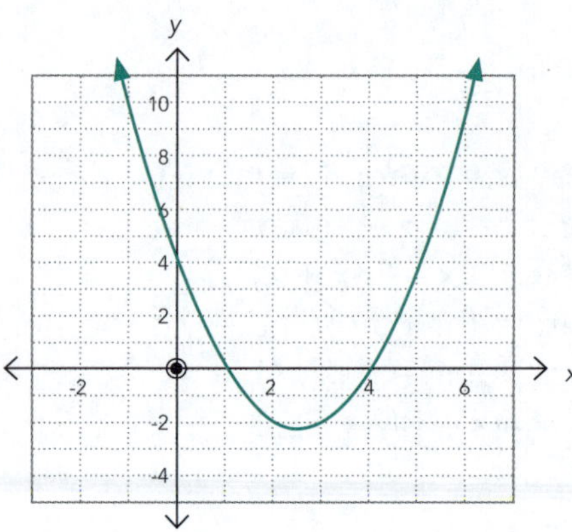

1 Mark all the integral points (•).
2 *x*-intercepts ⇒ equation must be

$y = a(x\_\_\_\_\_\_)(x\_\_\_\_\_\_)$

3 Substitute the co-ordinates of another integral point, e.g. (____, ____):

____

____

So the equation must be

y **=** __________________________

3

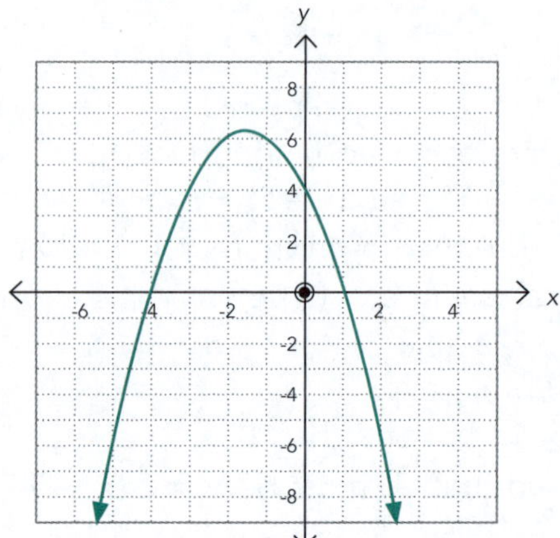

4

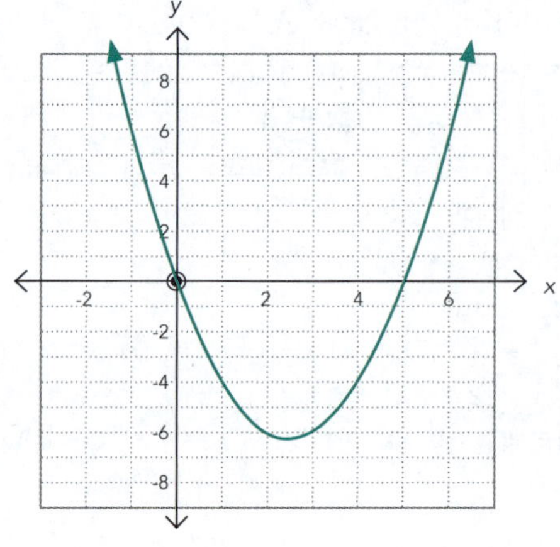

 ISBN: 9780170419376

5

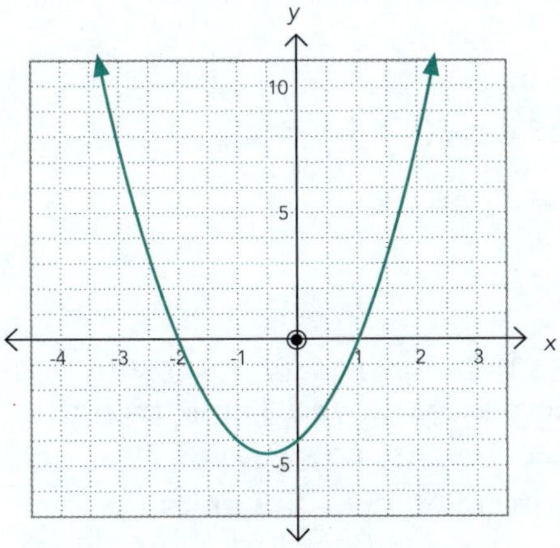
y
x
10
5
-5
-4
-3
-2
-1
1
2
3

6

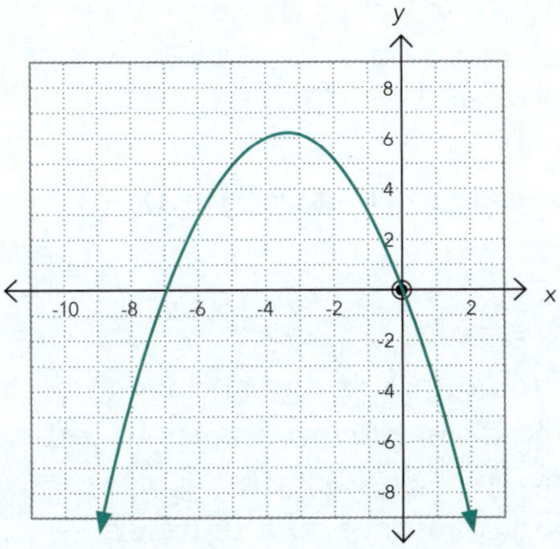
y
x
8
6
4
2
-2
-4
-6
-8
-10
-8
-6
-4
-2
2

7

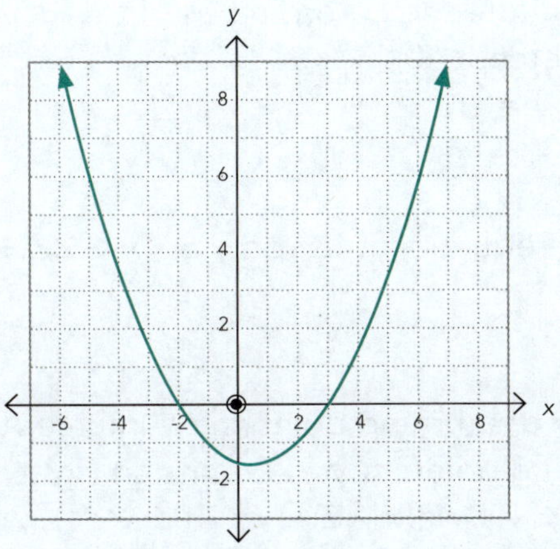
y
x
8
6
4
2
-2
-6
-4
-2
2
4
6
8

8

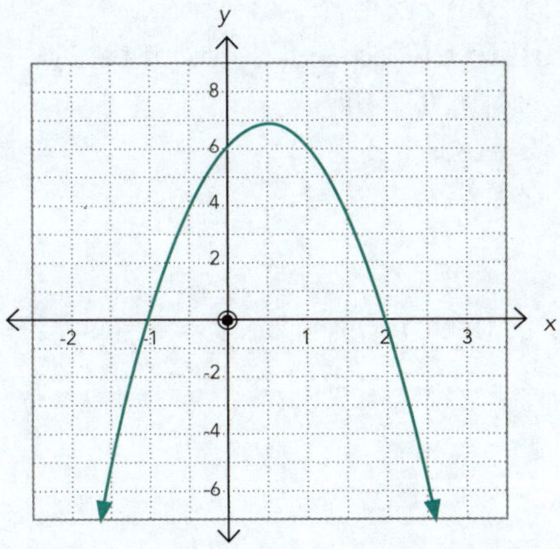
y
x
8
6
4
2
-2
-4
-6
-2
-1
1
2
3

2 The turning point

The equation takes the form $y = a(x \pm b)^2 \pm c$.

Write the equation of the following parabolas.

Examples:

1

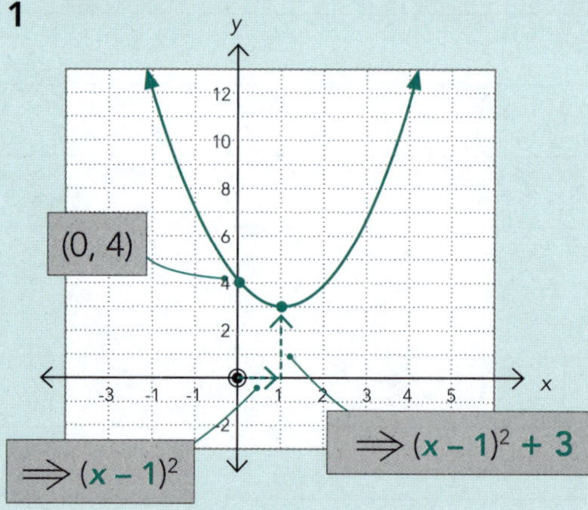

Steps:

1 Mark the turning point and *y*-intercept (•).

2 Turning point moved **1 unit to right**

$\Rightarrow y = a(x - 1)^2 \pm c$

3 Turning point moved **3 units up**

$\Rightarrow y = a(x - 1)^2 + 3$

4 Substitute the co-ordinates of the *y*-intercept, (0, 4):

$4 = a(0 - 1)^2 + 3$

$a = 1$

So the equation must be $y = (x - 1)^2 + 3$.

2

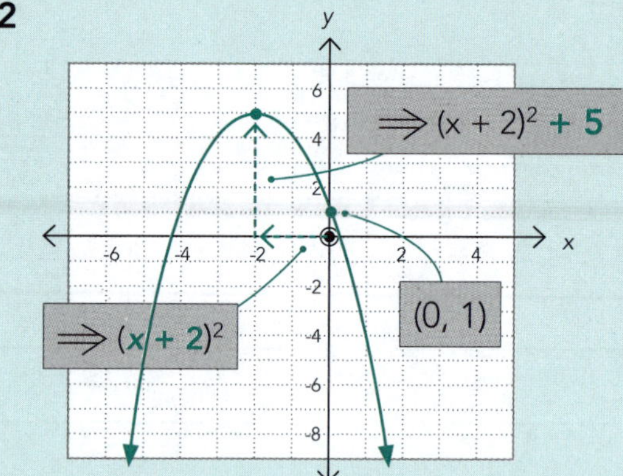

Steps:

1 Mark the turning point and *y*-intercept (•).

2 Turning point moved **2 units to left**

$\Rightarrow y = a(x + 2)^2 \pm c$

3 Turning point moved **5 units up**

$\Rightarrow y = a(x + 2)^2 + 5$

4 Substitute the co-ordinates of the *y*-intercept, (0, 1):

$1 = a(0 + 2)^2 + 5$

$-4 = 4a$

$a = -1$

So the equation must be $y = -(x + 2)^2 + 5$.

3

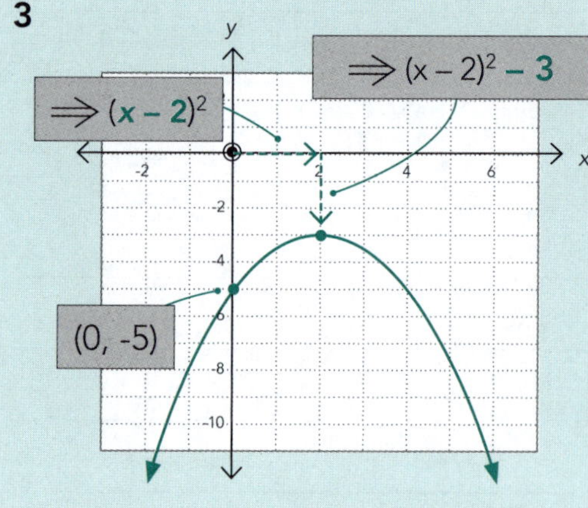

Steps:

1 Mark the turning point and *y*-intercept (•).

2 Turning point moved **2 units to right**

$\Rightarrow y = a(x - 2)^2 \pm c$

3 Turning point moved **3 units down**

$\Rightarrow y = a(x - 2)^2 - 3$

4 Substitute the co-ordinates of the *y*-intercept, (0, -5):

$-5 = a(0 - 2)^2 - 3$

$-2 = 4a$

$a = -\frac{1}{2}$

So the equation must be $y = -\frac{1}{2}(x - 2)^2 - 3$.

ISBN: 9780170419376

Write equations for the following parabolas.

1

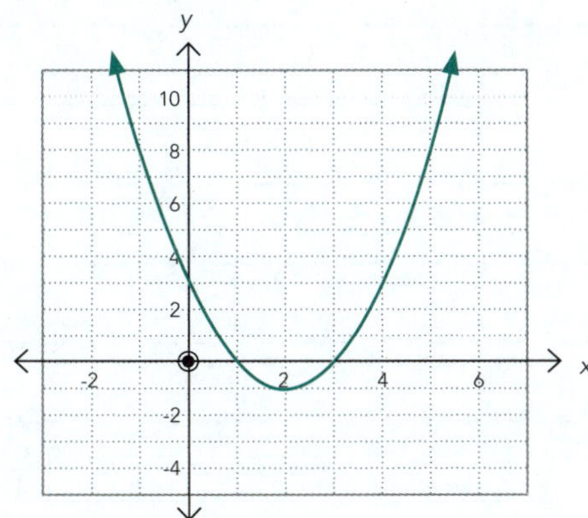

1 Mark all the integral points (•).

2 Turning point moved ___ unit(s) to ______

$y = a(x\_\_\_\_\_\_)^2 \pm c$

3 Turning point moved ___ unit(s) up/down

$y = a(x\_\_\_\_\_\_)^2$ ________

4 Substitute the co-ordinates of the *y*-intercept, (0, ___):

So the equation must be

y = ______________________________

2

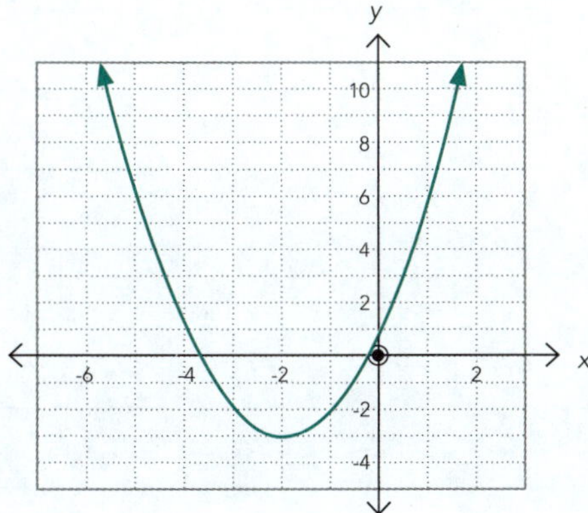

1 Mark all the integral points (•).

2 Turning point moved ___ unit(s) to ______

$y = a(x\_\_\_\_\_\_)^2 \pm c$

3 Turning point moved ___ unit(s) up/down

$y = a(x\_\_\_\_\_\_)^2$ ________

4 Substitute the co-ordinates of the *y*-intercept, (0, ___):

So the equation must be

y = ______________________________

3

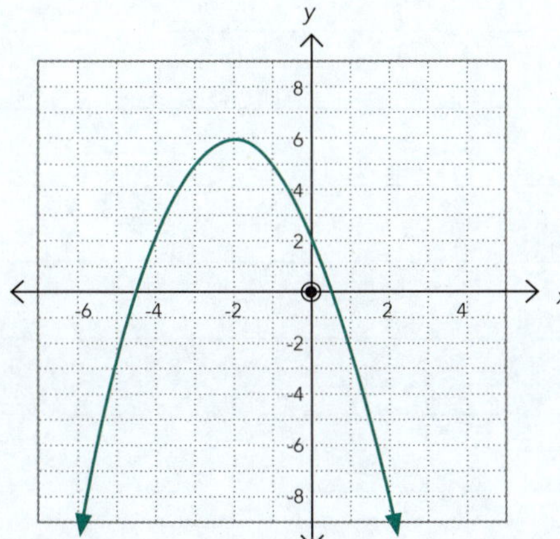

4

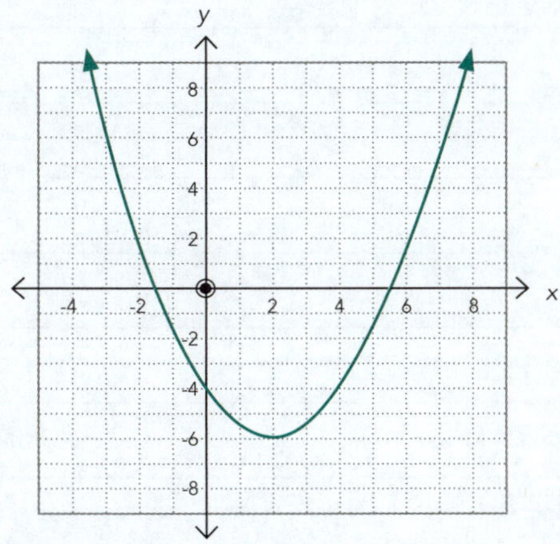

ISBN: 9780170419376

5

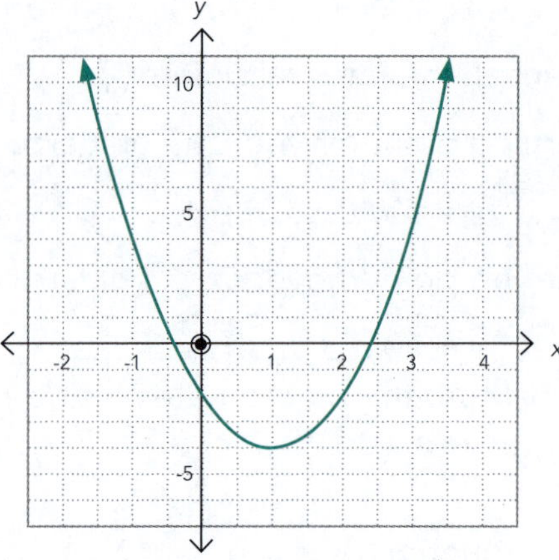

6

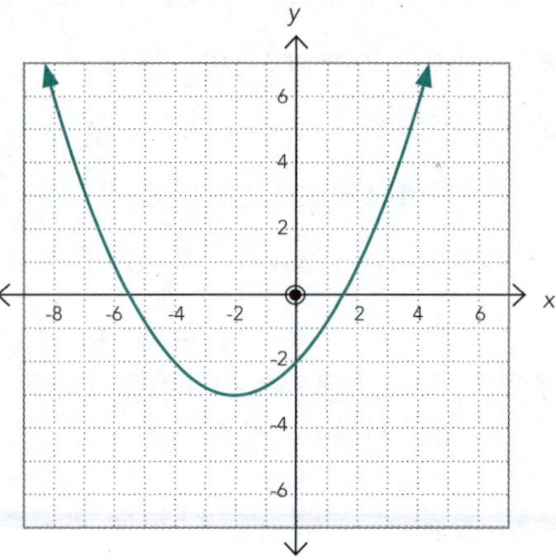

7

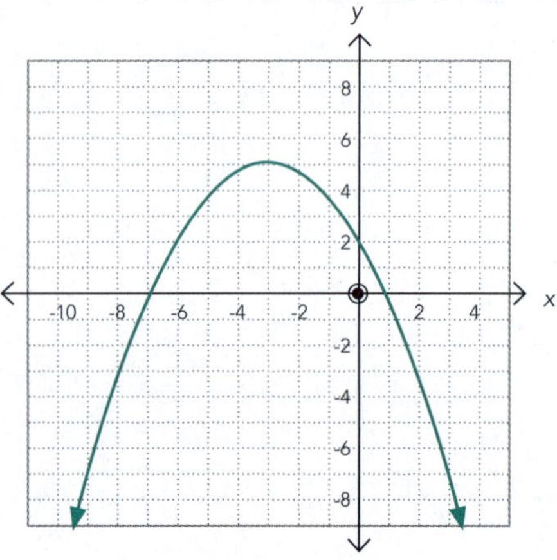

8

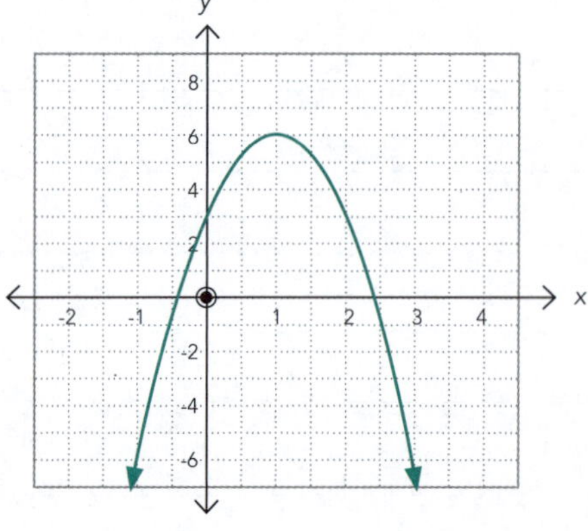

ISBN: 9780170419376

Translating, describing and comparing parabolas

- You need to be able to give the co-ordinates of important points on parabolas.

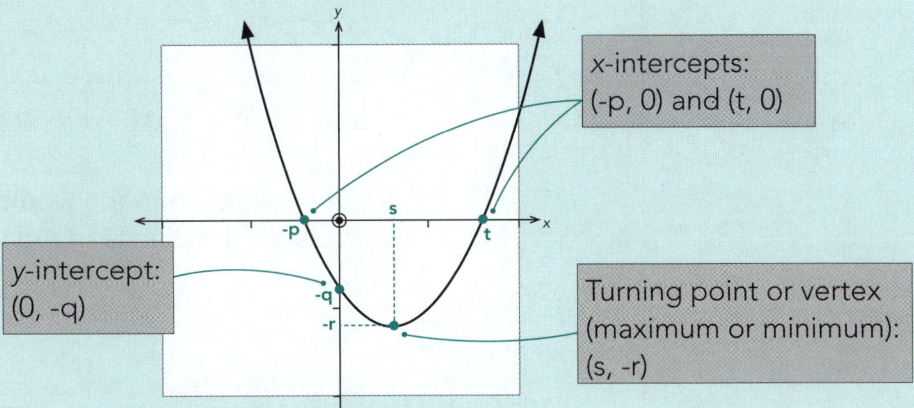

- You need to be able to compare parabolas using words.

Examples:

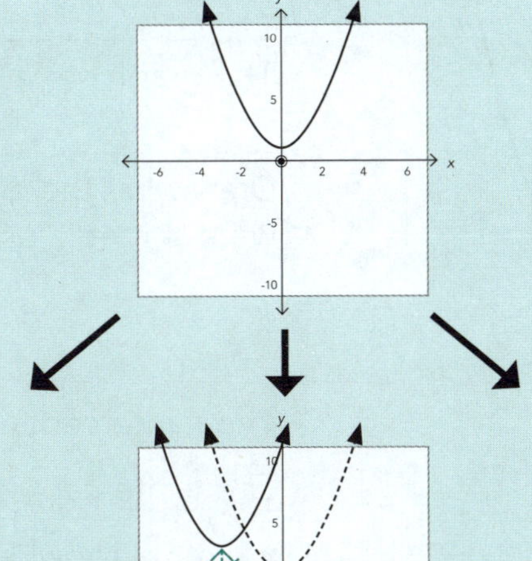

The graph has been **reflected** in the line $y = 1$.

The graph has been **translated left 3** units and **up 2** units.

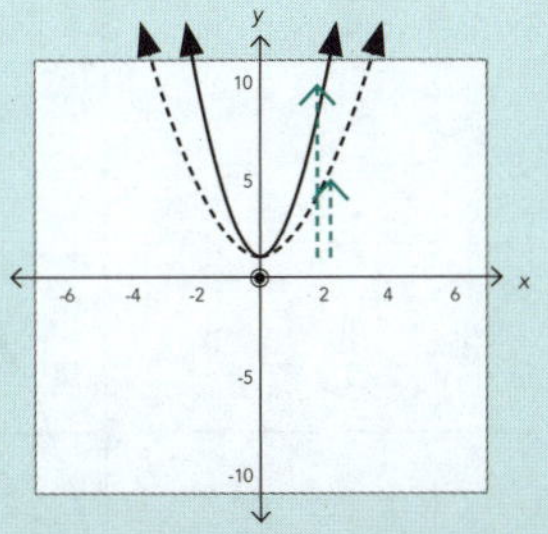

The graph goes up **twice as high**, or it is **twice as steep**.

- You need to be able to state the values of x where y is positive or negative.

Example:

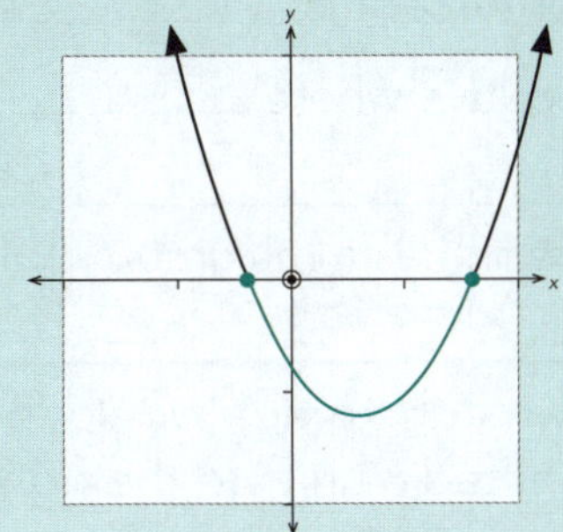

y is negative if x is between -2 and 8 (—) ($-2 < x < 8$).

y is positive if x is less than -2 or more than 8 (—) ($x < -2$ and $x > 8$).

ISBN: 9780170419376

Fill in the spaces below and draw the graphs required.

1

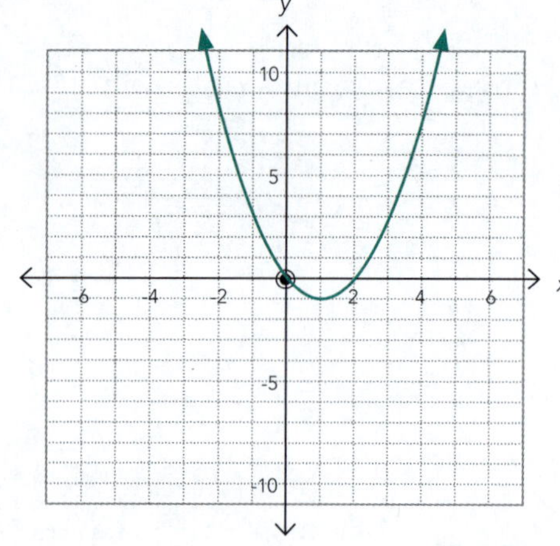

The x-intercepts are:________________

The y-intercept is: ________________

y is negative where:________________

____

The graph has a minimum point where:

____

Draw what the graph would look like if it were shifted 3 units to the left and 2 units down.

2

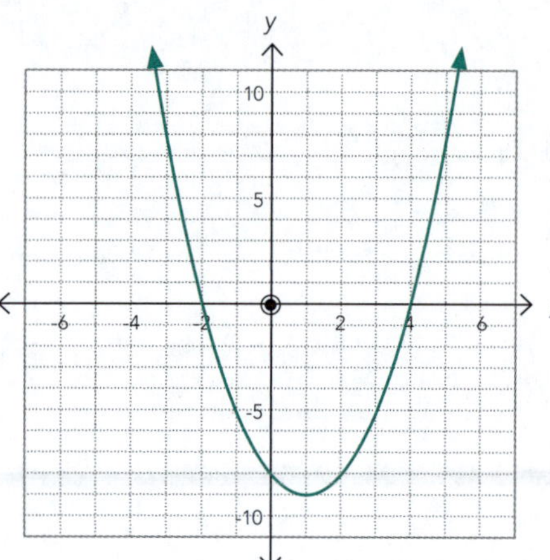

The x-intercepts are:________________

The y-intercept is: ________________

y is negative where:________________

____

The graph has a vertex where:

____

Draw what the graph would look like if it were shifted 2 units to the left and 3 units up.

3

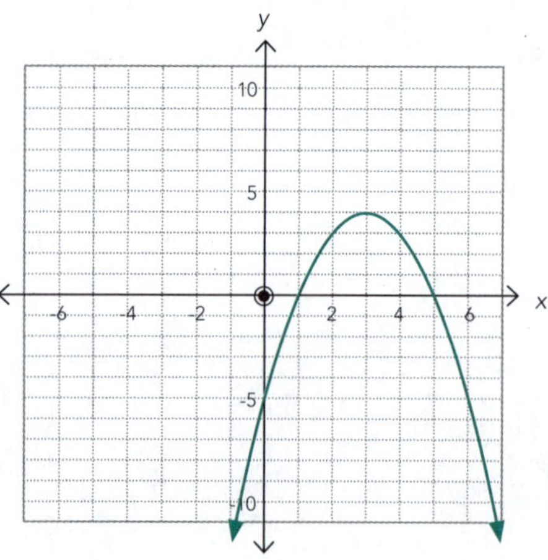

The x-intercepts are:________________

The y-intercept is: ________________

y is negative where:________________

____

The graph has a vertex where:

____

Draw what the graph would look like if it were shifted 3 units to the left and 1 unit down.

4

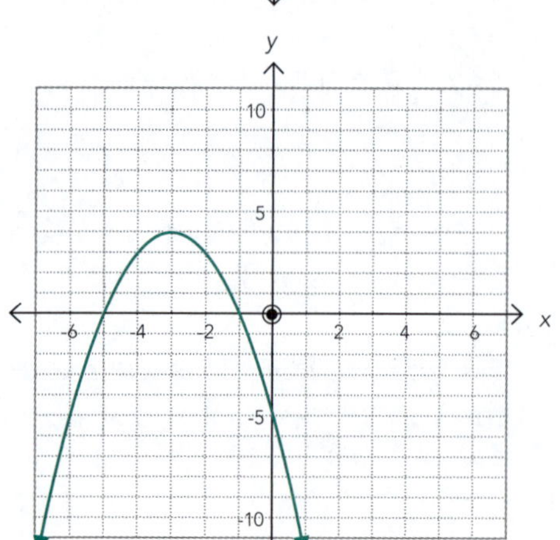

The x-intercepts are:________________

The y-intercept is: ________________

y is negative where:________________

____

The graph has a maximum point where:

____

Draw what the graph would look like if it were shifted 6 units to the right and 1 unit up.

ISBN: 9780170419376

Describe in words how the green graph compares with the black graph.

5

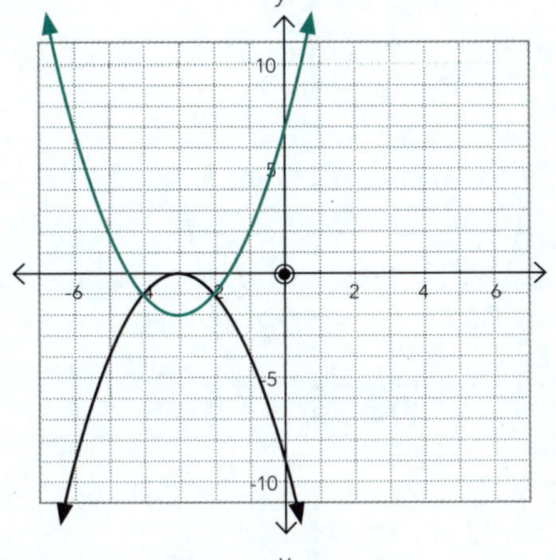

6

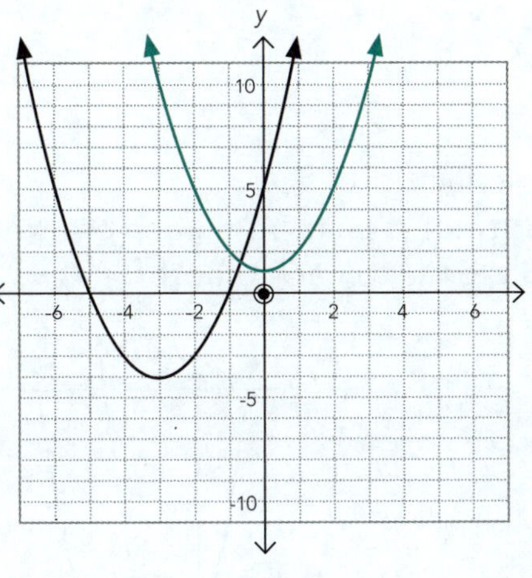

7

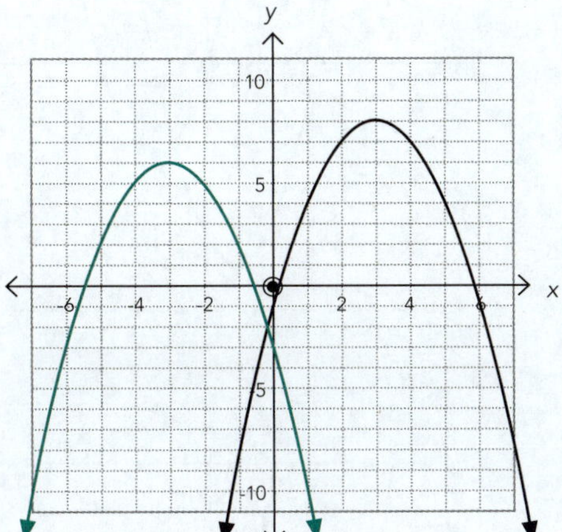

8

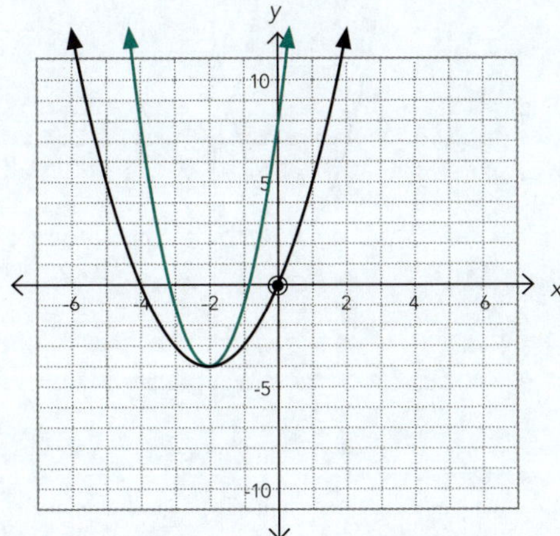

Writing equations for translated parabolas

1 To move a parabola up or down, add or subtract the required number of units.

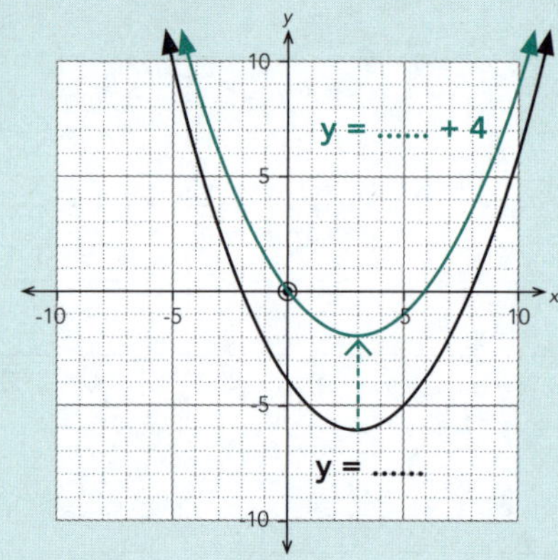

or

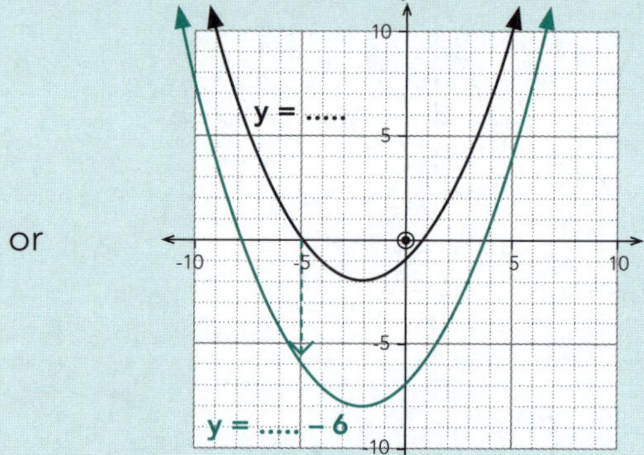

2 To move a parabola to the left or right:
Step 1: If it is not in factorised form, if possible factorise it.
Step 2: If it is moving p units to the **right**, **subtract** p units from each bracket.
If it is moving p units to the **left**, **add** p units to each bracket.

Examples:

1 Translate the graph of $y = (x - 2)(x + 4)$ **to the right 3 units** and **5 units up**.

$y = (x - 2)(x + 4)$ becomes $y = (x - 5)(x + 1) + 5$

3 units to the right ⇒ – 3

5 units up ⇒ add 5

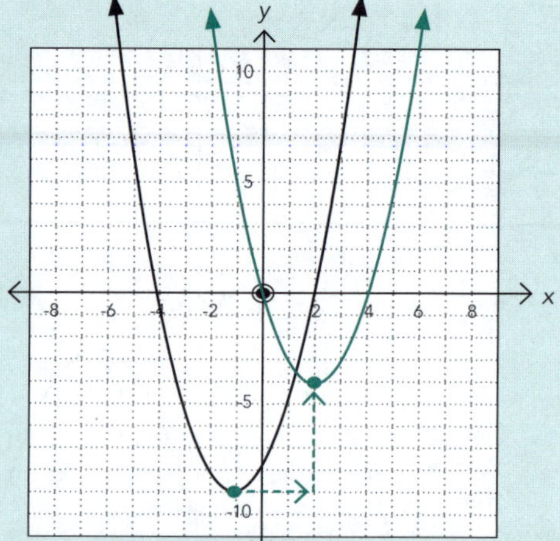

2 Translate the graph of $y = x^2 - 2x$ **to the left 4 units** and **3 units down**.

$y = x^2 - 2x = x(x - 2)$
$y = x(x - 2)$ becomes $y = (x + 4)(x + 2) - 3$

4 units to the left ⇒ + 4

3 units down ⇒ subtract 3

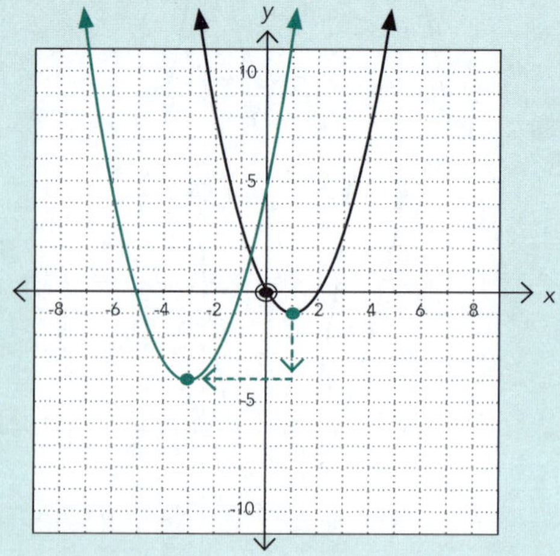

ISBN: 9780170419376

Draw the original graph, then draw the translated graph and write its equation.

1 $y = (x + 2)(x - 4)$ and translate it 3 units to the left and 6 units up.

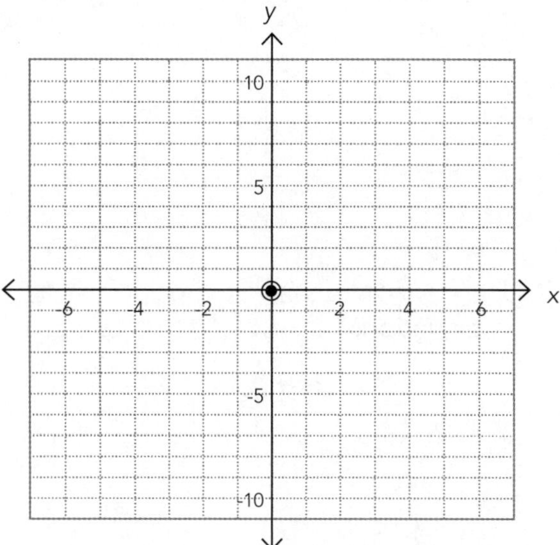

Equation: ______________________

2 $y = -(x - 2)(x + 4)$ and translate it 5 units to the right and 4 units down.

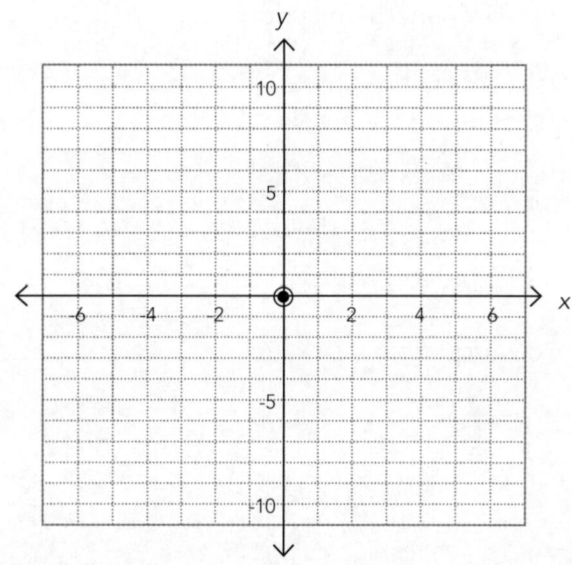

Equation: ______________________

3 $y = -x^2 + 4x$ and translate it 5 units to the left and 3 units down.

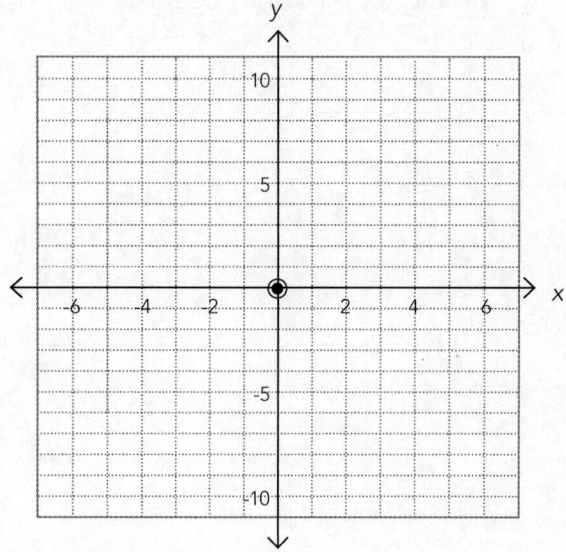

Equation: ______________________

ISBN: 9780170419376

4 $y = x^2 - 5$ and translate it 2 units to the right and 4 units up.

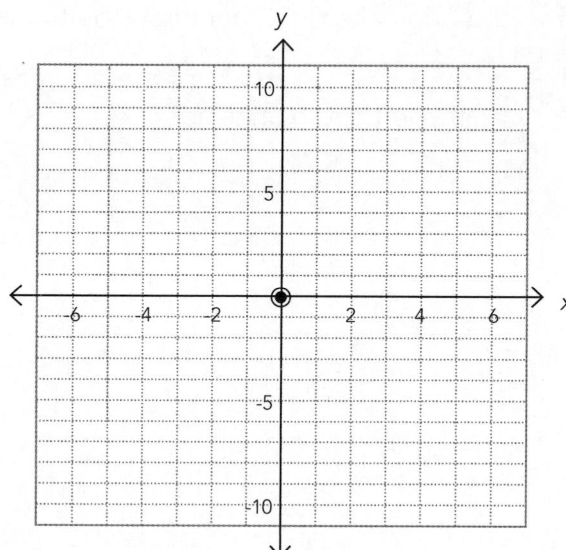

Equation: ______________________

5 $y = 7 - x^2$ and translate it 3 units to the left and 5 units down.

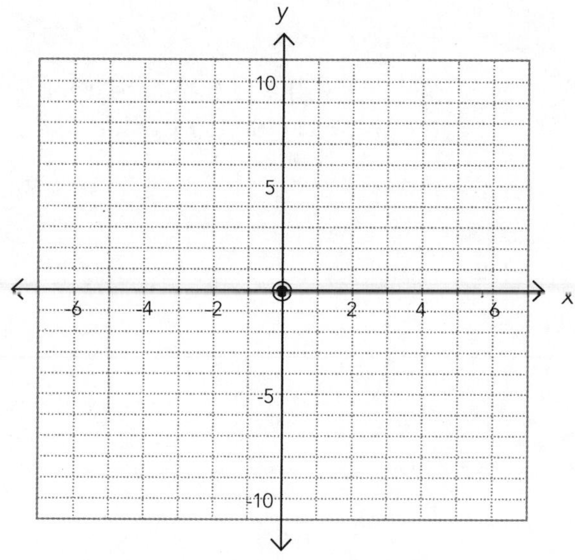

Equation: ______________________

6 $y = x^2 - 2x - 3$ and translate it 2 units to the right and 4 units up.

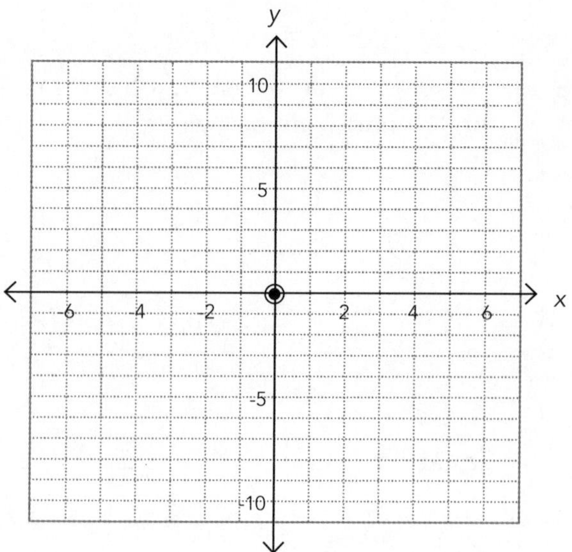

Equation: ______________________

ISBN: 9780170419376

Applications

Examples:

1 A feature of a skateboard park is to be modelled on a parabolic shape. It has a width of 10 m and its greatest depth is 0.5 m.

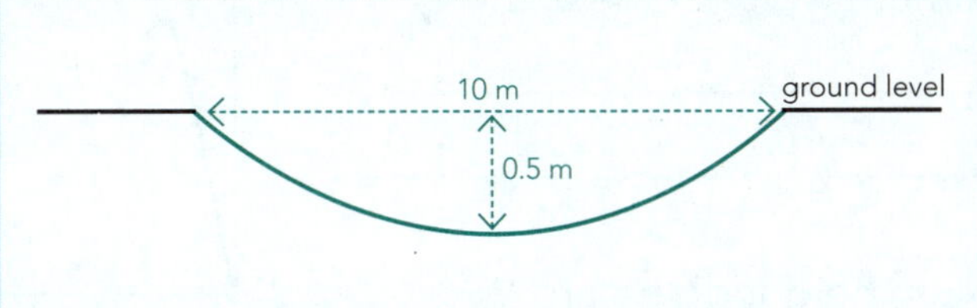

If ground level is represented by the *x*-axis, and the *y*-axis is at the left edge of the curved surface, calculate the equation for the parabola.

The parabola has *x*-intercepts where $x = 0$ and $x = 10$

$\Rightarrow$ equation must be $y = ax(x - 10)$

By symmetry, its greatest depth (0.5) must be at the turning point where $x = 5$

$\Rightarrow$ $-0.5 = a(5)(5 - 10)$

$-0.5 = -25a$

$a = 0.02$

$\therefore$ Equation is $y = 0.02x(x - 10)$.

2 The weight of apples that Morris picks in his orchard follows a quadratic model, $y = -0.01x(x - 16)$, where y is the weight in tonnes that is picked on any day, and *x* is the number of days since he started picking.

a For how many days does he pick apples?

He picks apples for 16 days, because if $x > 16$, the value of *y* becomes negative.

b On which day did he pick the most apples?

He picks the most apples on day 8 because $y = -0.01x(x - 16)$ forms an inverted parabola with *x*-intercepts at 0 and 16, so the midpoint must be halfway between those.

c What weight of apples was picked on the day when he picked the most?

On day 8 he picked $-0.01(8)(8 - 16) = 0.64$ tonnes.

d On which days did he pick 0.55 tonnes?

$$0.55 = -0.01x(x - 16)$$
$$55 = -x(x - 16)$$

so $x = 5$ or 11, so he picked 0.55 tonnes on days 5 and 11.

Answer the following.

1 A decorative arch is to be constructed for a party. It is parabolic, with a 1 m long horizontal row of lights below the highest point. The equation of the parabola is $y = -2.8x(x - 2)$.

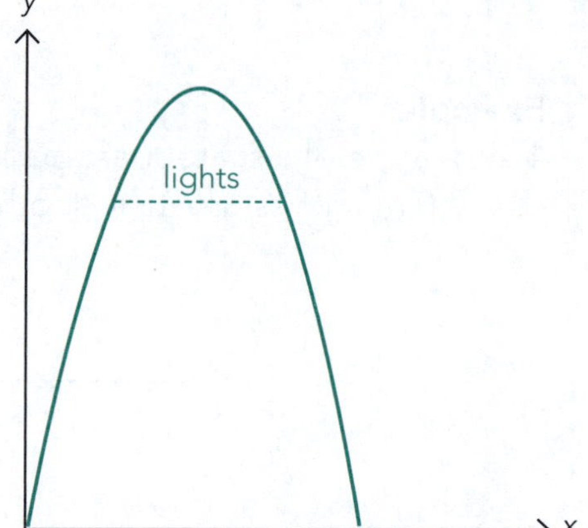

a Calculate the maximum width of the archway.

b What is the maximum height of the arch?

c Calculate the height of the horizontal row of lights.

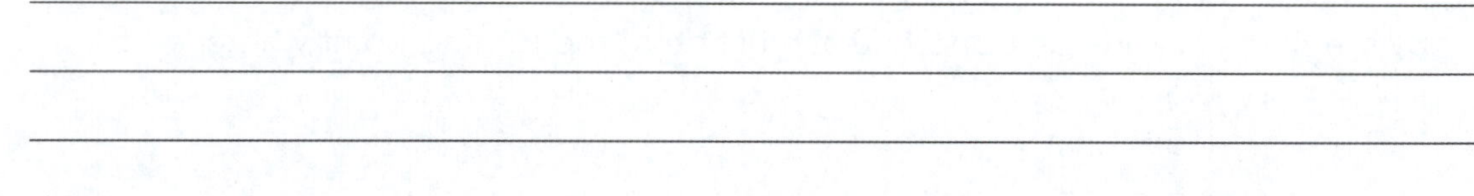

2 The base of on ornamental pond is modelled by the function $y = 0.1x(x - 8)$, where y is its depth (m) below ground level, and x represents the distance (m) from the left edge.

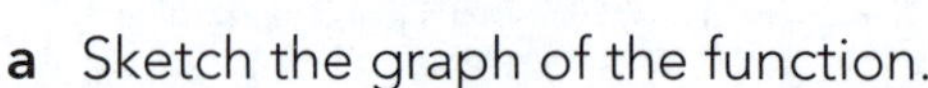

a Sketch the graph of the function.

b Calculate the maximum depth of the pond.

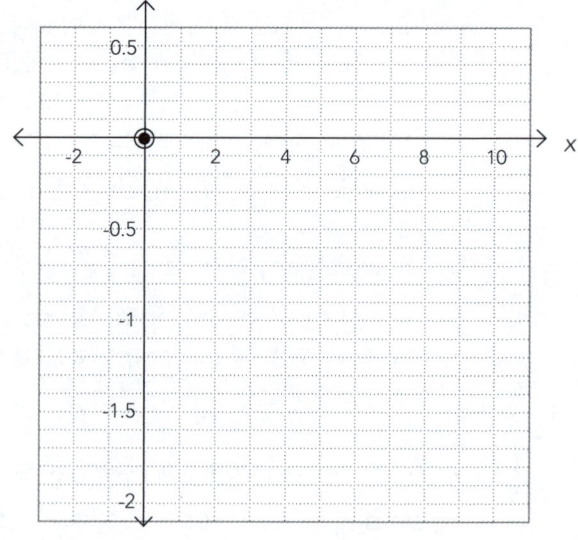

c How deep is the pond 1.5 m from the edge?

d If the width surface of the water is 7 m, calculate its distance below ground level.

ISBN: 9780170419376

3 As part of a confidence course, a rope is hung from points 6 m apart on a bar. It forms a parabolic curve. The lowest point on the rope is 2 m below the bar.

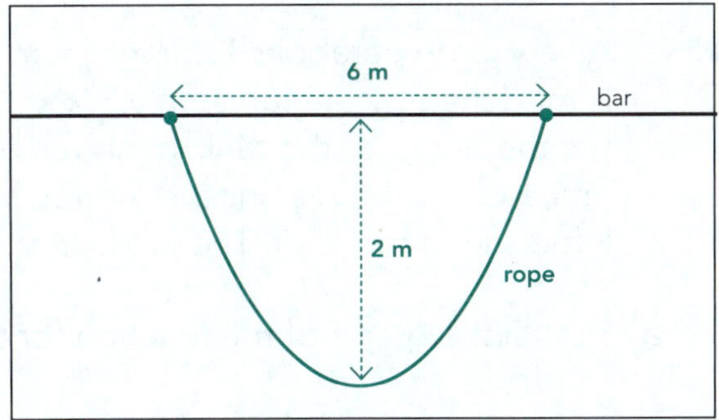

a If the left end of the rope is at the origin, find the equation for the parabola.

b Tane is standing on the bar at a point that is midway between the point of attachment and the point above the rope's lowest point. How far below his feet is the rope?

4 On another part of the confidence course, a rope is hung from two tree branches at points that are exactly 2 m above the ground. At its lowest point, the rope is 2 m horizontally from its point of attachment and 1 m above ground level.

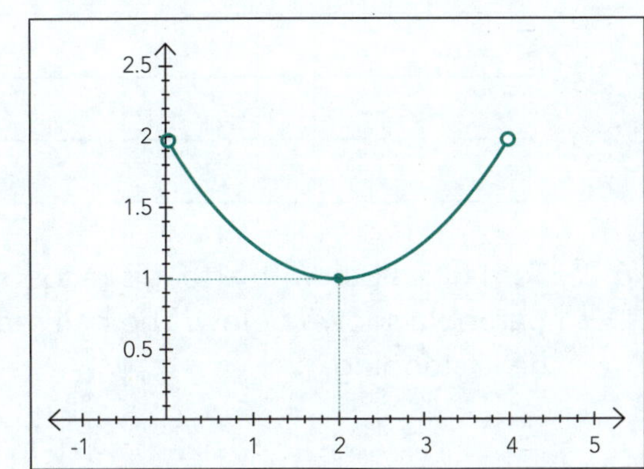

a Find the equation for the parabolic curve of the rope.

b Amy is 1.54 m high. If she stands at the point (0.5, 0), will her head touch the rope?

c The rope was tightened so that its lowest point was 1.5 m above the ground. Find the equation for the new parabolic curve of the rope.

ISBN: 9780170419376

5 A very large parabolic fish tank in an aquarium is modelled by the function $y = x(x - 3)$, where y is the depth of the tank in metres below the rim, and x is the distance in metres from the left edge of the tank. The rim is at the x-axis.

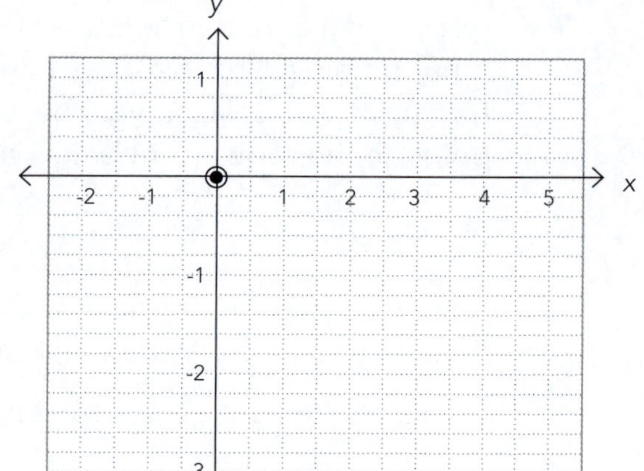

a Sketch the graph of the function for the tank.

b What is the maximum depth of the tank?

____

____

c The bottom of the tank will be filled with shingle. It will be filled to a level 2 m below the rim. Find the width of the top surface of the shingle.

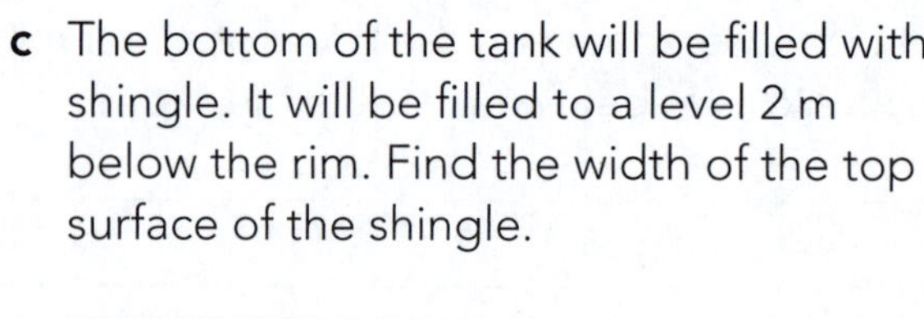

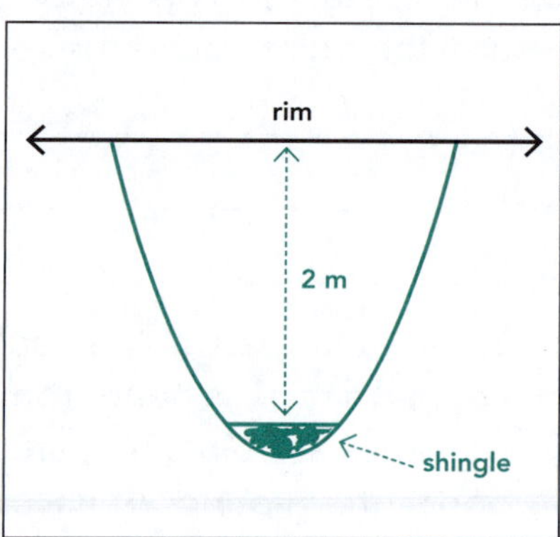

____

____

____

____

____

6 Tom hits a ball with a tennis racquet from a point on the y-axis, and it follows the parabola shown below. The ball reaches a peak of 5 m when it is 8 m away from where he is standing.

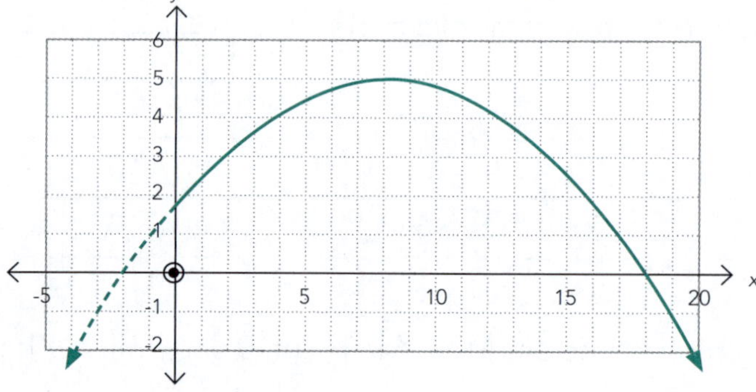

a Write the equation for the path of the ball.

____

____

b From what height did he hit the ball?

____

____

c How high was the ball when it was 4 m from where he was standing?

____

____

ISBN: 9780170419376

7 Freddie wants to make a triangular paddock for his calves. He uses an existing fence for one side of the paddock. For the other two sides he uses a total of 100 m electric fence wire. The paddock is in the shape of a right-angled triangle.

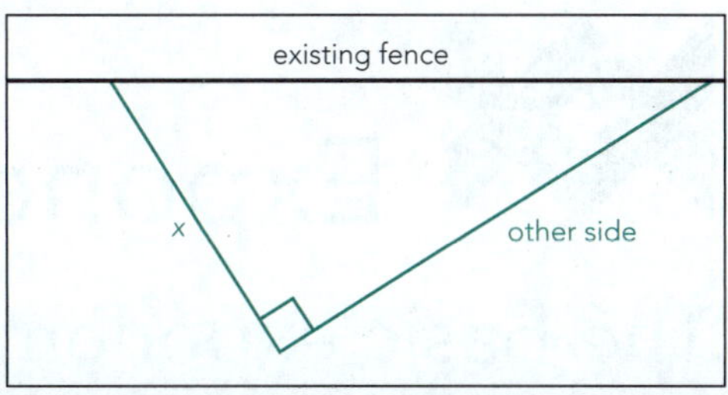

a The area of the paddock will depend on the length of x. The table shows some values that x could take. Complete the table using at least two different values for x.

x	Other side	Area (A)
10	90	450
20	80	800
30	70	1050

b The area of a right-angled triangle is given by
$A = \frac{1}{2}$(base)(height).
Write an equation in terms of A and x for calculating the area of the triangular paddock.

c How long is the shortest side when the area is at its maximum? Calculate the maximum area he can fence for his pigs.

8 A tunnel is constructed in a parabolic shape. Its left edge is 1 m from a marker post. At its peak, it is 9 m high, and this occurs 4 m horizontally from the marker post.

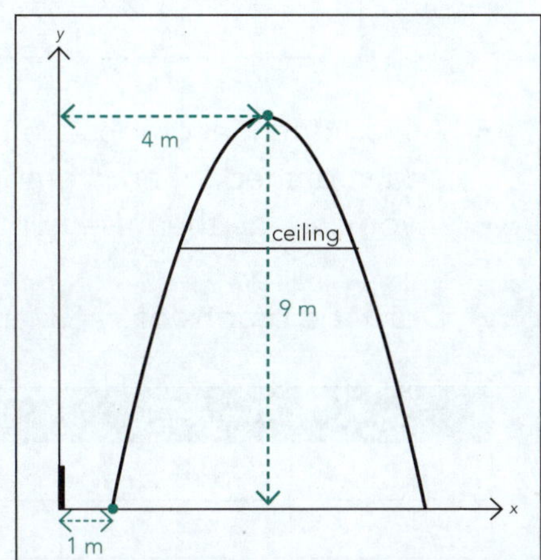

a Write an equation for this parabolic shape.

b How wide is the tunnel at ground level?

c A ceiling is constructed within the tunnel. It is 3.4642 m wide. At what height is the ceiling constructed?

ISBN: 9780170419376

Exponential graphs

The basic exponential graph, $y = p^x$

If you don't know what the graph looks like:

1 make a table
2 plot the points
3 join the points to form a smooth curve.

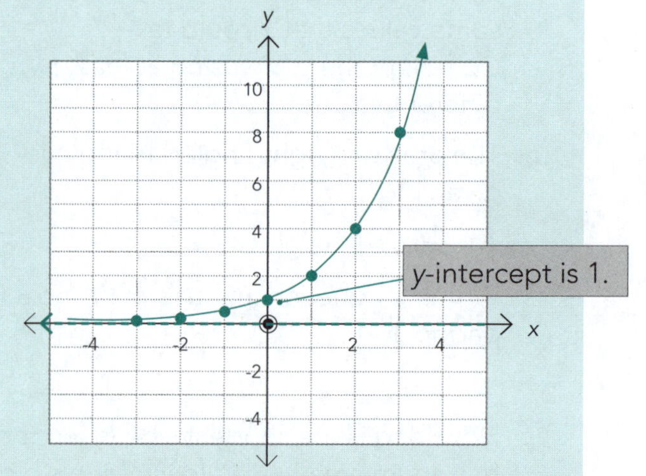

The curve approaches the x-axis very closely, but never reaches it. Such a line is called an **asymptote**.

Examples:

1 Draw the graph of $y = 2^x$.

x	y
3	$2^3 = 8$
2	$2^2 = 4$
1	$2^1 = 2$
0	$2^0 = 1$
-1	$2^{-1} = \frac{1}{2}$
-2	$2^{-2} = \frac{1}{2^2} = \frac{1}{4}$
-3	$2^{-3} = \frac{1}{2^3} = \frac{1}{8}$

(Going up the table, each value is x 2 the one below.)

- All exponential graphs are this shape, but they can be shifted, turned upside down and stretched, or any combination of these.
- If you change the base number, you change the shape of the curve.

2 Draw the graphs of $y = 3^x$ and $y = 5^x$.

x	$y = 3^x$	$y = 5^x$
3	$3^3 = 27$	$5^3 = 125$
2	$3^2 = 9$	$5^2 = 25$
1	$3^1 = 3$	$5^1 = 5$
0	$3^0 = 1$	$5^0 = 1$
-1	$3^{-1} = \frac{1}{3}$	$5^{-1} = \frac{1}{5}$
-2	$3^{-2} = \frac{1}{3^2} = \frac{1}{9}$	$5^{-2} = \frac{1}{5^2} = \frac{1}{25}$
-3	$3^{-3} = \frac{1}{3^3} = \frac{1}{27}$	$5^{-3} = \frac{1}{5^3} = \frac{1}{125}$

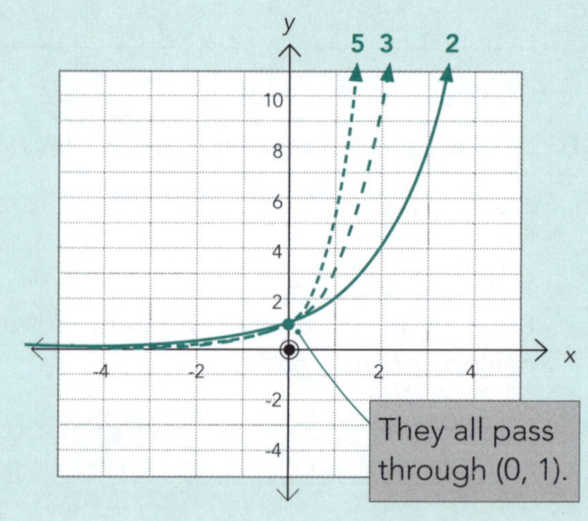

ISBN: 9780170419376

Translated exponential graphs

1 Vertical translation, $y = p^x \pm c$

Examples:

1 Draw the graph of $y = 2^x + 1$.

x	y
3	9
2	5
1	3
0	2
-1	$1\frac{1}{2}$
-2	$1\frac{1}{4}$
-3	$1\frac{1}{8}$

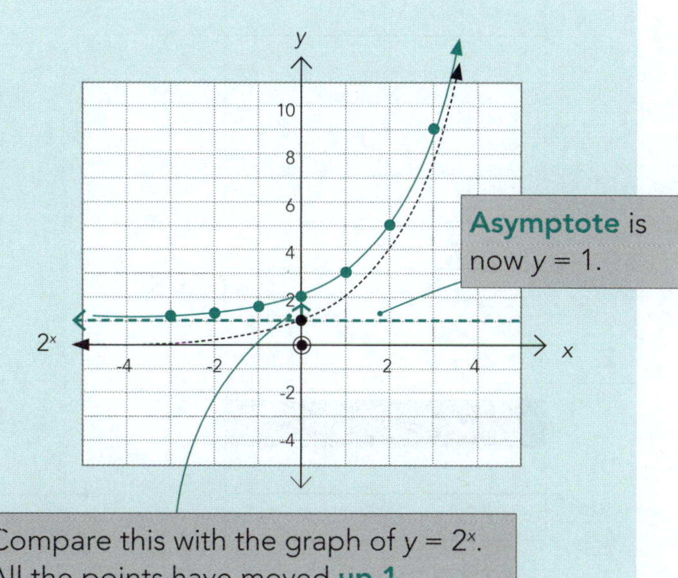

2 Draw the graph of $y = 2^x - 2$.

x	y
3	6
2	2
1	0
0	-1
-1	$-1\frac{1}{2}$
-2	$-1\frac{3}{4}$
-3	$-1\frac{7}{8}$

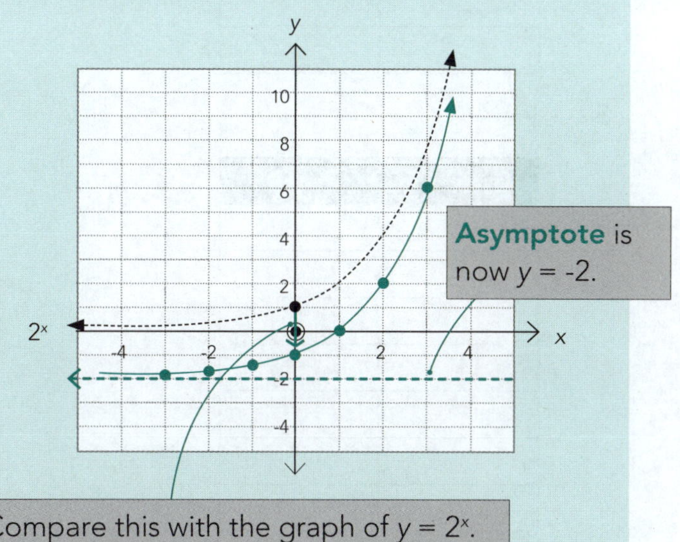

For graphs in the form $y = p^x \pm c$:
c is like an elevator — it moves the graph up or down by c units.
c also tells you where the horizontal asymptote is.

Complete the tables and draw graphs for the following equations.

1 $y = 2^x + 3$

x	y
2	
1	
0	
-1	
-2	
-3	
-4	

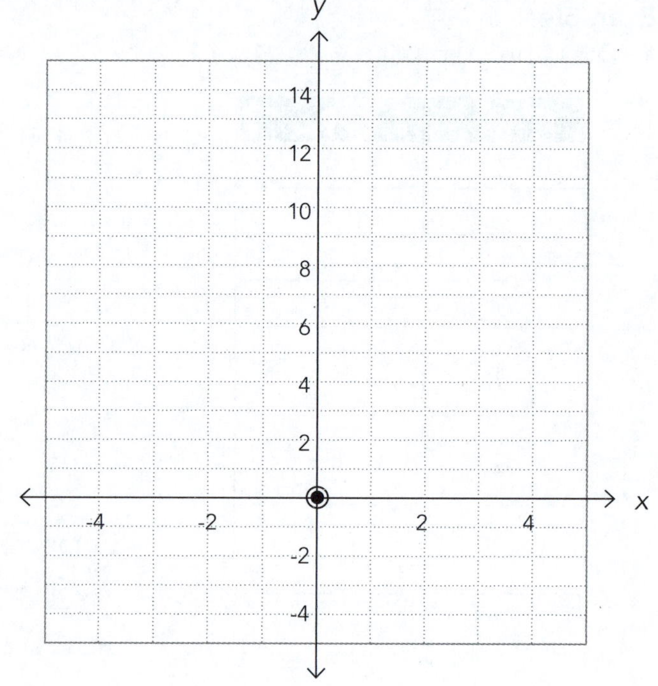

2 $y = 2^x - 1$

x	y
3	
2	
1	
0	
-1	
-2	
-3	

3 $y = 4^x$

x	y

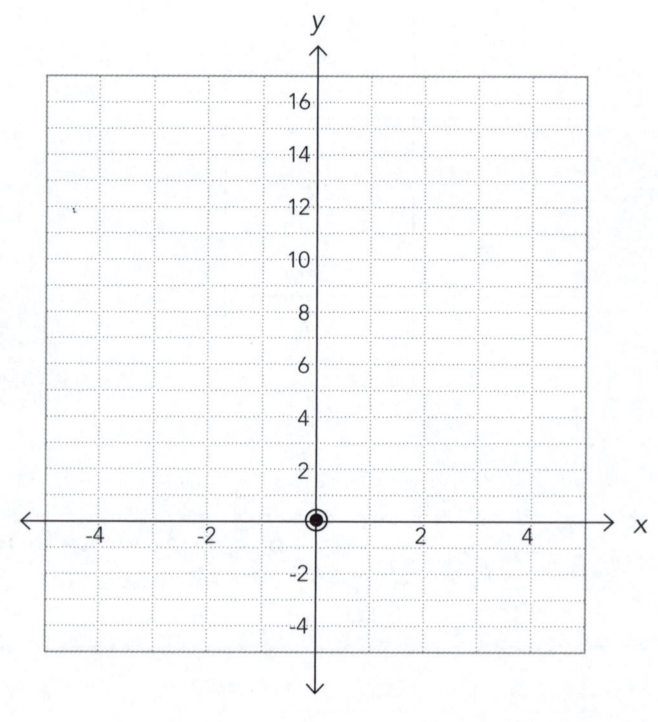

4 $y = 3^x - 4$

x	y

ISBN: 9780170419376

2 Horizontal translation, $y = p^{(x \pm b)}$

Examples:

1 Draw the graph of $y = 2^{(x+1)}$.

x	y
3	$2^4 = 16$
2	$2^3 = 8$
1	$2^2 = 4$
0	$2^1 = 2$
-1	$2^0 = 1$
-2	$2^{-1} = \frac{1}{2}$
-3	$2^{-2} = \frac{1}{2^2} = \frac{1}{4}$

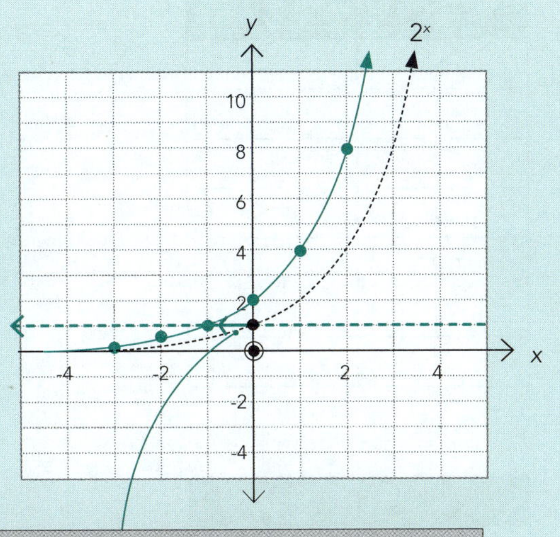

Compare this with the graph of $y = 2^x$.
All the points have moved **left 1**.

2 Draw the graph of $y = 2^{(x-2)}$.

x	y
5	$2^3 = 8$
4	$2^2 = 4$
3	$2^1 = 2$
2	$2^0 = 1$
1	$2^{-1} = \frac{1}{2}$
0	$2^{-2} = \frac{1}{2^2} = \frac{1}{4}$
-1	$2^{-3} = \frac{1}{2^3} = \frac{1}{8}$

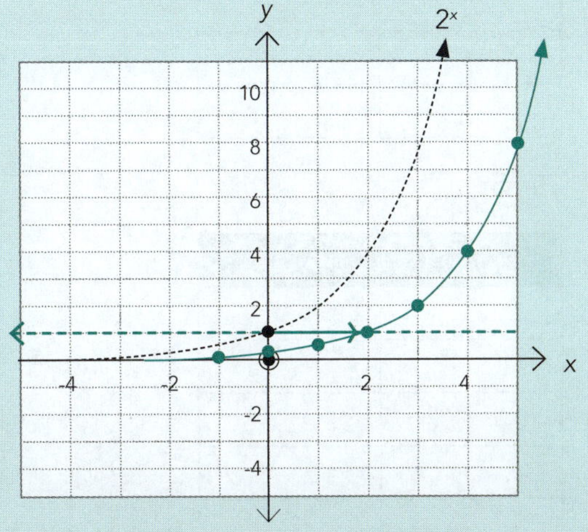

Compare this with the graph of $y = 2^x$.
All the points have moved **right 2**.

For graphs in the form $y = p^{(x \pm b)}$:
+ b moves the graph left and – b moves the graph right.

ISBN: 9780170419376

Complete the tables and draw graphs for the following equations.

1 $y = 2^{(x+3)}$

x	y
1	
0	
-1	
-2	
-3	
-4	
-5	

2 $y = 2^{(x-1)}$

x	y
3	
2	
1	
0	
-1	
-2	
-3	

3 $y = 3^{(x+1)}$

x	y

4 $y = 3^{(x-1)}$

x	y

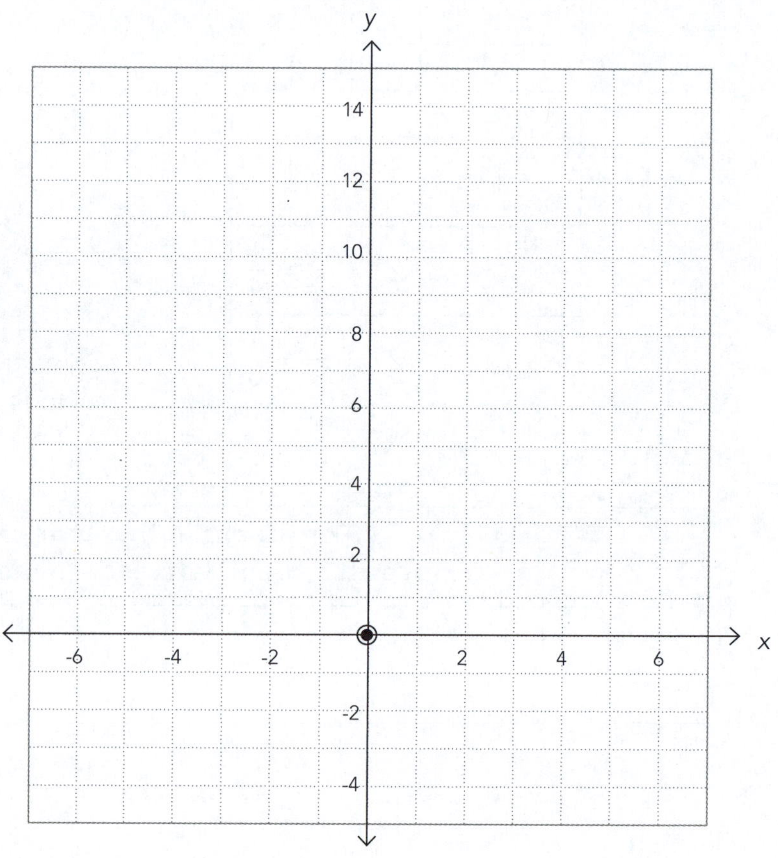

ISBN: 9780170419376

3 Combinations, $y = p^{(x \pm b)} \pm c$

The vertex of a parabola is the turning point.

Examples:

1 Draw the graph of $y = 2^{(x+1)} + 3$.

x	y
3	19
2	11
1	7
0	5
-1	4
-2	$3\frac{1}{2}$
-3	$3\frac{1}{4}$

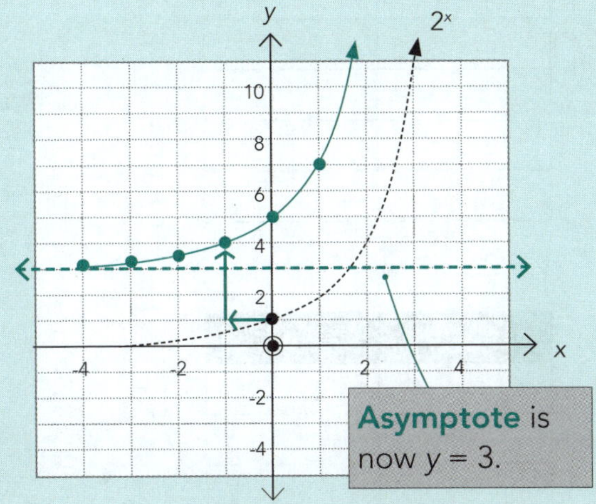

$y = 2^{(x+1)} + 3$

+ 1 ⟹ move all points **left 1**.

+ 3 ⟹ move all points **up 3**.

You will notice a similar pattern to translating parabolas. However, exponential graphs lack symmetry, so you will probably need to draw tables.

2 Draw the graph of $y = 2^{(x-2)} - 3$.

x	y
5	5
4	1
3	-1
2	-2
1	$-2\frac{1}{2}$
0	$-2\frac{3}{4}$
-1	$-2\frac{7}{8}$

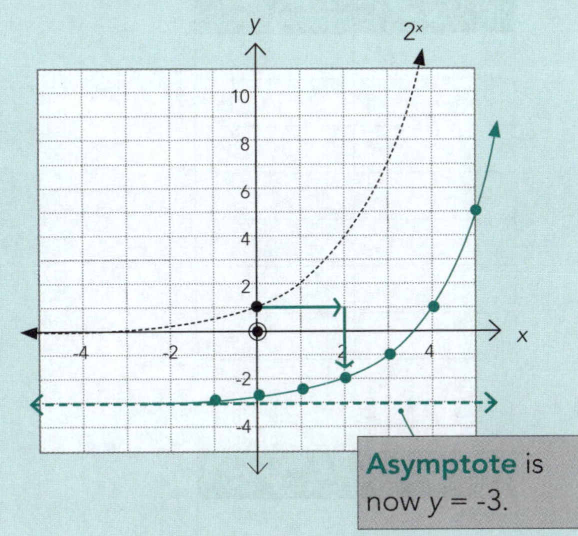

$y = 2^{(x-2)} - 3$

– 2 ⟹ move all points **right 2**.

– 3 ⟹ move all points **down 3**.

For graphs in the form $y = p^{(x \pm b)} \pm c$:
+ b moves the graph left and
– b moves the graph right
+ c moves the graph up and
– c moves the graph down.

ISBN: 9780170419376

Draw graphs for the following equations.

1 $y = 2^{(x-2)} + 1$

x	y

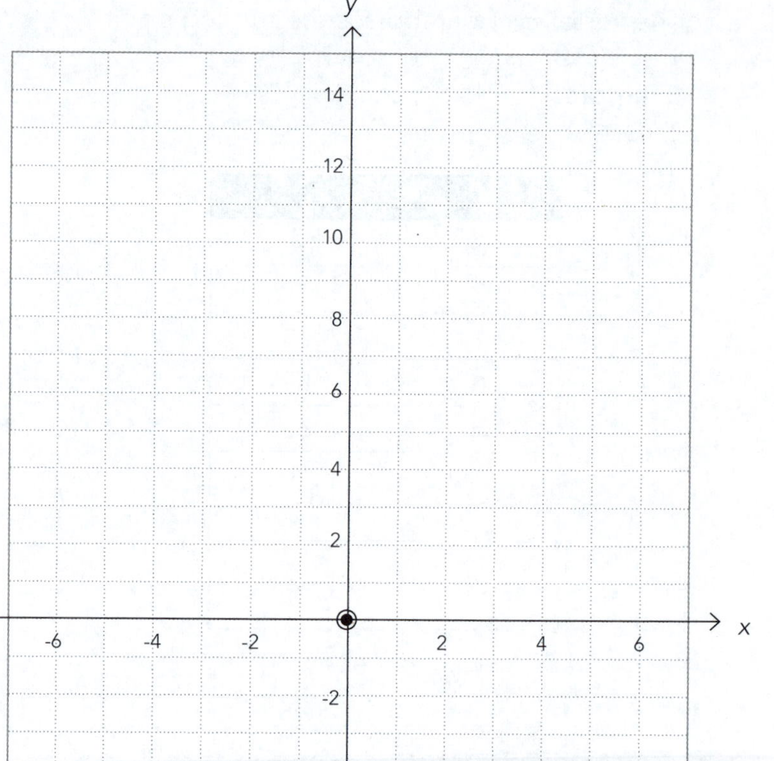

2 $y = 2^{(x+1)} + 2$

x	y

3 $y = 2^{(x+3)} - 1$

x	y

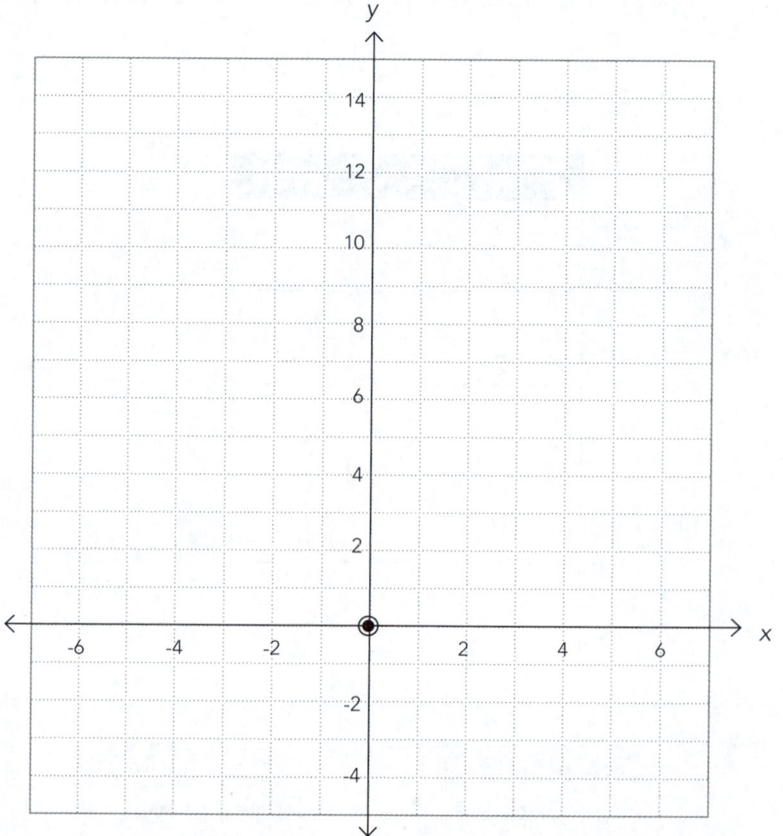

4 $y = 3^{(x-1)} + 2$

x	y

ISBN: 9780170419376

Inverted exponential graphs, $y = -p^{(x \pm b)} \pm c$

Remember that $y = -x^2$ is the same as $y = x^2$ except that the graph is reflected in the x-axis.

Examples:

1 Draw the graph of $y = -2^x$.

x	y
3	-8
2	-4
1	-2
0	-1
-1	$-2^{-1} = -\frac{1}{2}$
-2	$-2^{-2} = -\frac{1}{2^2} = -\frac{1}{4}$
-3	$-2^{-3} = -\frac{1}{2^3} = -\frac{1}{8}$

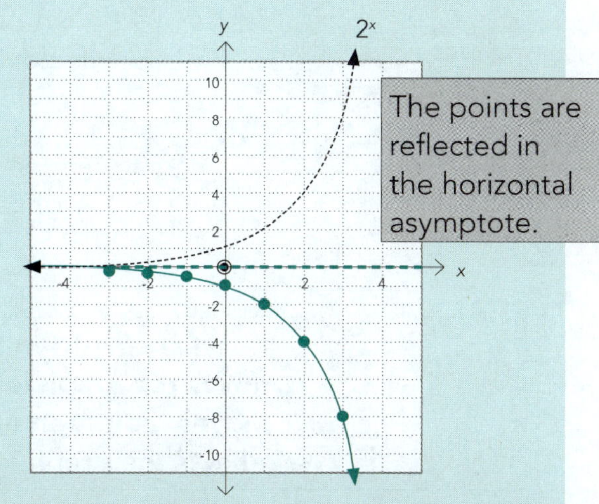

Compare this with the graph of $y = 2^x$. All the points are **reflected in the horizontal asymptote**.

2 Draw the graph of $y = -2^x + 3$.

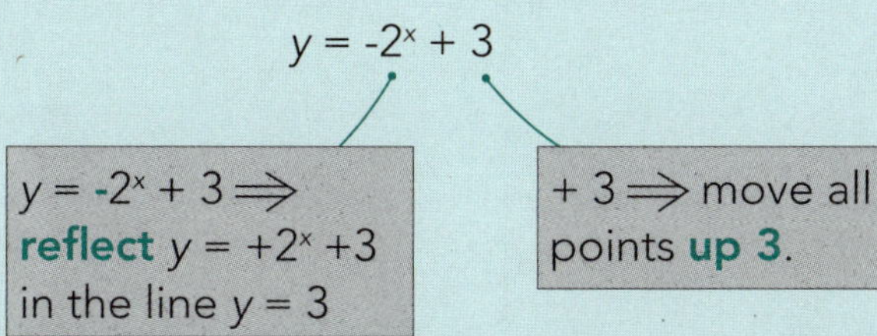

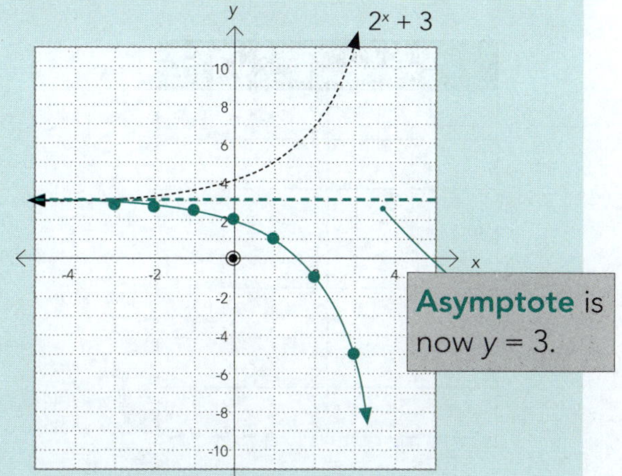

3 Draw the graph of $y = -2^{(x+1)}$.

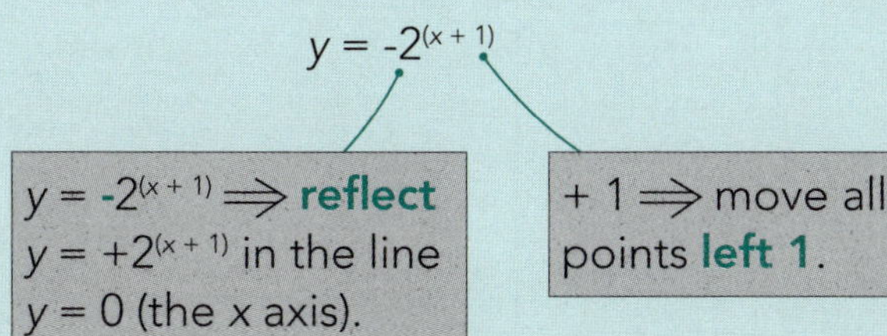

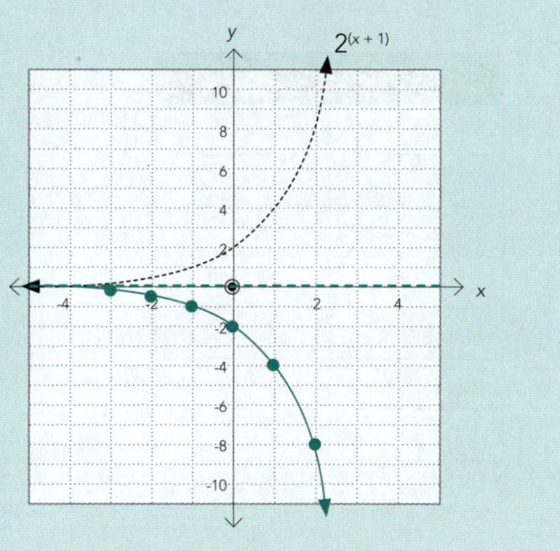

ISBN: 9780170419376

4 Draw the graph of $y = -2^{(x-2)} - 1$.

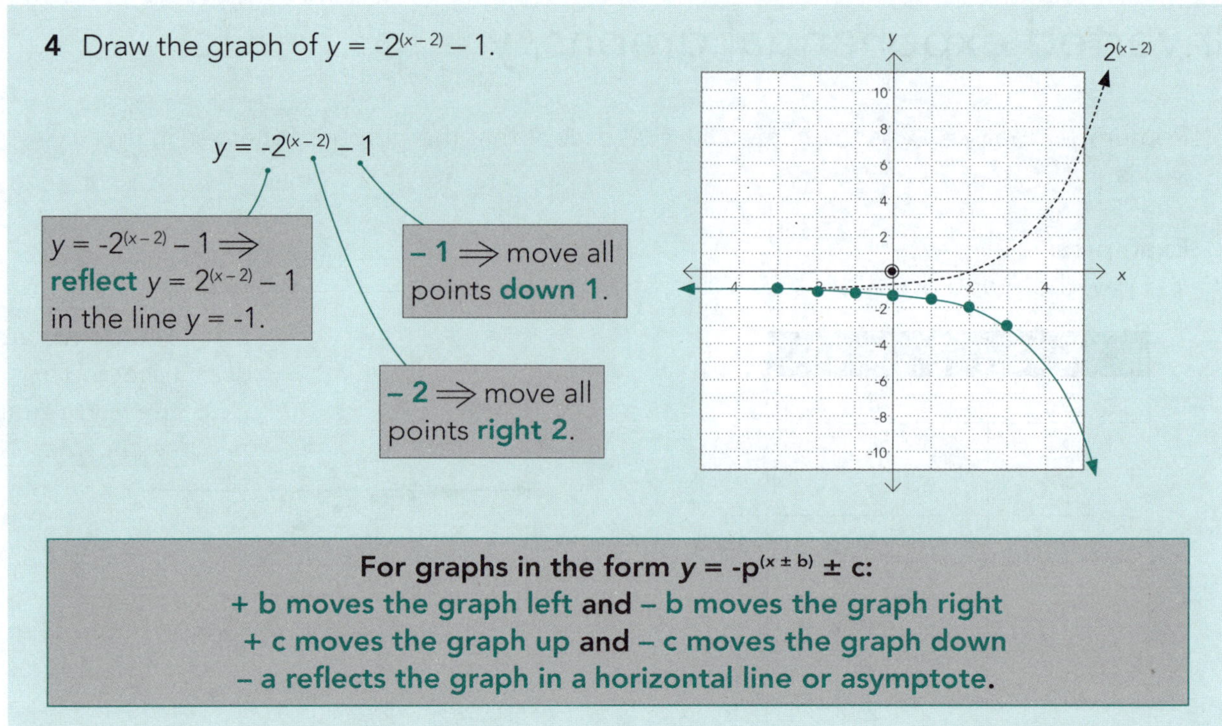

For graphs in the form $y = -p^{(x \pm b)} \pm c$:
+ b moves the graph left and – b moves the graph right
+ c moves the graph up and – c moves the graph down
– a reflects the graph in a horizontal line or asymptote.

Draw graphs for the following equations.

1 $y = -2^{(x-1)} + 2$

x	y

2 $y = -2^{(x+2)} - 1$

x	y

ISBN: 9780170419376

Writing equations for exponential graphs

- You will probably be asked to write equations only for $y = +p^{(x \pm b)} \pm c$.
- You are unlikely to be asked for **p** values other than **2**.

Examples:

1

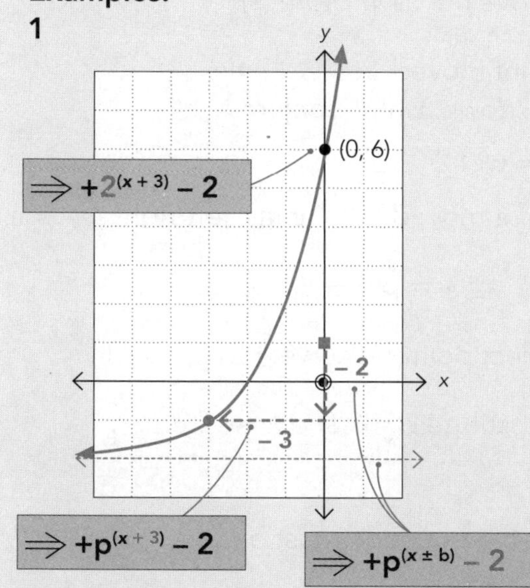

Steps:

1. Draw the asymptote. It is at y = -2
   $\Rightarrow y = p^{(x \pm b)} - 2$
2. Mark the point (0, 1) (■). Draw arrows from this to the point where the curve is 1 unit above the asymptote (•).
3. Point moved **2 units down** confirms that
   $y = p^{(x \pm b)} - 2$
4. Point moved **3 units to left**
   $y = p^{(x+3)} - 2$
5. Select a point on the curve that has 'easy' co-ordinates, e.g. (**0**, 6).
   Let **p = 2**, and substitute **x = 0** to see if the equation is true.
   $y = 2^{(0+3)} - 2$
   $= 8 - 2$
   $= 6$

So the equation must be $y = +2^{(x+3)} - 2$.

2

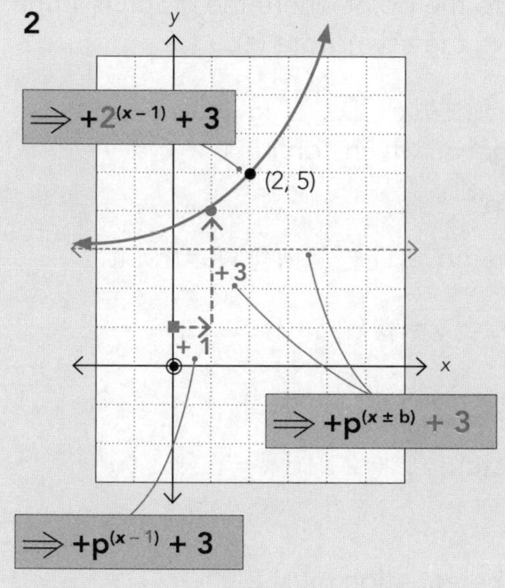

Steps:

1. Draw the asymptote. It is at y = +3
   $\Rightarrow y = p^{(x \pm b)} + 3$
2. Mark the point (0, 1) (■). Draw arrows from this to the point where the curve is 1 unit above the asymptote (•).
3. Point moved **3 units up** confirms that
   $y = p^{(x \pm b)} + 3$
4. Point moved **1 unit to right**
   $\Rightarrow y = p^{(x-1)} + 3$
5. Select a point on the curve that has 'easy' co-ordinates, e.g. (**2**, 5).
   Let **p = 2**, and substitute **x = 2** to see if the equation is true.
   $y = +2^{(2-1)} + 3$
   $= 2 + 3$
   $= 5$

So the equation must be $y = 2^{(x-1)} + 3$.

ISBN: 9780170419376

Write equations for the following exponential graphs.

1

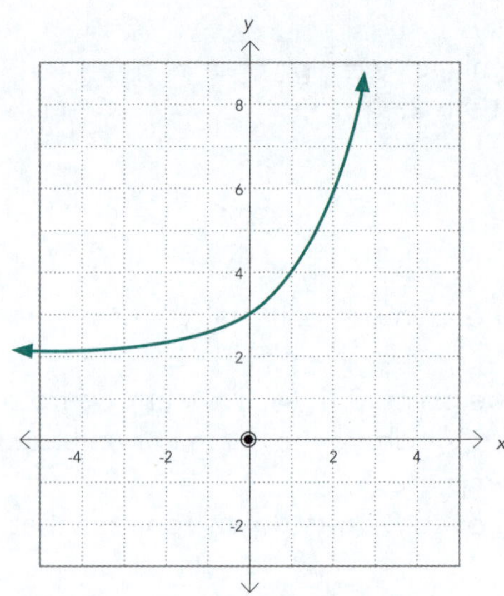

1 Asymptote is at $y =$ _____ $\Rightarrow$

$y = p^{(x \pm b)}$ _____

2 Mark the point (0, 1) (■). Draw arrows from this to the point where the graph is 1 unit above the asymptote (•).

3 Point moved _____ unit(s) up/down, which confirms

$y = p^{(x \pm b)}$ _____

4 Point moved ____ unit(s) left/right

$\Rightarrow y = p^{(x \text{\_\_\_\_})}$ _____

5 Select point on curve: (_____, _____).

Substitute p = 2 and $x =$ _____

$y =$

$=$

So the equation must be

$y =$ ________________

2

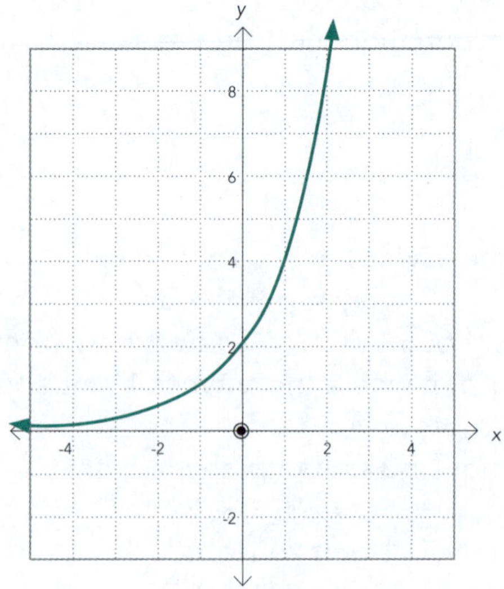

1 Asymptote is at $y =$ _____ $\Rightarrow$

$y = p^{(x \pm b)}$ _____

2 Mark the point (0, 1) (■). Draw arrows from this to the point where the graph is 1 unit above the asymptote (•).

3 Point moved _____ unit(s) up/down, which confirms

$y = p^{(x \pm b)}$ _____

4 Point moved ____ unit(s) left/right

$\Rightarrow y = p^{(x \text{\_\_\_\_})}$ _____

5 Select point on curve: (_____, _____).

Substitute p = 2 and $x =$ _____

$y =$

$=$

So the equation must be

$y =$ ________________

 ISBN: 9780170419376

3

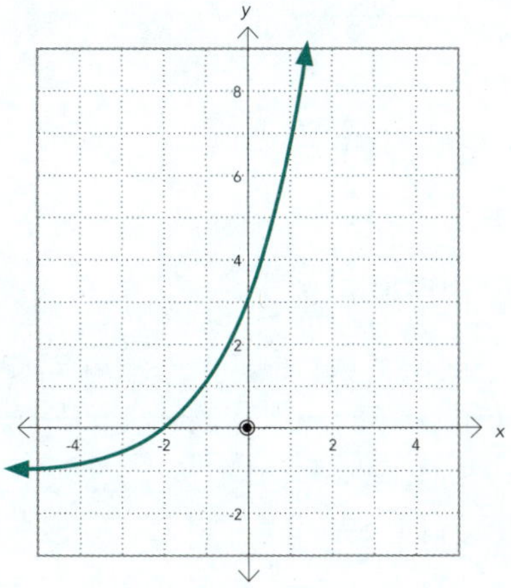

4

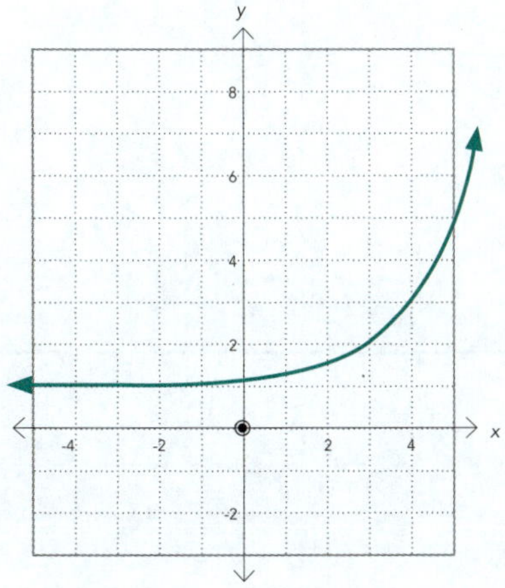

5

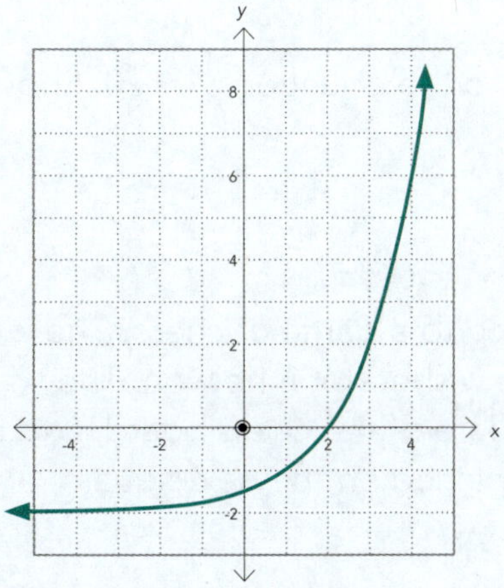

6

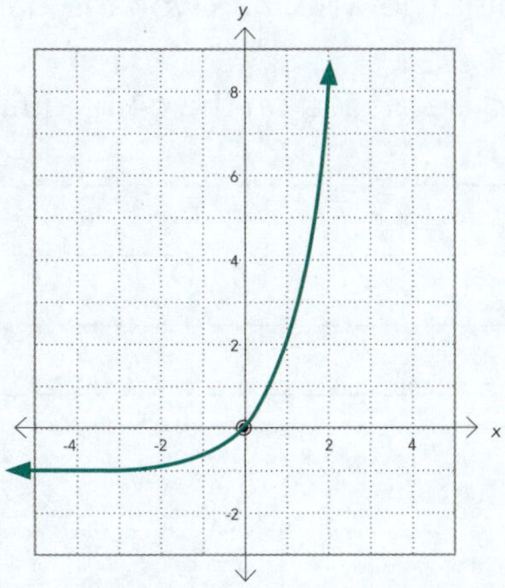

Applications and problems

Answer the following.

1 a Complete the table below, and use it to draw the graph of $y = 3^n$.

n	3^n
-1	
0	
1	
2	
3	

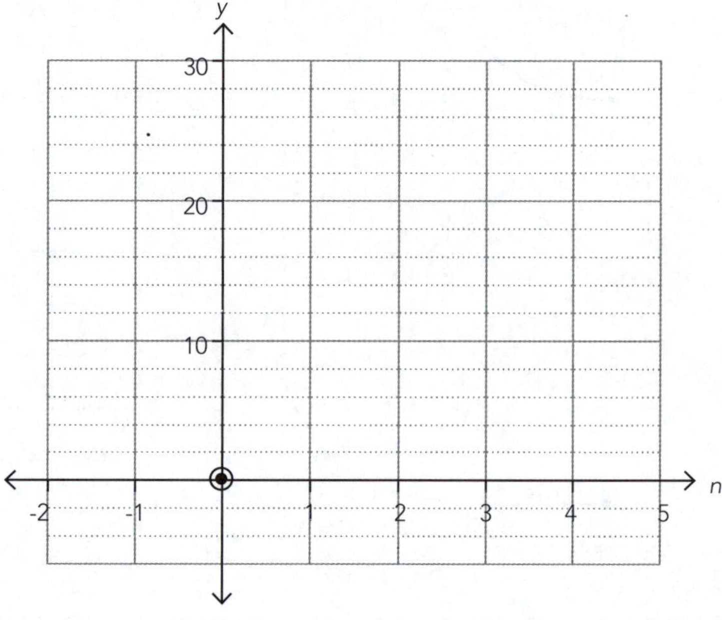

b Write down the co-ordinates of the y-intercept: y intercept = ____________________

c Use your graph to find an approximate solution to the equation $3^n = 20$. Show how you have done this.

$n \approx$ ____________________

2 In an Indian legend, a wise man challenged a king to a game of chess. The king was so rich that he offered the wise man anything he wished for if he won. The wise man asked for one grain of rice to be placed on a square of the chess board, and each day double the number of grains of rice were to be placed on the next square, and so on for each square on the board (64).

The king agreed to this, thinking he had a bargain. The wise man won the game.

Calculate the number of grains of rice that would be placed on the 64th square.

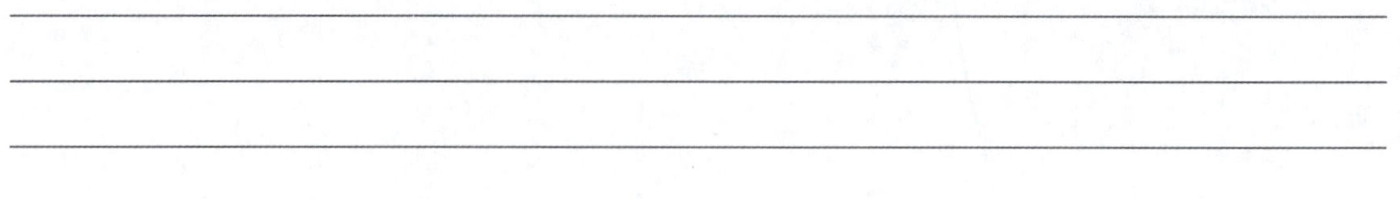

 ISBN: 9780170419376

3 a A bacterial colony covers 5 mm^2 on day 0. Its area doubles each day. Complete the table below to show the area it covers on each of the following days.

Day (d)	0	1	2	3	4
Area (mm^2) (A)	5	10			

Fill in the gaps to show how you could calculate the area of the colony on a particular day.

b Area on day ______ = 5 x 2 x 2 x 2 x 2 x 2

= 5 x $2^{\_\_}$

= ______

c Use the pattern in **b** to help you write an equation for this relationship:

A = ____________________

d Plot the values in the table on the graph below.

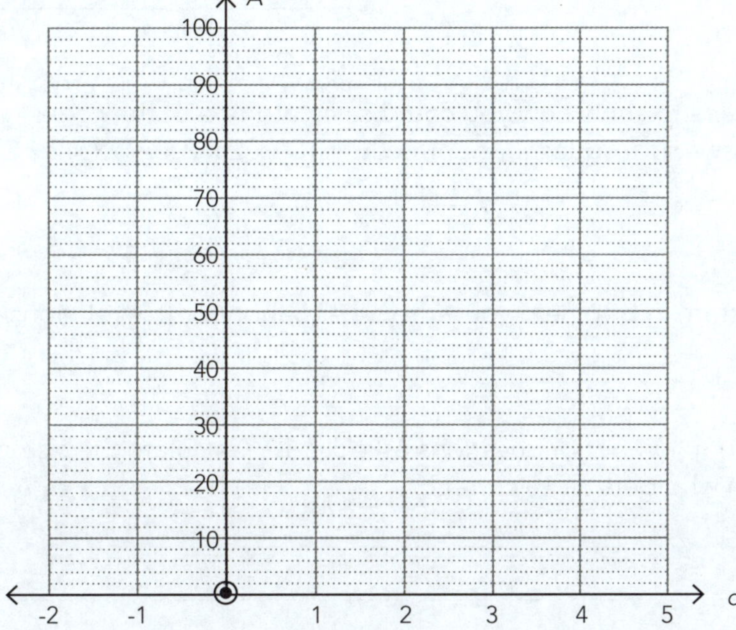

e Use your graph to estimate when the colony had an area of 50 mm^2.

d = ____________________

f What was the area of the colony the day before day 0?

Area = __________ mm^2

g Describe what would stay the same on the graph and what would change if the colony tripled (became three times bigger) each day.

____

____

____

ISBN: 9780170419376

4 a On a TV quiz game, the contestant wins $100 for the first correct answer, and for each correct answer after that their prize doubles. Complete the table below to show how their prize grows with each winning question and plot the values on the graph.

q	Prize ($)
1	100
2	200
3	
4	
5	

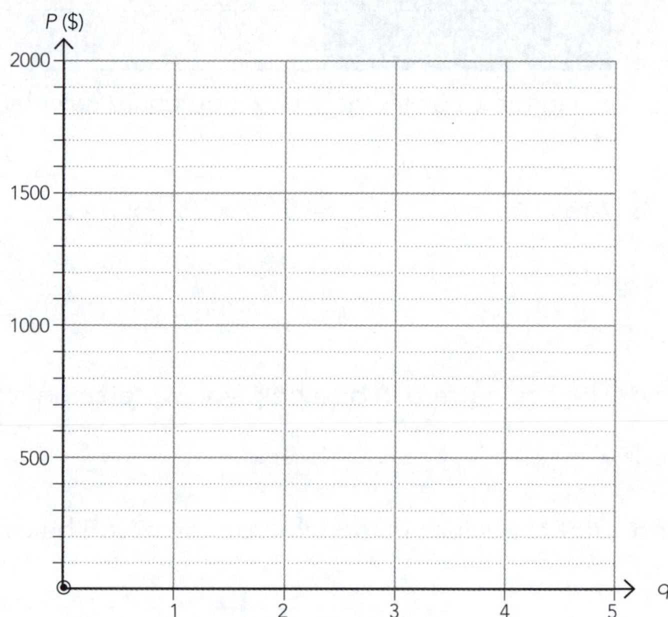

b Fill in the gaps to show how you could calculate one of the prizes.

Prize for answering 7 questions correctly = 100 x 2 x 2 x 2 x 2 x 2 x 2

= 100 x 2 ___

= ________

c Use the pattern in **b** to help you write an equation for this relationship:

P = ____________________

d The maximum number of questions asked is 10. Calculate the size of the prize won by a person who gets all 10 correct.

____

____

e Modify the formula that you found in **c** in order to work out the prize won in the following situations.

i A similar game with a first prize of $100, but with 15 questions.

Maximum prize = ____________________

ii A similar game with a first prize of $200, but the contestant gets only 7 questions correct.

Prize = ____________________

ISBN: 9780170419376

Piecewise functions

These occur when there are **different** rules for finding y, depending on the value of x.

Example: The cost of having T-shirts printed on both the front and the back depends on how many are ordered. If the order is for fewer than 20 T-shirts, the printing costs \$15 per shirt. If it is for more than 20 but fewer than 40, printing costs \$10 per shirt. For 40 or more T-shirts, the cost of printing is \$7 per shirt.

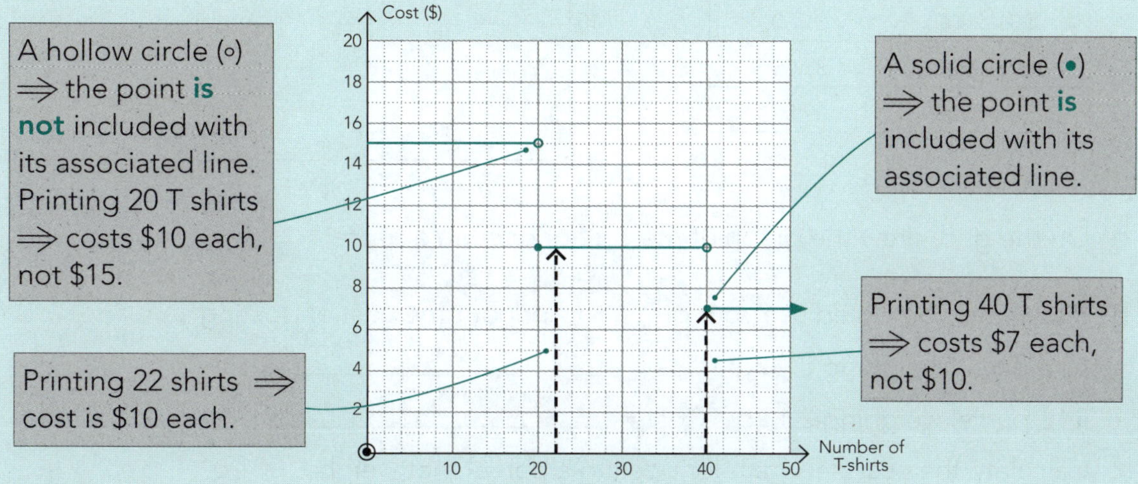

The scale of charges is different for printing a small logo on one side only. If the order is for fewer than 20 T-shirts, the printing costs \$8 per shirt. If it is for more than 20 but fewer than 40, printing costs \$5 per shirt. For 40 or more T-shirts, the cost of printing is \$3 per shirt.

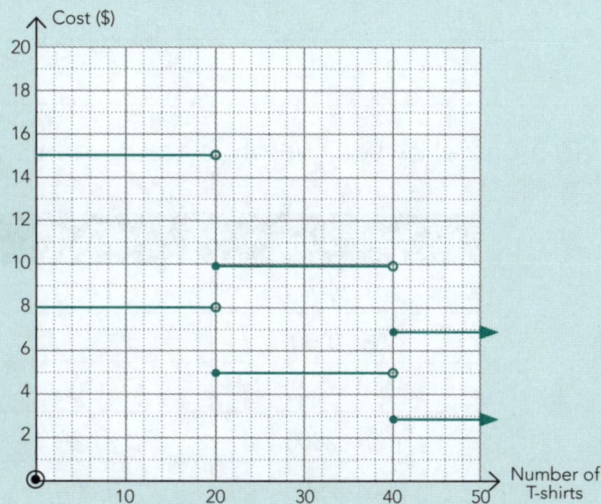

Describe how the graph for printing on both sides compares with that for printing just a logo:

- The y-intercept is at 15 for printing on both sides, but it is at 8 for printing a logo.
- The 'steps' are greater for printing on both sides — between 19 and 20 shirts the cost drops \$5 compared with \$3 for just logos.
- Between 39 and 40 shirts, the cost drops \$3 compared with \$2 for just logos.

Answer the following.

1 The cost of posting a parcel by air (weighed to the nearest gram) is shown in the table below.

Weight (g)	Cost ($)
0–500	17.00
501–1000	21.50
1001–1500	26.00
1501–2000	31.50
2001–2500	35.00
2501–3000	39.50

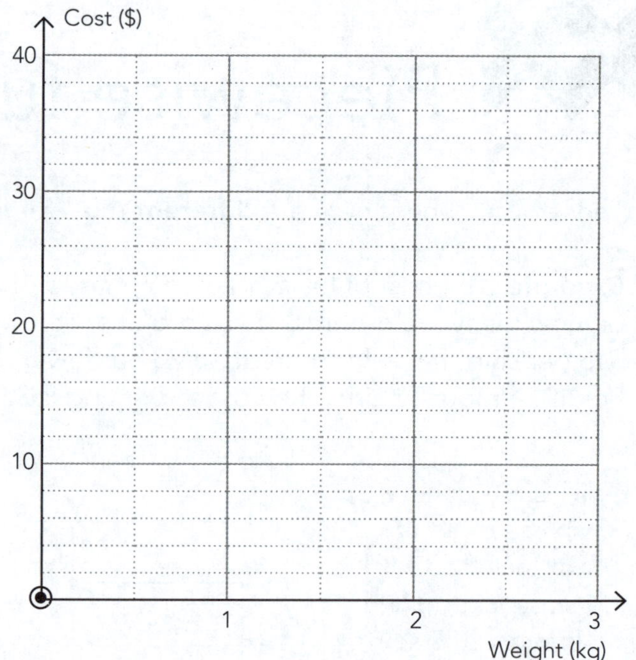

a On the grid, draw the graph of the cost of posting a parcel.

b Show how you would use your graph to work out the cost of posting

i a parcel weighing 0.9 kg: Cost = ______________________

ii a parcel weighing 2.1 kg: Cost = ______________________

c Calculate the cost per gram for posting a parcel that weighs 1001 g.

Cost = ____

d Compare the cost per gram of posting a 1001 g parcel with the cost per gram of posting a 1499 g parcel.

____

____

e The cost of posting a parcel by sea (weighed to the nearest gram) is shown in the table below.

Weight (g)	Cost ($)
0–500	12.00
501–1000	15.00
1001–1500	18.00
1501–2000	21.00
2001–2500	24.00
2501–3000	27.00

If a graph were drawn for the cost of posting a parcel by sea, describe the similarities and differences between the graphs of the costs of post by air and post by sea.

____

____

____

ISBN: 9780170419376

2 A school is having its magazines printed. The cost of printing each magazine depends on how many are printed. The table below shows the prices quoted by Pete's Printing.

Number of copies (n)	Cost per copy ($)
0–199	5.40
200–499	4.60
500–999	3.10
1000–1999	2.50
⩾ 2000	2.10

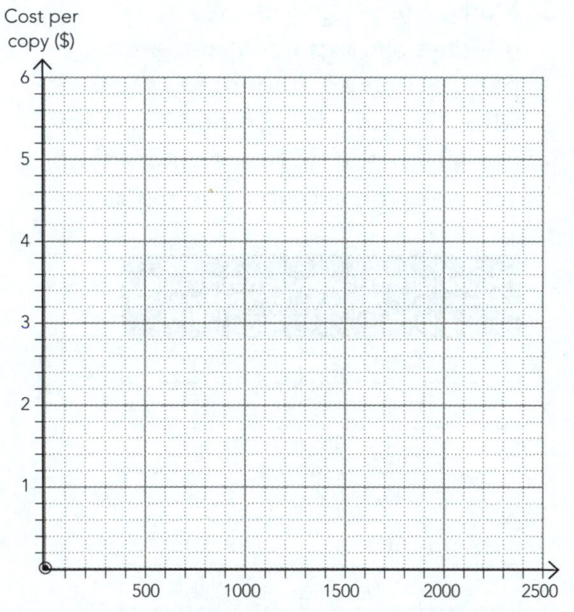

a On the grid, draw the graph of the cost of printing each magazine.

b Show how you would use your graph to work out the cost per copy of printing

i 600 magazines: Cost = ____________________

ii 1900 magazines: Cost = ____________________

3 The graph shows the value of a new car throughout its first seven years. The value decreases as soon as it is driven out of the car yard where it was bought, and then decreases more with each year of its life.

Age (years)	Value ($)
new	
< 1	
< 2	
< 3	
< 4	
< 5	
< 6	
< 7	

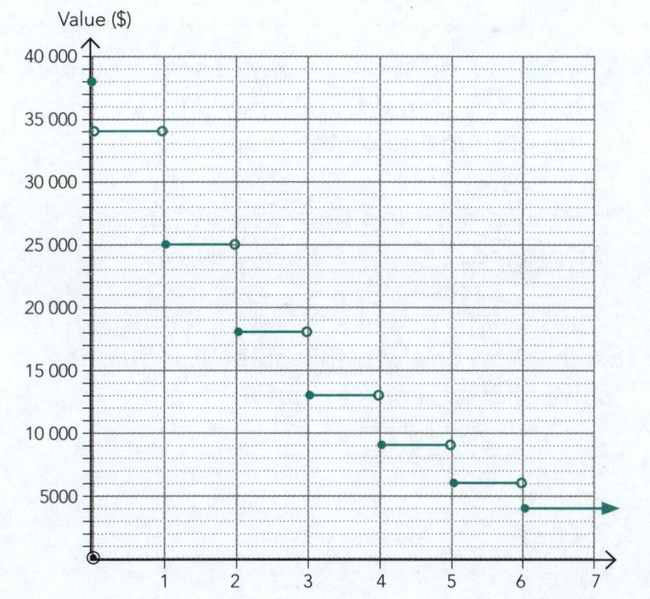

a Complete the table.
(Note: '< 2' means 1 year old or more but less than 2 years old.)

b Describe how the value of the car changes during the first year of its life.

____

____

____

ISBN: 9780170419376

4 a Marco prunes grapevines in his holidays. He is paid a fixed amount per day plus an amount for each whole row of vines pruned. Each row has 40 vines. If he prunes more than 160 vines, he is paid more per row.

Number of vines pruned (n)	Amount paid ($)
1–40	$18
41–80	$50
81–120	$82
121–160	$114
161–200	$150
201–240	$186
241–280	$222

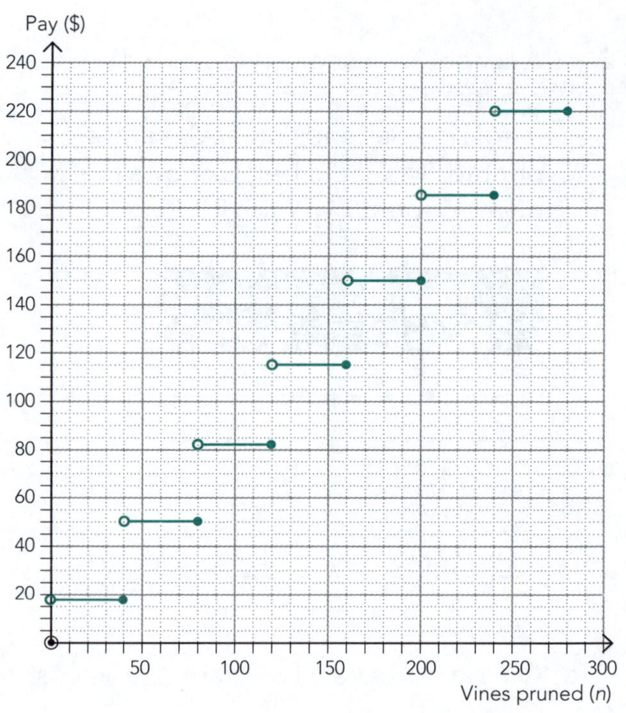

b If Marco pruned fewer than 160 vines on his first day, explain how his pay is calculated.

____

____

c He worked out that if he pruned 161 vines, he was paid more per vine than if he pruned 199 vines. Explain why. Show calculations to support your answer.

____

____

d A neighbouring vineyard pays a set amount for each vine pruned. Their pay rate is shown by the dashed line on the graph.

How much does this vineyard pay for each vine pruned?

____

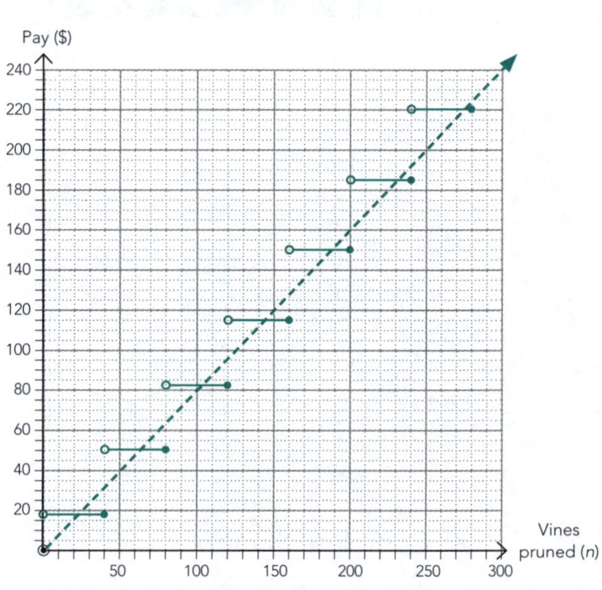

e Explain how and why this graph is different to the original graph in part **a**.

____

____

____

____

____

____

f Give an example of a number of vines that Marco could have pruned that would result in more pay if he worked for the neighbours

____

 ISBN: 9780170419376

Practice questions

Practice question one

a Elani walked 2 km from home to her school.

- To start with, she walked at a constant speed for 20 minutes until she reached her friend's place, which was 1600 m from her home.
- Her friend wasn't ready, so Elani had to wait there for 16 minutes before they set off together for school.
- They walked the rest of the way at a constant speed of 25 metres per minute.
- Elani's little sister walked to school with their mother. They followed the same route. They left at the same time as Elani, but took 40 minutes to get there, walking at the same speed the entire way.
- Elani's big brother left on his skateboard 20 minutes after the rest of the family. He travelled at 100 m per minute for the first 10 minutes, then, realising he was late, he travelled the last kilometre in 8 minutes.

Fully investigate this situation to find out:

- who arrived at school first, and when each group arrived
- when and where the groups passed each other.

Write down equations for each section of all the journeys.

b **i** Write an equation for the graph shown here.

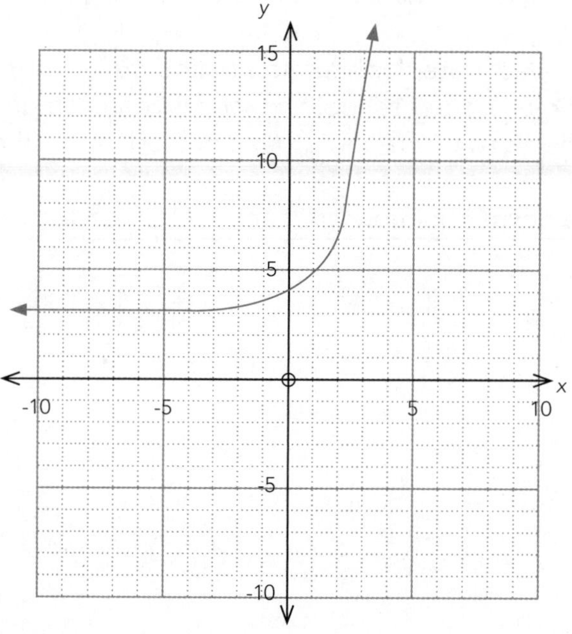

ii State the new equation if the graph above is reflected in the x-axis.

ISBN: 9780170419376

Practice question two

An engineer is designing a tunnel, which will become a walkway within the concrete walls of a large power station.

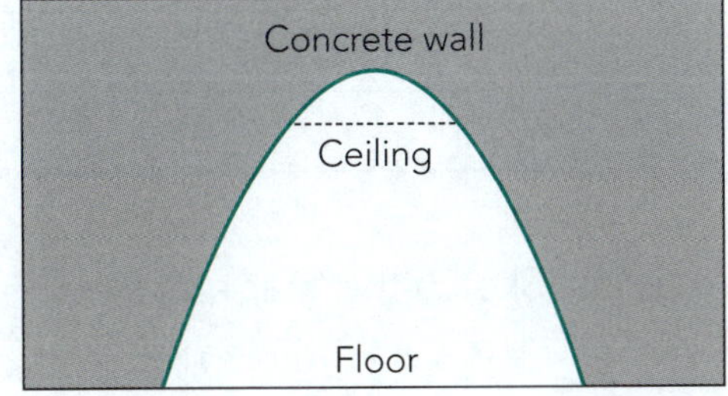

- The cross-section of the tunnel will be in the shape of a parabola.
- Its floor will start 2 m from the left side of the concrete wall.
- The tunnel floor will be 6 m wide.
- The tunnel's highest point will be 4.5 m above the floor.

Recommend a sensible model for the shape of the tunnel, remembering that it will be in the shape of a parabola.

i ______________________________

____

ii A horizontal ceiling is to be built centrally into the tunnel. The ceiling must be 3 m wide. How high is the ceiling above the floor?

____

____

____

____

____

ISBN: 9780170419376

iii The graph is then translated p units down and q units to the left.
Write down its new equation, and the co-ordinates of the vertex.

b i Sketch the graph of $y = \dfrac{3x^2 + 7x}{2}$. Give the co-ordinates of all intercepts.

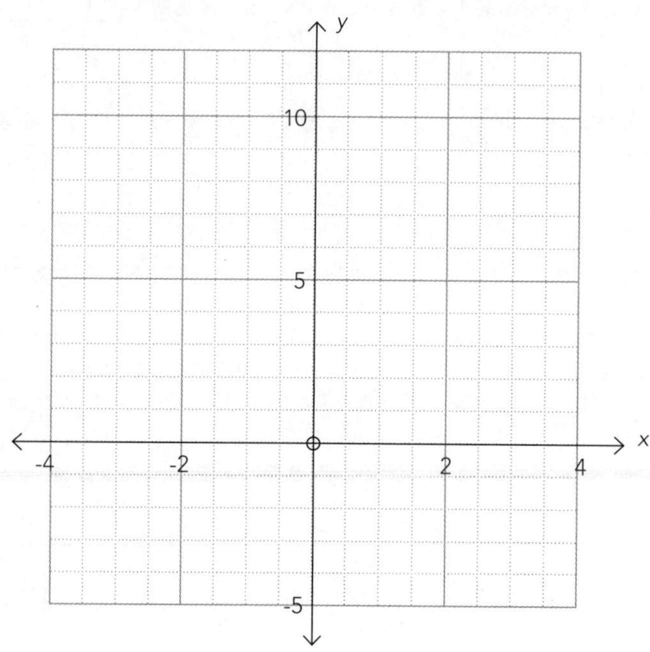

ii Olllie has made some patterns with buttons:

Pattern 1 Pattern 2 Pattern 3

Ollie knows that $B = \dfrac{3n^2 + 7n}{2}$ is the equation for the **total** number of buttons (B) needed for making **one of each** pattern, up to pattern n.
How would the graph of the relationship between B and n differ from the graph you drew in **i**? Give reasons for your answer.

ISBN: 9780170419376

Practice question three

a A landscaper need to buy some kowhai trees. He can buy them from three nurseries: Tom's Trees, Pita's Plants or Grant's Garden Centre.

Tom's Trees charges:

- $24 for trees with a height of 0.5 m or less
- $36 for trees that are over 0.5 m and up to and including 1 m
- $60 for trees that are over 1 m high but less than 1.5 m
- $90 for all trees with a height of 1.5 m or more.

Pita's Plants charges an average of $4 for every 0.1 m of height.

Grant's Garden Centre charges $48 for all their kowhai trees, regardless of height.

The landscaper needs to buy trees that range in height between 0.3 m and 2 m. Make recommendations on who he should buy trees from, based on their cost.

b **i** A 50 cm high kowhai tree was planted at the start of May. It didn't grow at all through the winter, but from the start of September, its height increased by about 4% per month.

After the first four months, the height of the kowhai tree can be modelled by $H = 50 \times 1.04^{m-4}$, where m is the number of months since the tree was planted.

The landscaper checks the tree at the start of every month. He puts in a stake to support the tree when it reaches a height of 60 cm. Investigate the growth of the tree, and when the landscaper will need to put in a stake.

ii The landscaper likes kowhai trees to be 800 cm by the end of their first year. The growth rate of kowhai trees is fairly consistent at 4% per month. How high would the tree need to be when it was planted if this was to be achieved?

 ISBN: 9780170419376

Answers

Straight lines (pp. 6–29)

Co-ordinates revision (p. 6)

a (3, 4) **b** (8, 6)
c (-4, 2) **d** (7, -4)
e (-7, -3) **f** (0, 9)
g (5, -10) **h** (-9, -8)
i (6, 8) **j** (0, -6)
k (-7, 10) **l** (7, 0)
m (-3, -1) **n** (-8, 0)
o (-9, 5) **p** (0, 0)

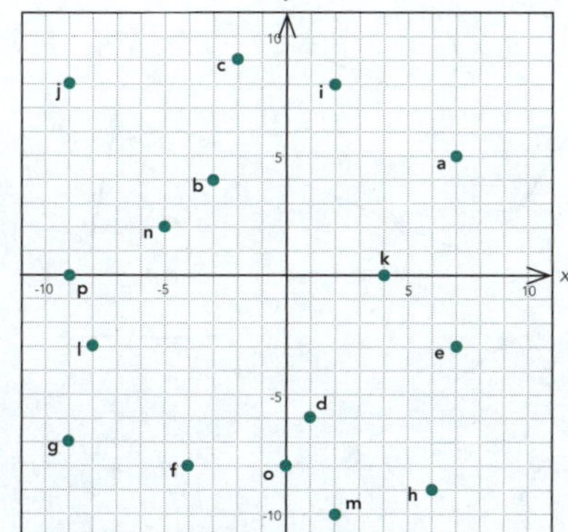

Linear patterns with discrete data (pp. 7–10)

1

Pattern # (n)	# of buttons (B)
1	5
2	9
3	13
4	**17**
5	**21**
6	**25**

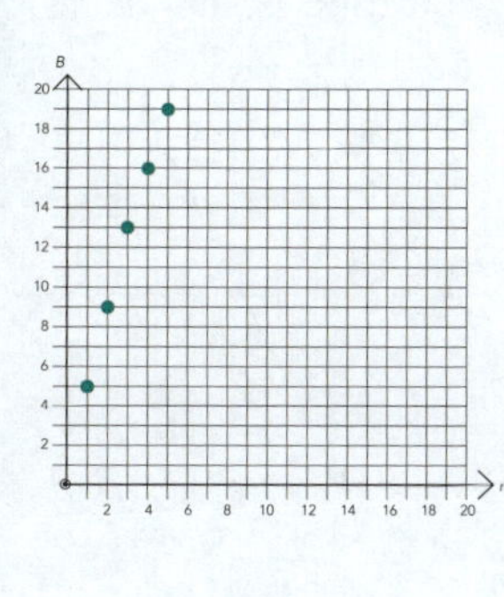

Equation: $B = 4n + 1$

30th pattern ⟹ $B = 121$

$B = \mathbf{4}n + \mathbf{1}$

4 because 4 more buttons are needed for each extra pattern.

1 because pattern number 0 would be just 1 button.

2

Age (n)	# of friends (F)
1	4
2	5
3	6
4	**7**
5	**8**
6	**9**

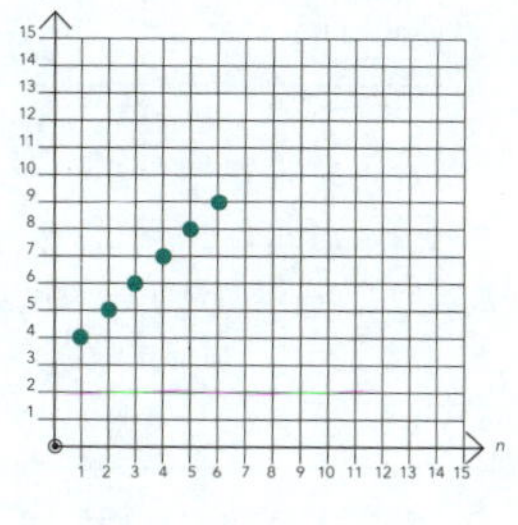

Equation: $F = 1n + 3$

18th birthday ⟹ $F = 21$

$F = \mathbf{1}n + \mathbf{3}$

1 because each year she is allowed 1 more friend.

3 because when she was 0 she could have had 3 friends!

3

Pattern # (n)	# of matches (M)
1	4
2	7
3	10
4	**13**
5	**16**
6	**19**

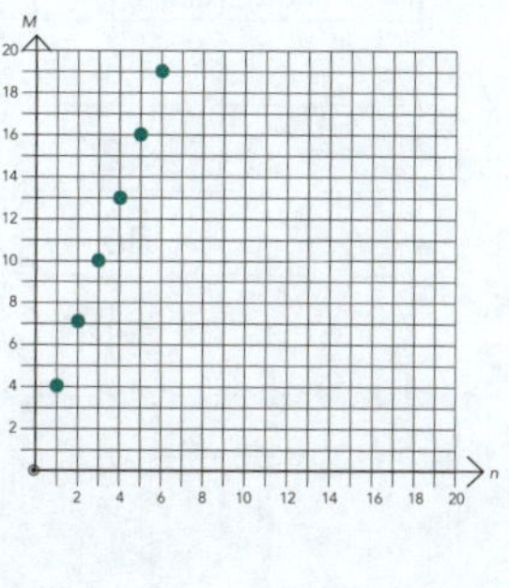

Equation: $M = 3n + 1$

25th pattern ⟹ $M = 76$

$M = \mathbf{3}n + \mathbf{1}$

3 because 3 more matches are needed for each extra pattern.

1 because pattern number 0 would be just 1 match.

ISBN: 9780170419376

4

# of Excellence credits (n)	\$ earned (D)
1	55
2	60
3	65
4	**70**
5	**75**
6	**80**

Equation: $D = 5n + 50$

20 Excellence credits ⟹ $D = 150$

$D = \mathbf{5}n + \mathbf{50}$

5 because he gets \$5 more for each Excellence credit.

50 because if he passed NCEA Level 1 and got no Excellence credits, he would get \$50.

5

# of tables (n)	# of guests (G)
1	**6**
2	**10**
3	**14**
4	**18**
5	**22**
6	**26**

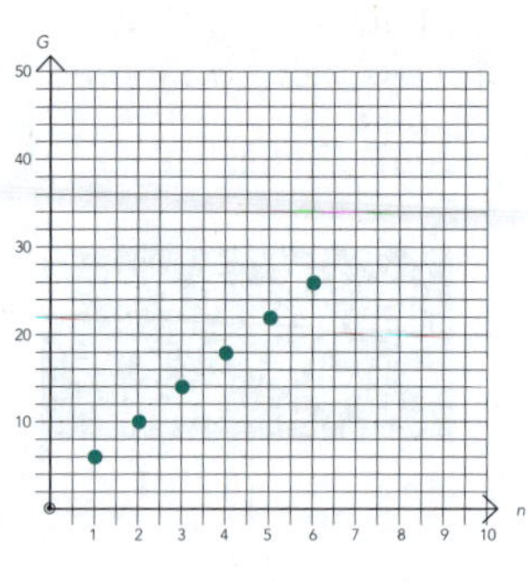

Equation: $G = 4n + 2$

10 smaller tables ⟹ $G = 42$

50 guests ⟹ $n = 12$

$G = \mathbf{4}n + \mathbf{2}$

4 because adding each extra table means she can seat 4 more guests.

2 because pattern number 0 would have 2. *Or* every arrangement of small tables has 2 people sitting on the left and right ends.

6

# of weeks (n)	\$ owed (O)
1	**\$480**
2	**\$460**
3	**\$440**
4	**\$420**
5	**\$400**
6	**\$380**

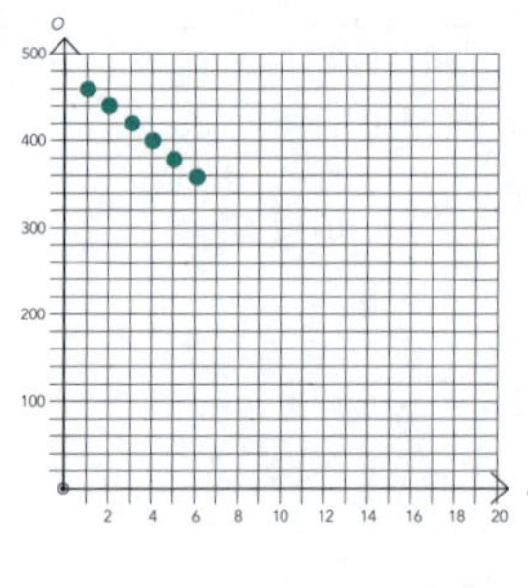

Equation: $O = -20n + 500$

12 weeks aftger starting ⟹ $O = 260$

He owes \$40 ⟹ $n = 23$

$O = \mathbf{-20}n + \mathbf{500}$

-20 because he pays \$20 off his debt each week.

500 because he owed his mother that at the start.

The gradient of a line (pp. 11–13)

A $\frac{3}{2}$ B 2 C $\frac{1}{5}$ D 0

E $-\frac{3}{4}$ F $-\frac{5}{2}$ G 1

H Undefined I $\frac{2}{3}$ J $-\frac{1}{7}$

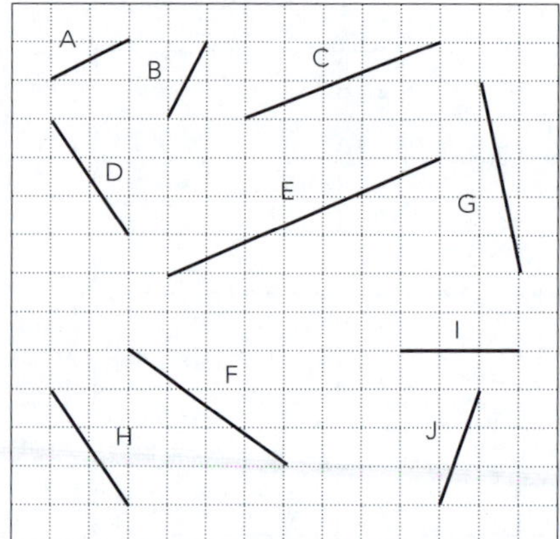

Drawing straight lines — continuous data (pp. 14–21)

1 Plotting points using the equation (pp. 14–16)

1

2

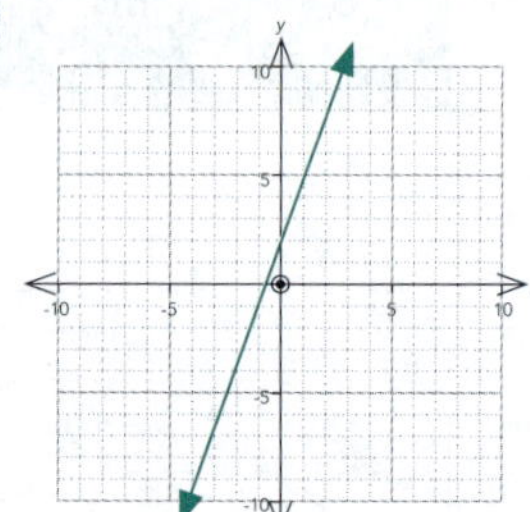

3

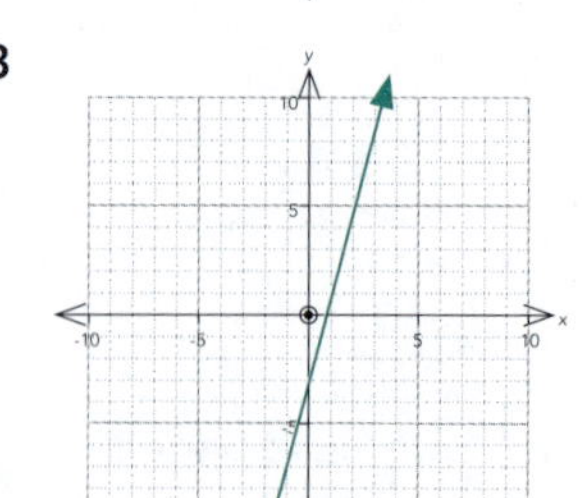

4

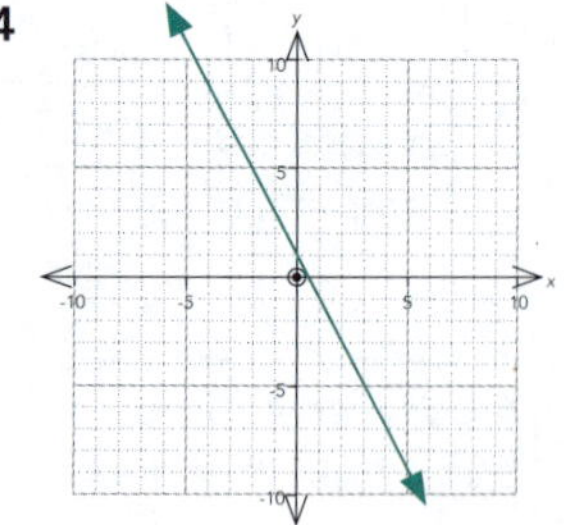

5

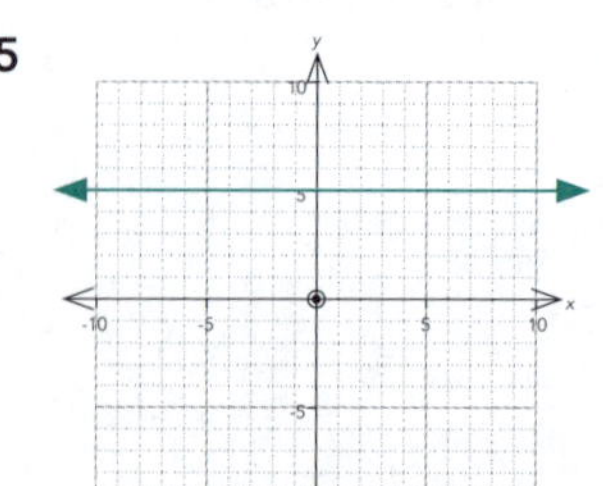

6

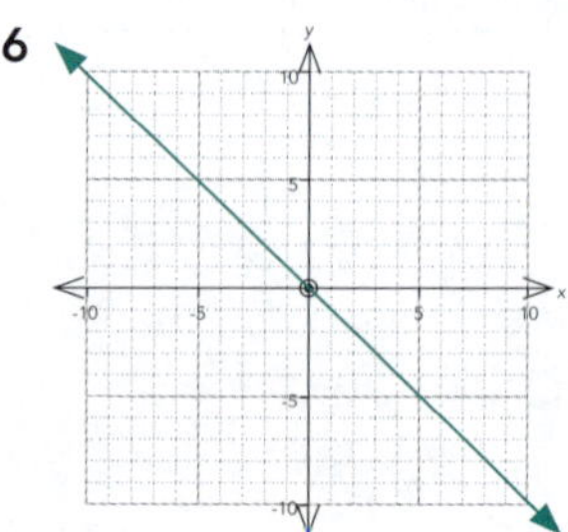

ISBN: 9780170419376

2 Using the y-intercept and the gradient (pp. 17–18)

1 & 2

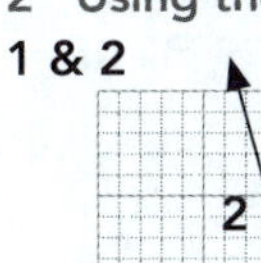

3

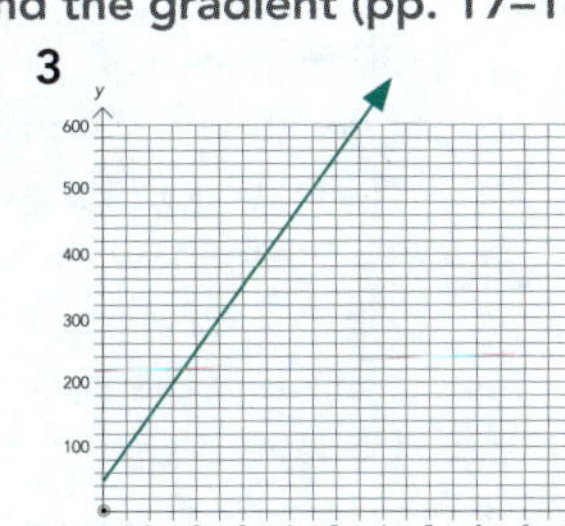

4

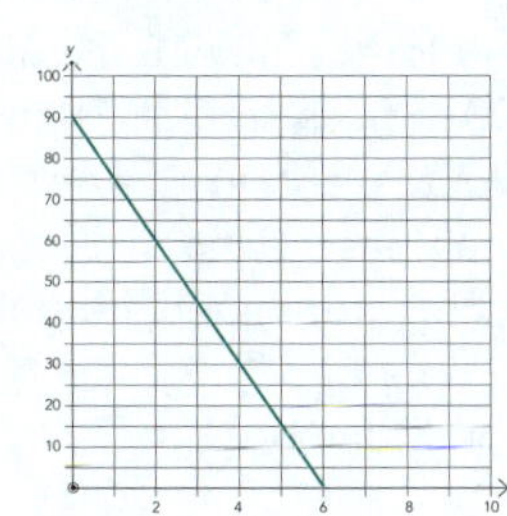

5

6

8

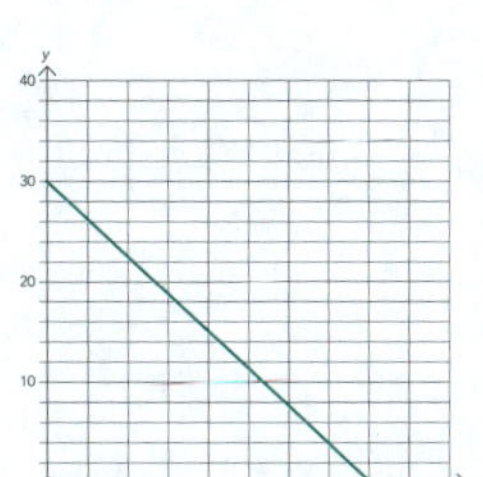

4 Horizontal and vertical lines (p. 21)

1

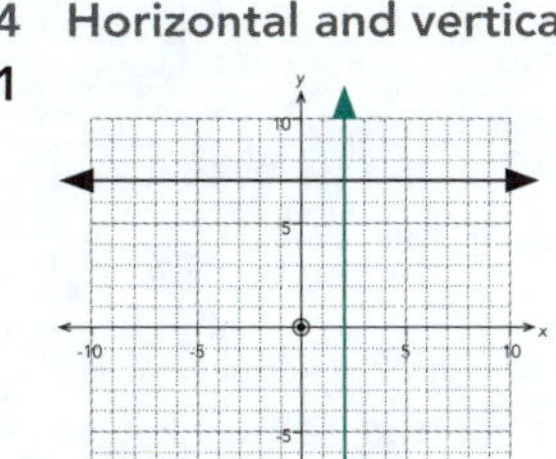

2

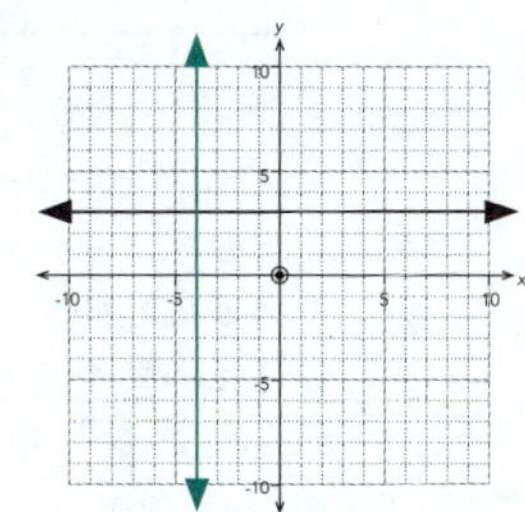

3

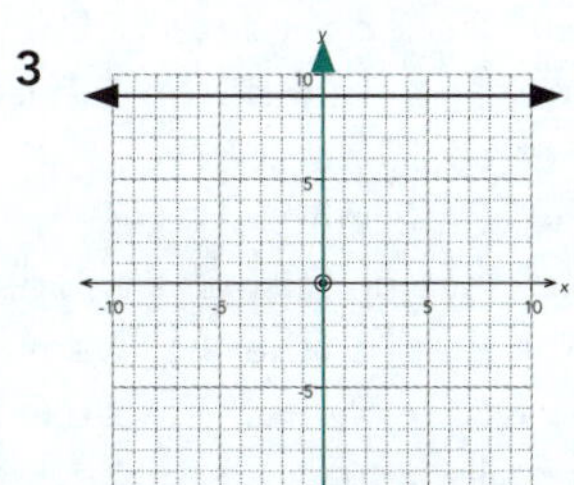

4

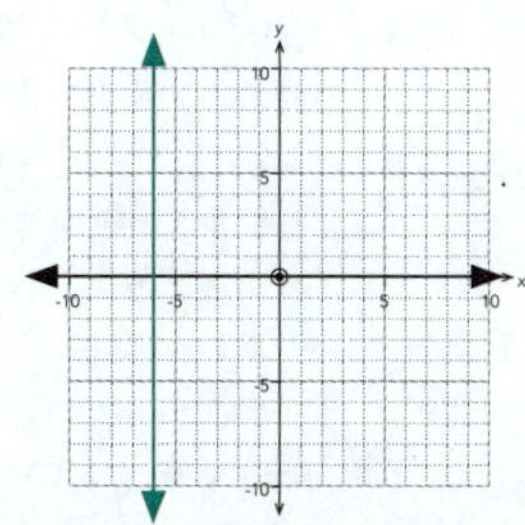

3 Using the x- and y-intercepts (pp. 19–20)

1 & 2

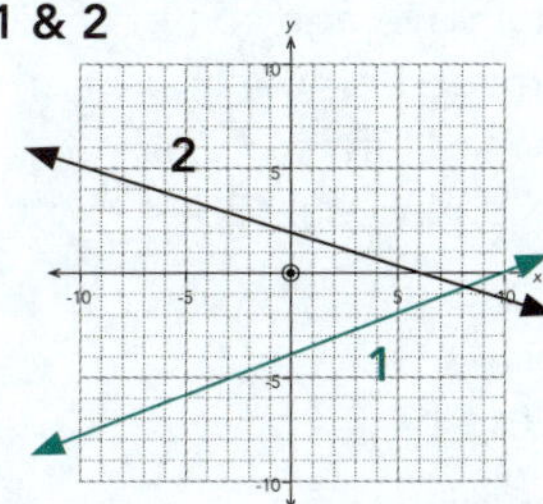

3

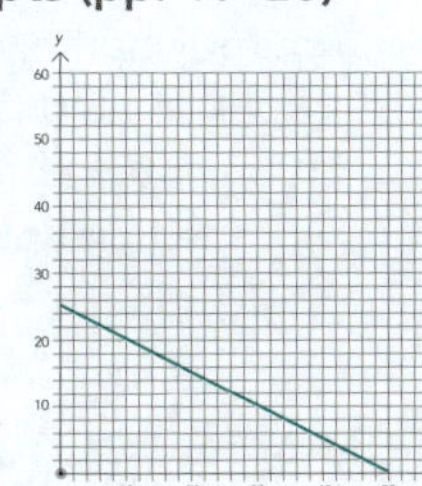

4

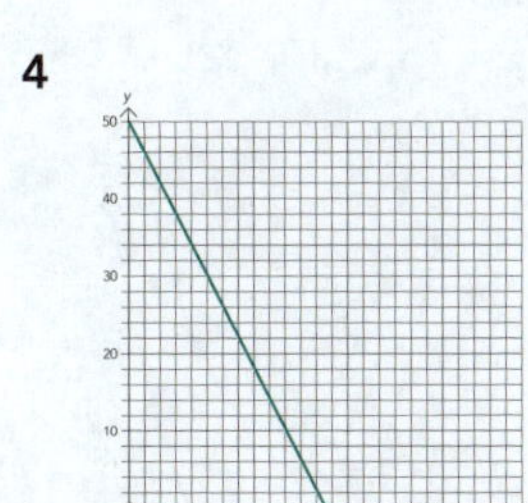

5

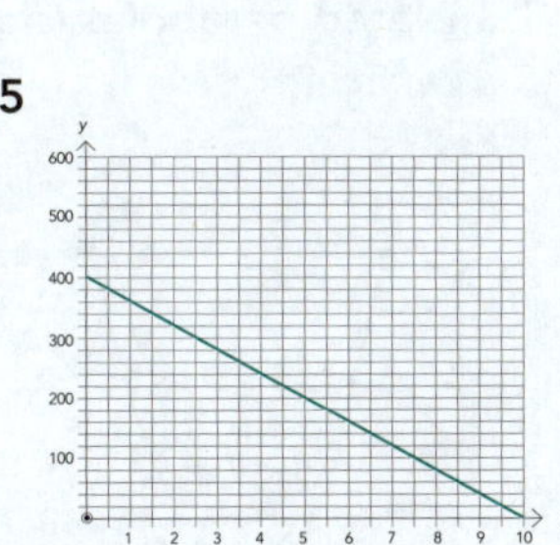

6

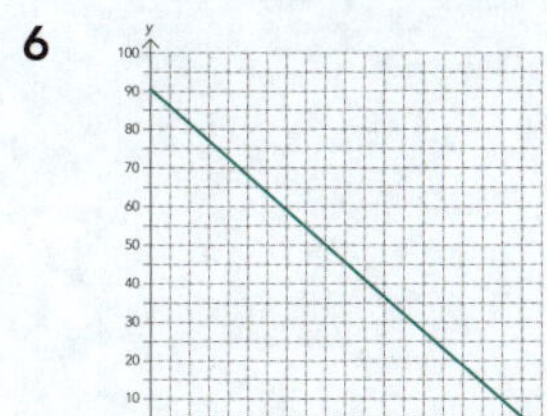

7

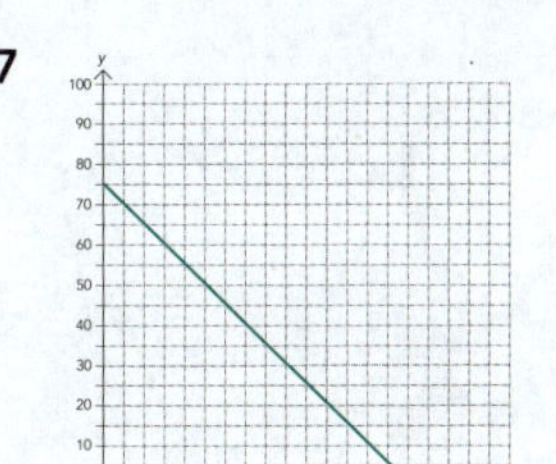

Writing equations from graphs (pp. 22–23)

1	$y = 2x + 3$	2	$y = -x - 3$
3	$y = -3x + 1$	4	$y = -2x + 14$
5	$y = -5x + 75$	6	$y = -6x + 90$
7	$y = -\frac{1}{3}x + 30$	8	$y = -\frac{2}{5}x + 36$

Applications (pp. 24–28)

1 a $T = 50n + 100$ b $25

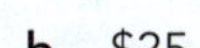

c After 18 weeks

d

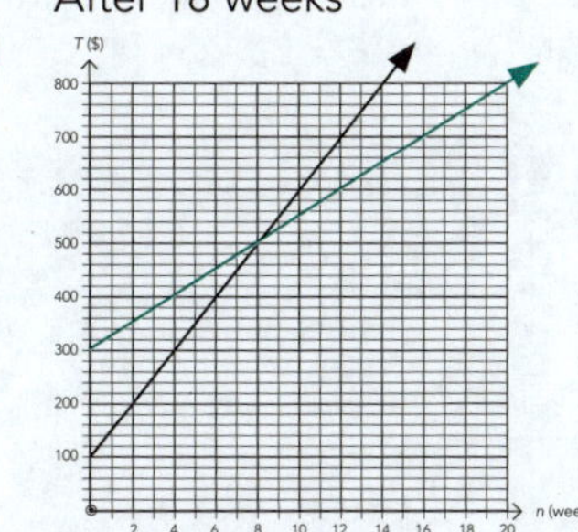

e $T = 25n + 300$

f After 8 weeks. $n = 8$ at the point where the two lines cross.

g Isaac starts with $300, whereas Arapeta starts with $100. These are shown by the constants in the equations and the y-intercepts on the graphs. Isaac starts from a point that is $215 above the point where Arapeta starts.

Isaac saves $25 per week, whereas Arapeta saves $50 per week. These values form the coefficients of n in the equations, and the gradients on the graphs. Arapeta's graph is steeper because he saves more each week.

2 a $C = 0.75k + 80$

b $7.50 per 10 km

c

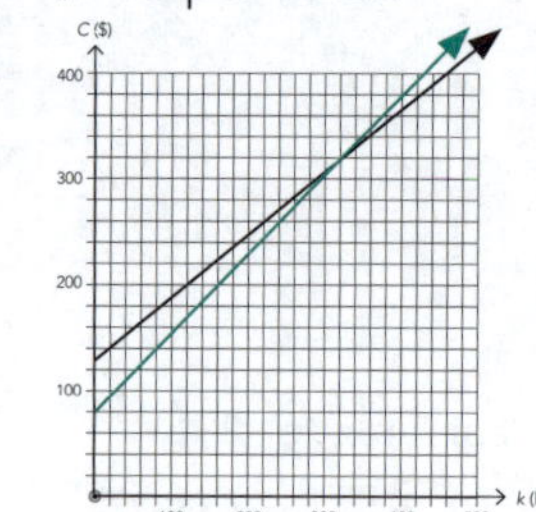

d 300 km. This is shown by the point of intersection of the two lines.

e $C = 0.60k + 125$

f The basic fee charged by Vic's Vans is $80, while that charged by Rogue Rentals is $125. These values form the *y*-intercepts on the graphs, and are the constants in the equations. In addition to the basic fee, Vic's Vans charges $0.75 per kilometre driven, while Rogue Rentals charges $0.60 per kilometre. These values form the coefficients of the *k* term in the equations. They are also the values of the gradients on the graphs. The Vic's Vans graph is steeper than Rogue Rentals, because they charge more per kilometre.

3 a

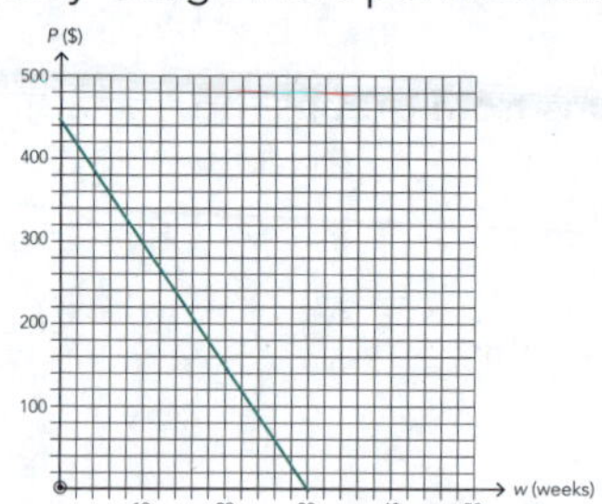

b $270

c After 30 weeks. This is shown by the intercept on the *w*-axis (where $P = 0$).

d

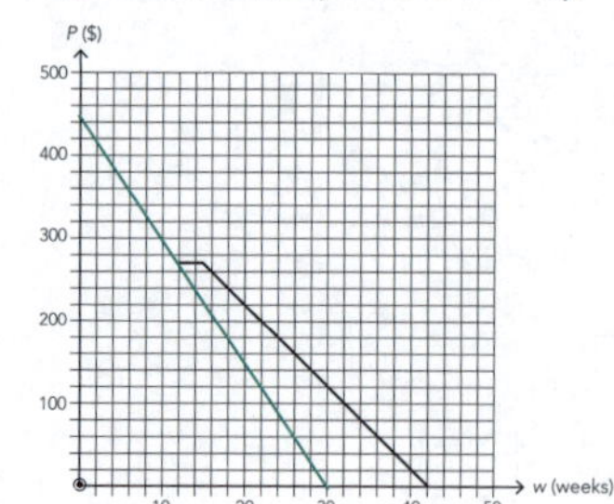

e 42 weeks

f $P = -15w + 450$

$P = 270$

$P = -10w + 420$

4 a Hannah: $D = -150T + 3600$

Chris: $D = -60T + 1800$

b Hannah lives 3600 m from school, and she travelled to school at a constant speed of 150 m/min. Hannah arrived at school 24 minutes after they left home.

Chris lives 1800 m from school, and he travelled to school at a constant speed of 60 m/min. Chris arrived at school 30 minutes after they left home.

c Hannah skateboards because she goes at 150 m/min, while Chris walks at 60 m/min.

d 20 minutes after they left home, they were the same distance from school (600 m), and Hannah passed Chris.

e Hannah's trip was the same as on Monday. Chris's trip started the same as on Monday — he moved at 60 m/min for the first 10 minutes, when he was still 1200 m from school. Then he stopped for six minutes, and just as he started walking, Hannah passed him. He continued walking at 60 km/min until he got to school after a total time of 36 minutes, 6 minutes later than on Monday.

5 a $0 \leq T < 1$: $D = 84T$

$1 \leq T < 2.5$: $D = 84$

b Between 1 h and 2 h 30 min after leaving and between 3 h and 3 h 20 min after leaving.

c A: -84

B: 0

C: -50.4

d They left Sam's grandmother's 1 h 30 min after they arrived (2 h 30 min after leaving home). They drove at an average speed of 84 kph for 30 min, then stopped for 20 minutes when they were 42 km from home. The rest of the journey home was at an average speed of 50.4 kph, and they arrived home 4 hours and 10 minutes after they had left.

e For the first hour and during phase A — both at 84 kph.

Parabolas (pp. 29–61)

Translated parabolas (pp. 29–35)

1 Vertical translation, $y = x^2 \pm c$ (pp. 30–32)

1 & 2

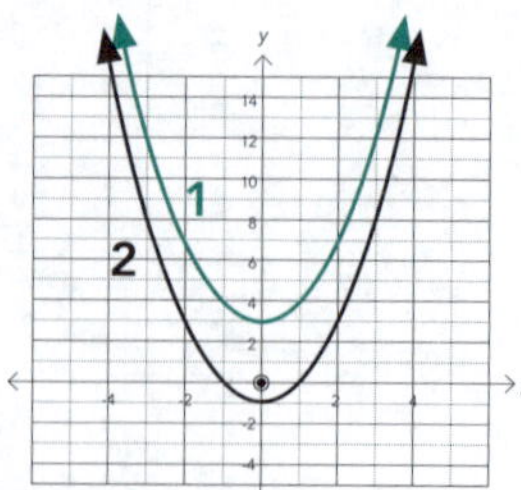

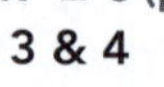

3 & 4

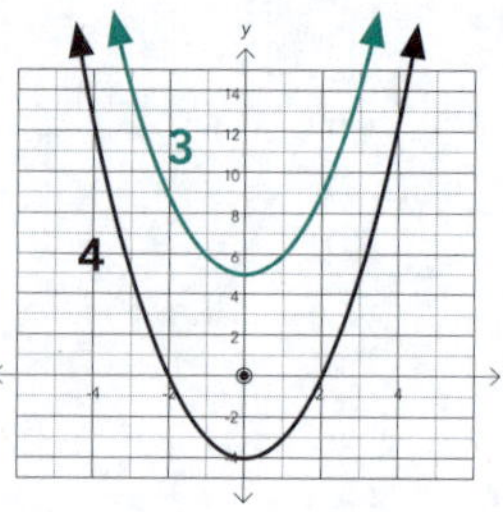

5 & 6

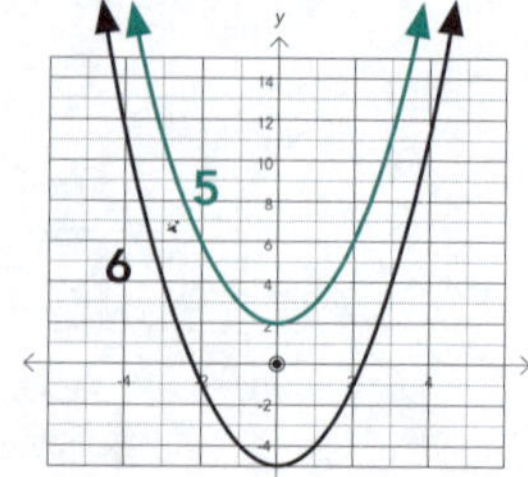

ISBN: 9780170419376

2 Horizontal translation, $y = (x \pm b)^2$ (pp. 32–33)

1 & 2

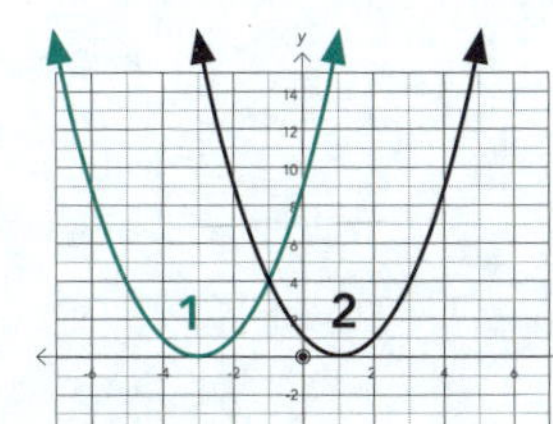

3 & 4

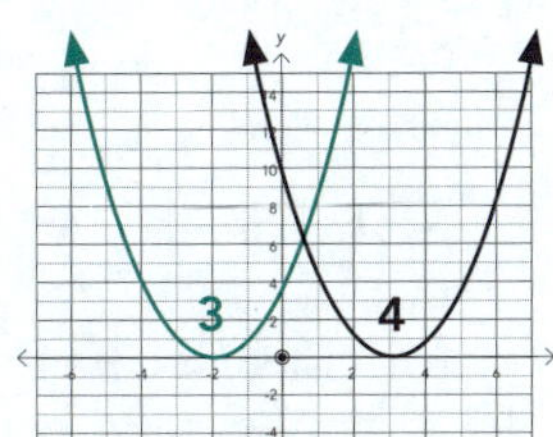

3 Combinations, $y = {}^{(x \pm b)2} \pm c$ (pp. 34–35)

1 & 2

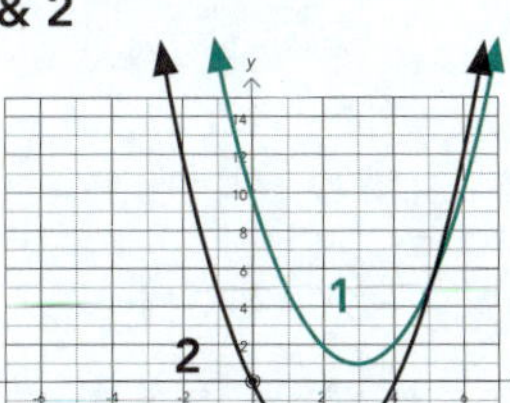

3 & 4

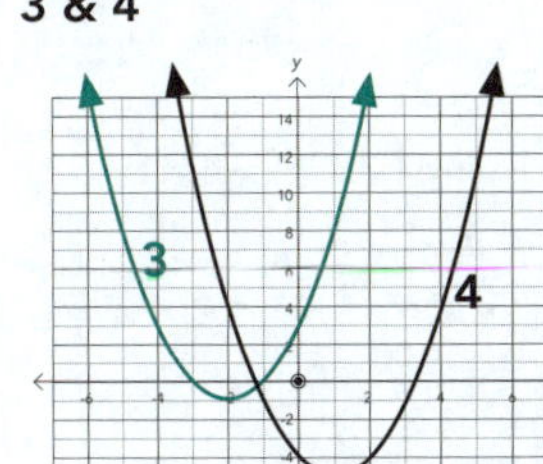

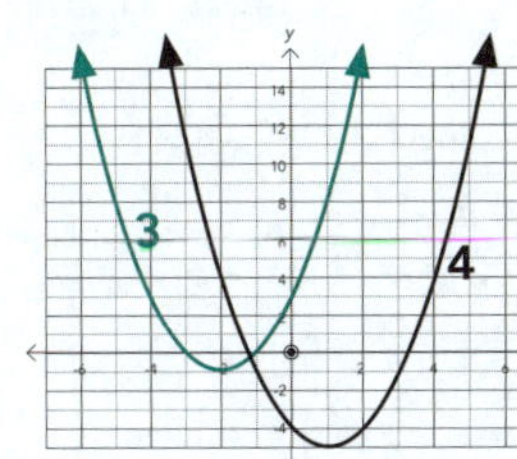

5 & 6

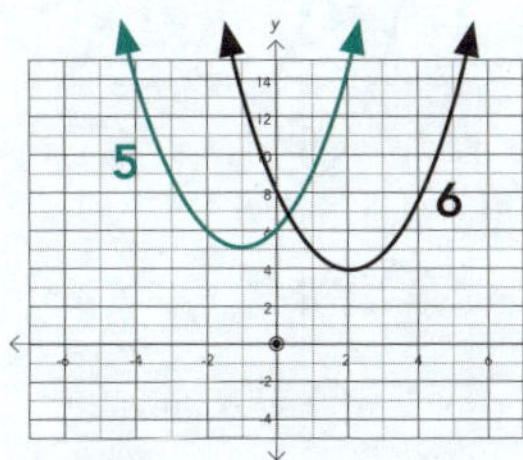

Inverted parabolas, $y = ax^2$….., where a is negative (pp. 36–37)

1

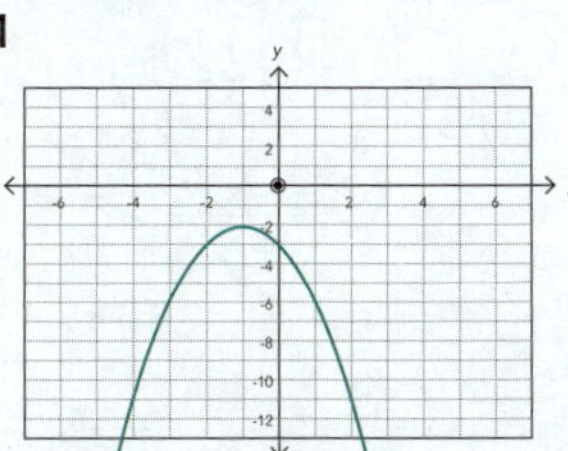

2

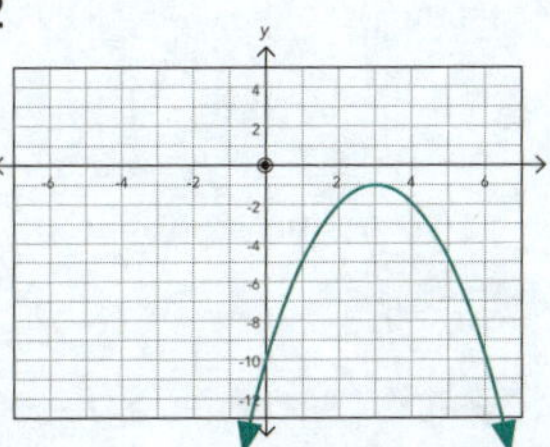

3

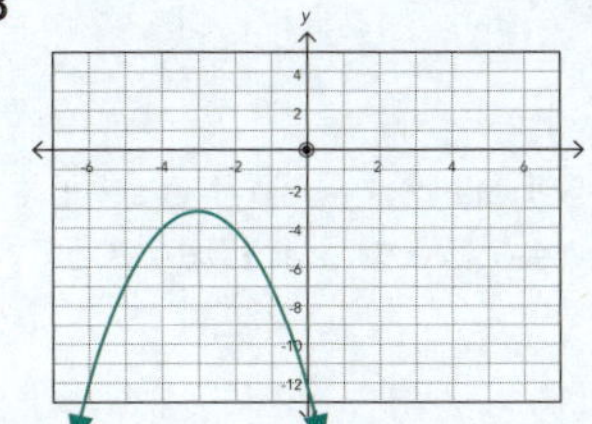

4

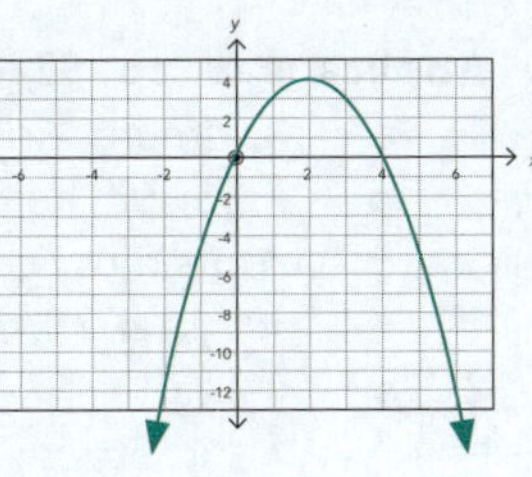

Mixing it up (p. 38)

1 & 2

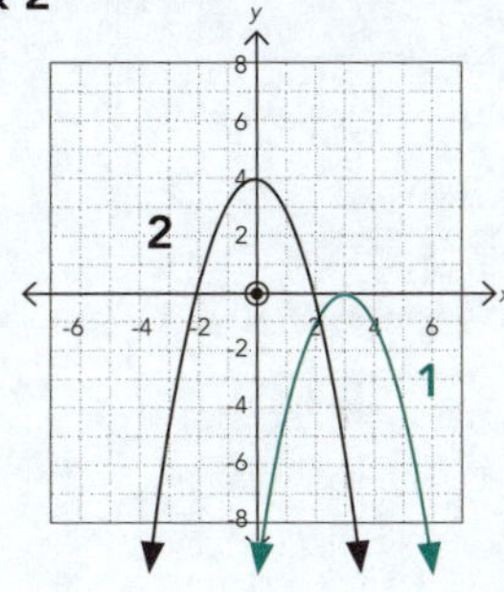

3 & 4

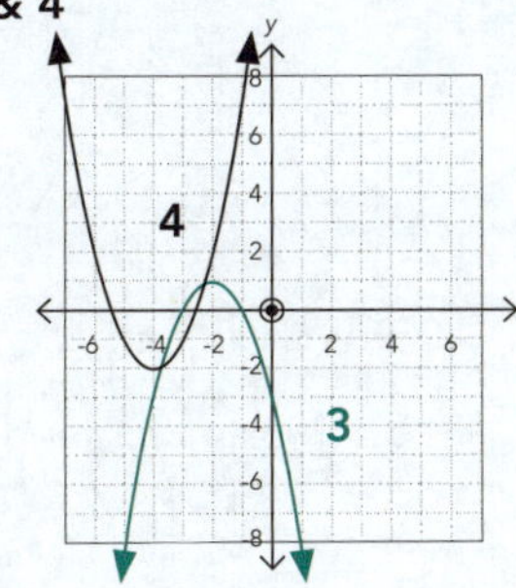

5 & 6

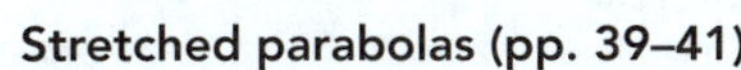

Stretched parabolas (pp. 39–41)

1

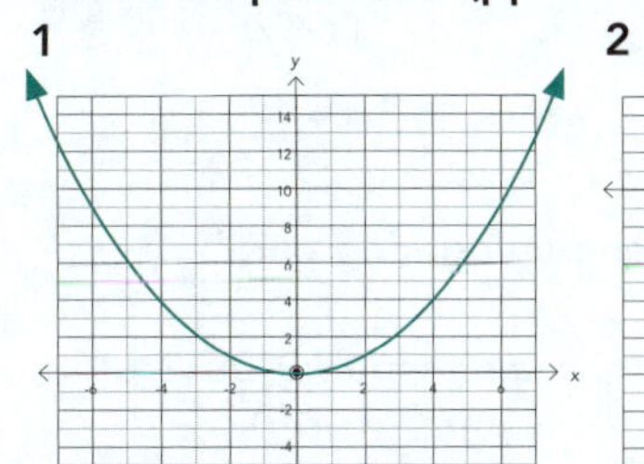

2

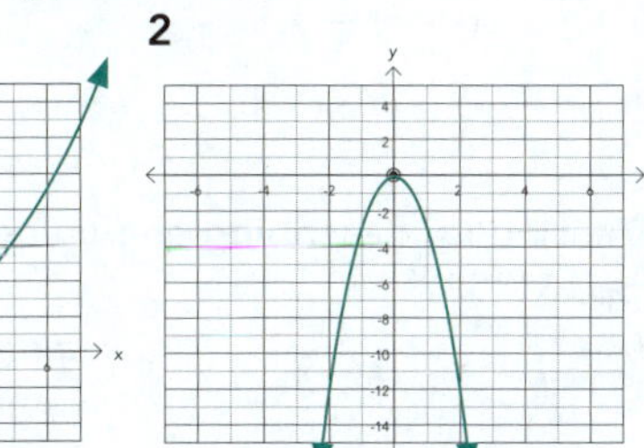

3 **4**

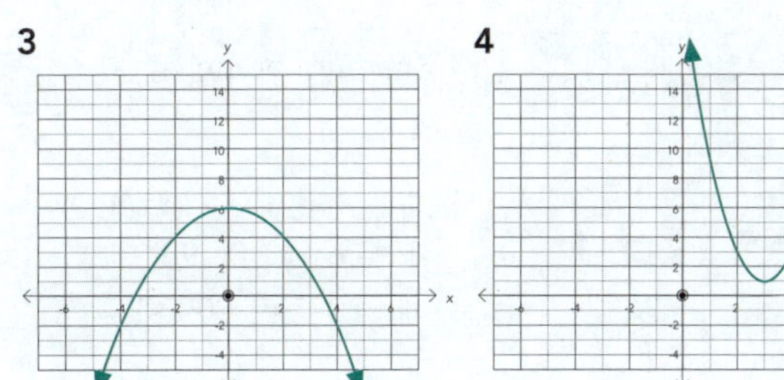

Plotting parabolas with the form $y = a(x \pm p)(x \pm q)$ (pp. 42–44)

1

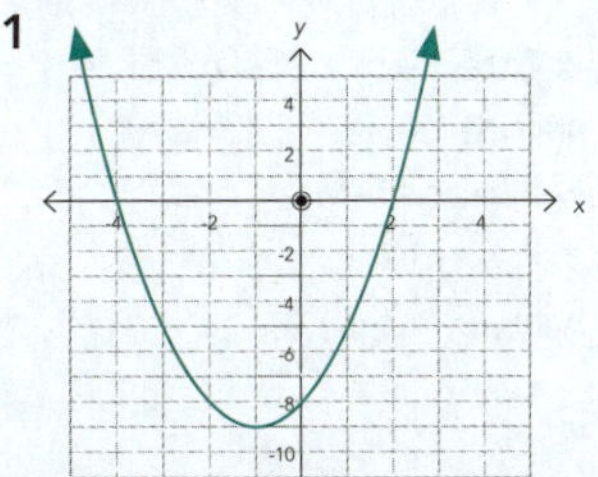

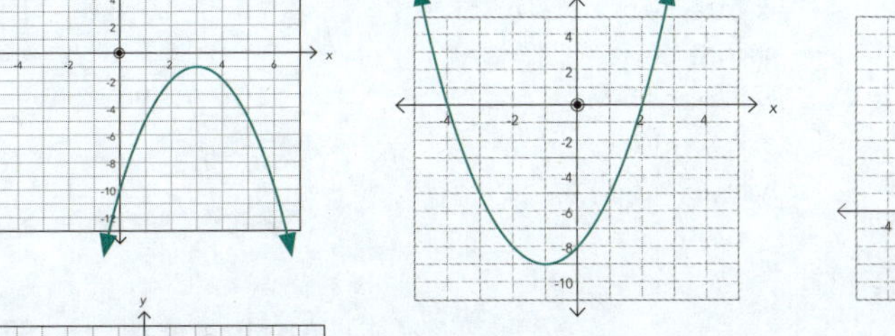

2

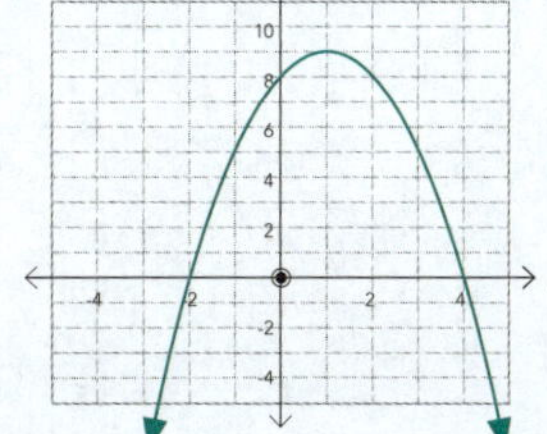

3

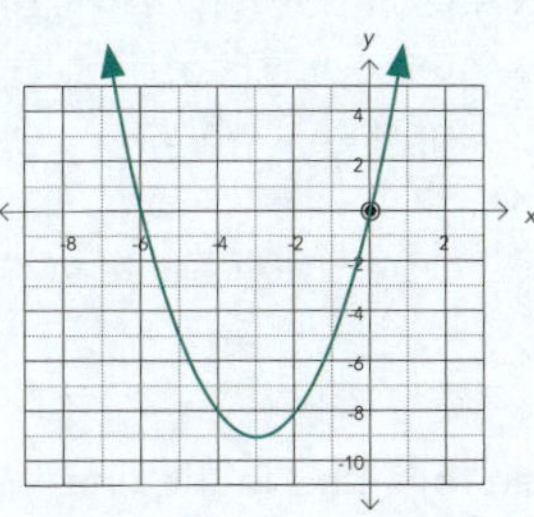

4

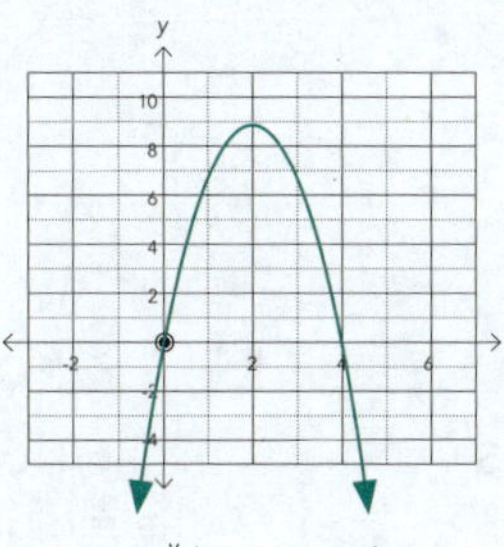

5

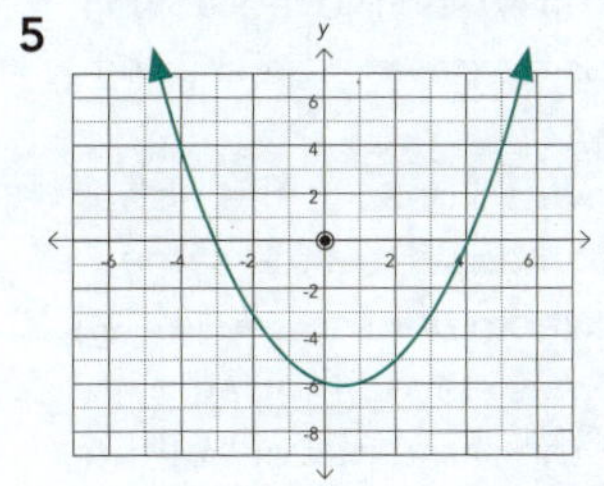

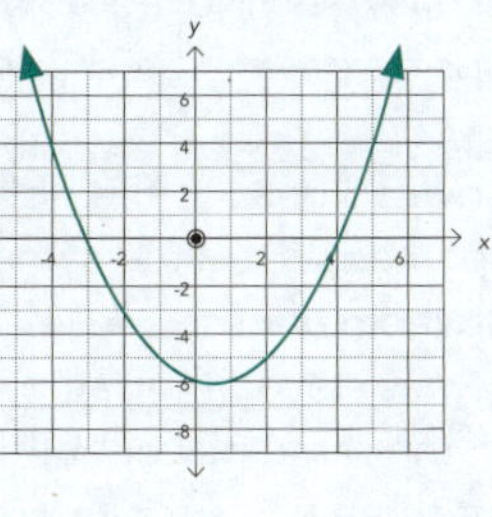

6

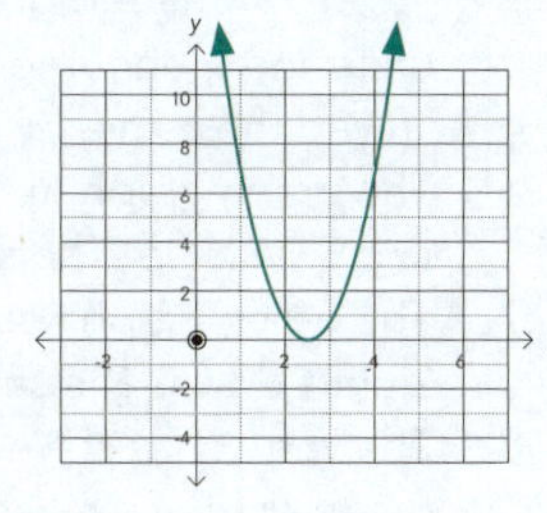

Writing equations for parabolas (pp. 45–50)

1 The x-intercepts (pp. 46–48)

1 $y = (x + 1)(x - 4)$
2 $y = (x - 1)(x - 4)$
3 $y = -(x - 1)(x + 4)$
4 $y = x(x - 5)$
5 $y = 2(x - 1)(x + 2)$
6 $y = -\frac{1}{2}x(x + 7)$
7 $y = \frac{1}{4}(x - 3)(x + 2)$
8 $y = -3(x + 1)(x - 2)$

2 The turning point (pp. 48–50)

1 $y = (x - 2)^2 - 1$
2 $y = (x + 2)^2 - 3$
3 $y = -(x + 2)^2 + 6$
4 $y = \frac{1}{2}(x - 2)^2 - 6$
5 $y = 2(x - 1)^2 - 4$
6 $y = \frac{1}{4}(x + 2)^2 - 3$
7 $y = -\frac{1}{3}(x + 3)^2 + 5$
8 $y = -3(x - 1)^2 + 6$

Translating, describing and comparing parabolas (pp. 51–53)

1

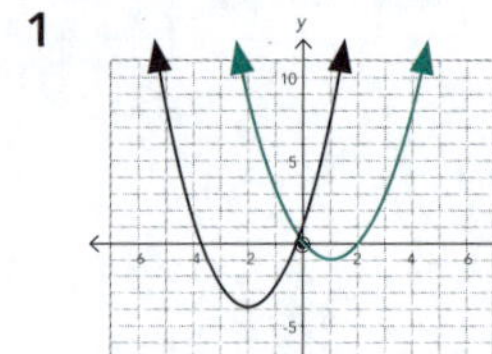

x-intercepts: (0, 0), (2, 0)
y-intercept: (0, 0)
y is negative where:
$0 < x < 2$
Minimum point: (1, -1)

2

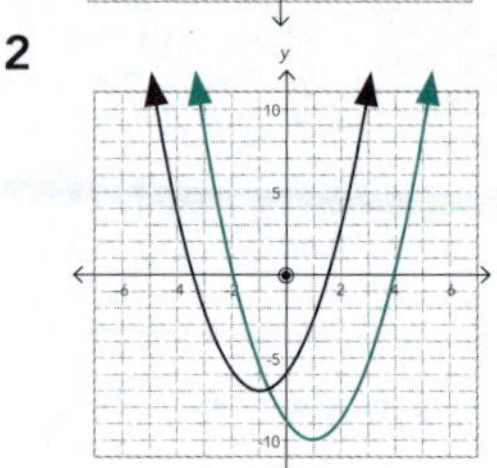

x-intercepts: (-2, 0), (4, 0)
y-intercept: (0, -9)
y is negative where:
$-2 < x < 4$
Vertex: (1, -10)

3

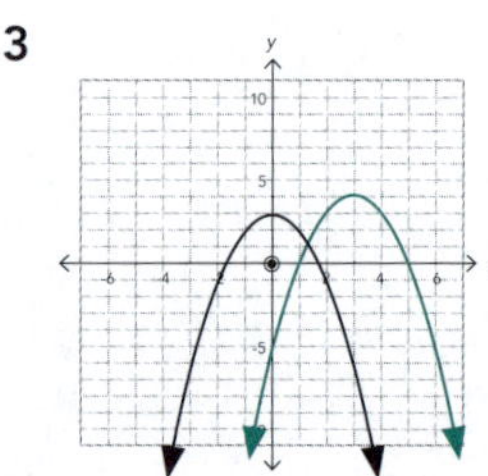

x-intercepts: (1, 0), (5, 0)
y-intercept: (0, -5)
y is negative where:
$x < 1$ and $x > 5$
Vertex: (3, 4)

4

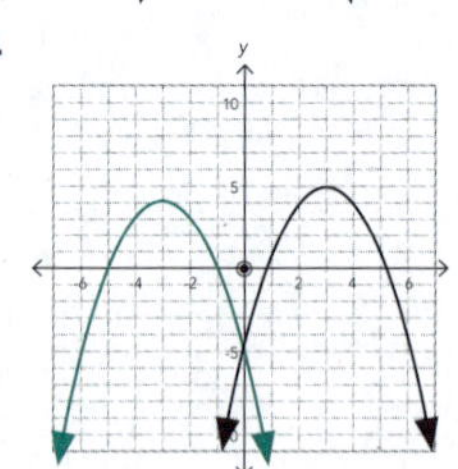

x-intercepts: (-1, 0), (-5, 0)
y-intercept: (0, -5)
y is negative where:
$x < -5$ or $x > -1$
Maximum point: (-3, 4)

5 The green graph has been reflected in the line $y = -1$. *Or* the red graph has been moved down 2 units and then turned upside down. The shape has stayed the same.

6 The green graph has moved 3 units to the right and 5 units up. The shape has stayed the same.

7 The green graph has moved 6 units to the left and 2 units down. The shape has stayed the same.

8 The vertex has stayed in the same place, but the green graph increases at three times the rate of the black graph.

Writing equations for translated parabolas (pp. 54–56)

1 $y = (x + 5)(x - 1) + 6$
or
$y = x^2 + 4x + 1$

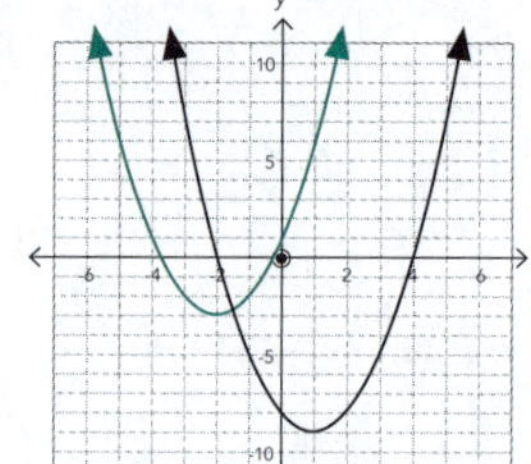

2

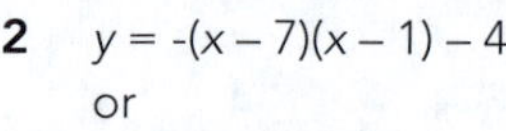

$y = -(x - 7)(x - 1) - 4$
or

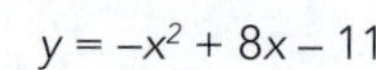

$y = -x^2 + 8x - 11$

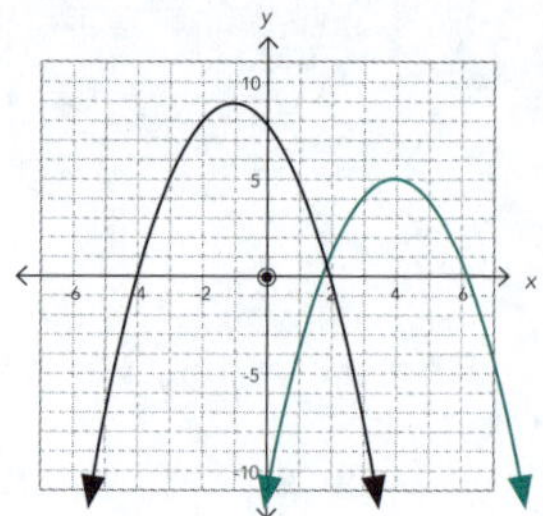

3 $y = -(x + 5)(x + 1) - 3$
or
$y = -x^2 - 6x - 8$

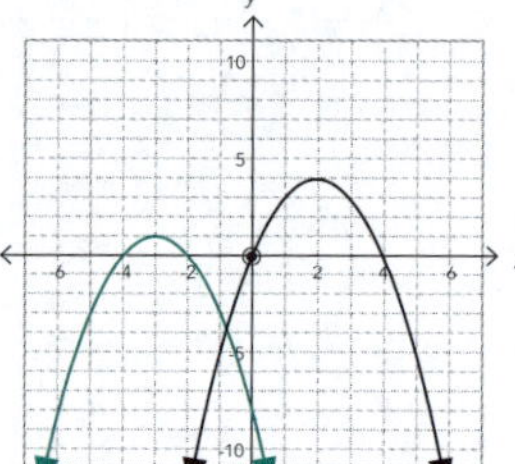

4 $y = (x - 2)^2 - 1$
or
$y = x^2 - 4x + 3$

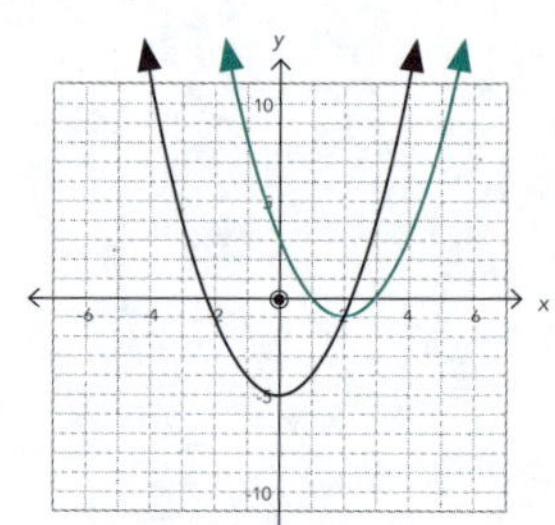

5 $y = 2 - (x + 3)^2$
or
$y = -x^2 - 6x - 7$

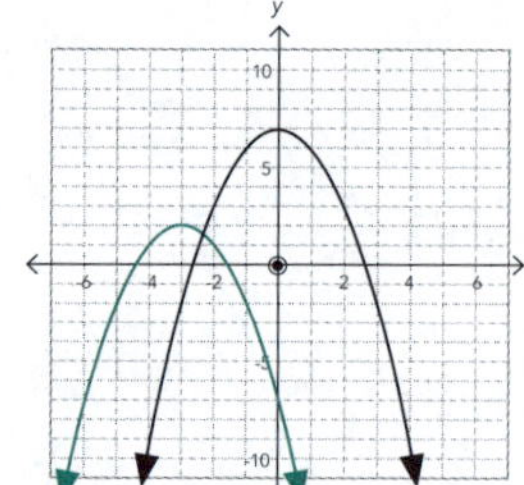

6

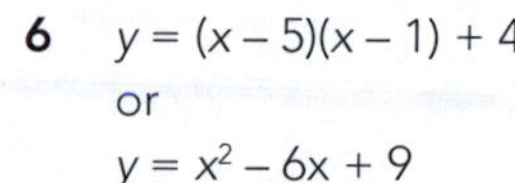

$y = (x - 5)(x - 1) + 4$
or
$y = x^2 - 6x + 9$

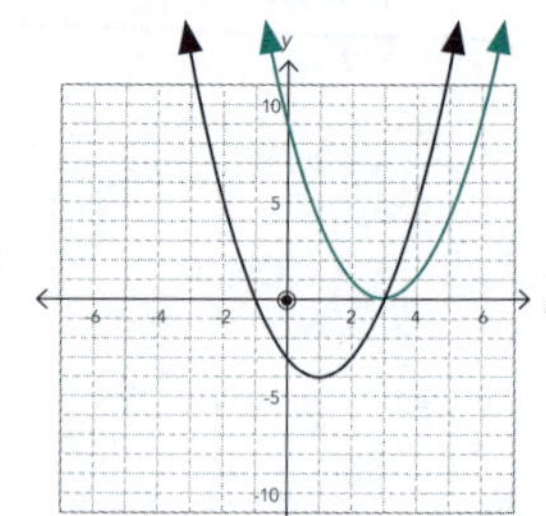

Applications (pp. 57–61)

1
a Maximum width = 2 m
b Maximum height is where $x = 1$, so it is 2.8 m.
c Lights must go between $x = 0.5$ and $x = 1.5$. Height = 2.1 m

2
a

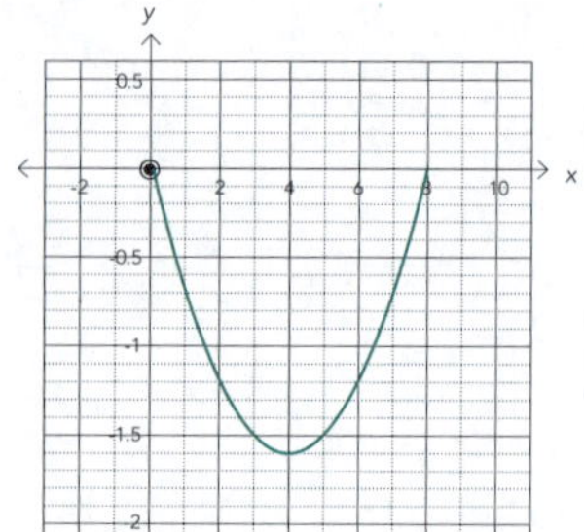

b Maximum depth where $x = 4$, so depth = 1.6 m.
c $x = 1.5 \Longrightarrow$ depth = 0.975 m

ISBN: 9780170419376

d Width = 7 m $\Rightarrow$ x = 0.5 or 7.5, so y = -0.375.
So the surface of the water is 0.375 m below ground level.

3 a 6 m apart $\Rightarrow$ y = ax(x – 6)
Lowest point at (3, -2) $\Rightarrow$ a = $0.\dot{2}$k
Equation is y = $0.\dot{2}$x(x – 6)

b x = 1.5 $\Rightarrow$ rope is 1.5 m below the bar.

4 a Turning point at (2, 1) $\Rightarrow$ y = a$(x – 2)^2$ + 1
y-intercept at (0, 2) $\Rightarrow$ a = 0.25
Equation is 0.25$(x – 2)^2$ + 1

b x = 0.5 $\Rightarrow$ y = 1.5625 m so her head will not touch the rope.

c Turning point at (2, 1.5) $\Rightarrow$ y = a$(x – 2)^2$ + 1.5
y-intercept at (0, 2) $\Rightarrow$ a = 0.125
Equation is y = 0.125$(x – 2)^2$ + 1.5

5 a

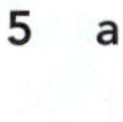

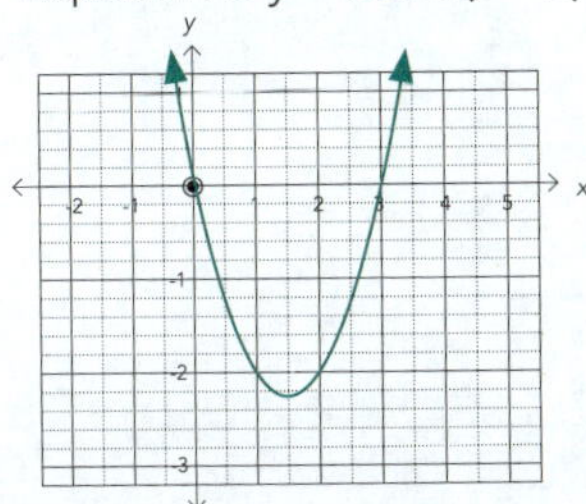

b Maximum depth (where x = 1.5) is 2.25 m.

c -2 = x(x – 3) $\Rightarrow$ x^2 – 3x + 2 = 0
So x = 1 or 2.
Width of shingle = 2 – 1 = 1 m

6 a y = -0.05(x + 2)(x – 18)

b x = 0 $\Rightarrow$ height = 1.8 m

c x = 4 $\Rightarrow$ height = 4.2 m

7 a

x	Other side	Area (A)
40	60	1200
50	50	1250
60	40	1200
70	30	1050
		Etc.

b $A = \frac{1}{2}x(100 - x)$

c Maximum area is when x = 50 m.
Area = 1250 m^2

8 a y = a$(x – 4)^2$ + 9 or y = -(x – 1)(x – 7)
Passes through (1, 0) $\Rightarrow$ a = -1
Equation is y = -$(x – 4)^2$ + 9

b By symmetry, x-intercepts must be at (1, 0) and (7, 0) ∴ tunnel must be 6 m wide.

c 3.4642 m wide $\Rightarrow$ value for x = 4 – 3.4642 ÷ 2
= 2.2679
∴ y = 6, so ceiling is 6 m high.

Exponential graphs (pp. 62–76)

Translated exponential graphs (pp. 63–68)

1 Vertical translation, $y = p^x \pm c$ (pp. 63–64)

1 & 2

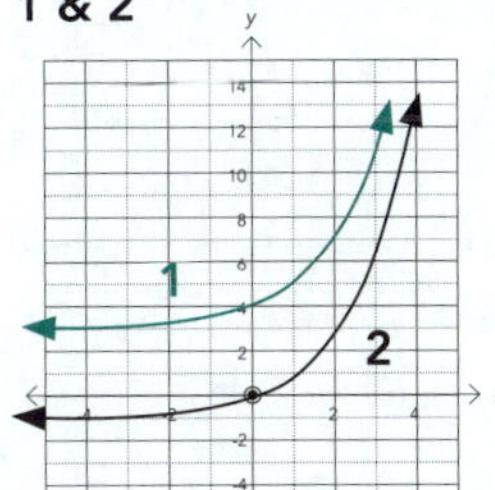

3 & 4

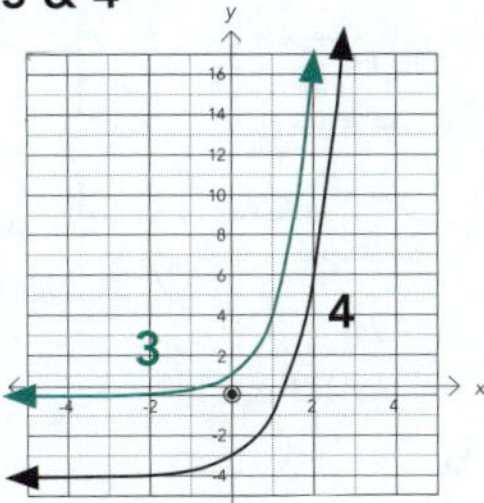

2 Horizontal translation, $y = p^{(x \pm b)}$ (pp. 65–66)

1 & 2

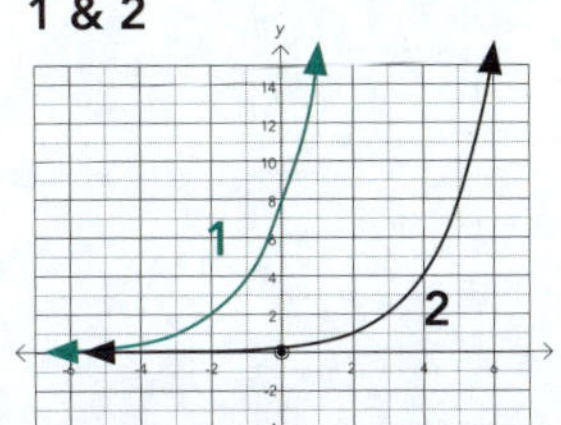

3 & 4

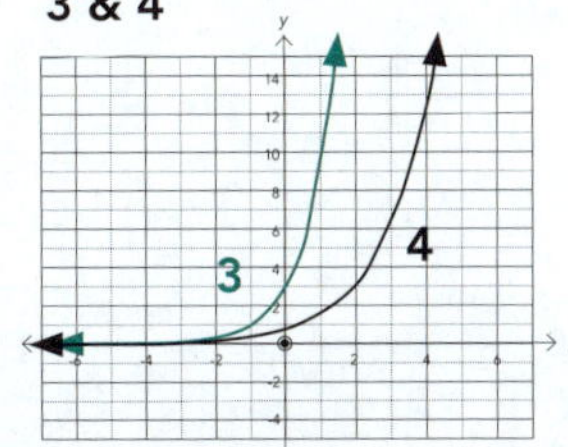

3 Combinations, $y = p^{(x \pm a)} \pm c$ (pp. 67–68)

1 & 2

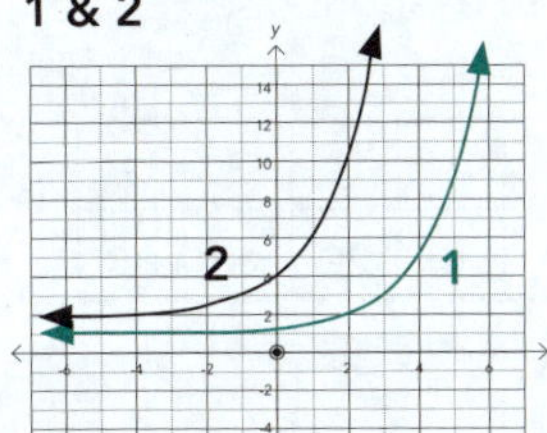

3 & 4

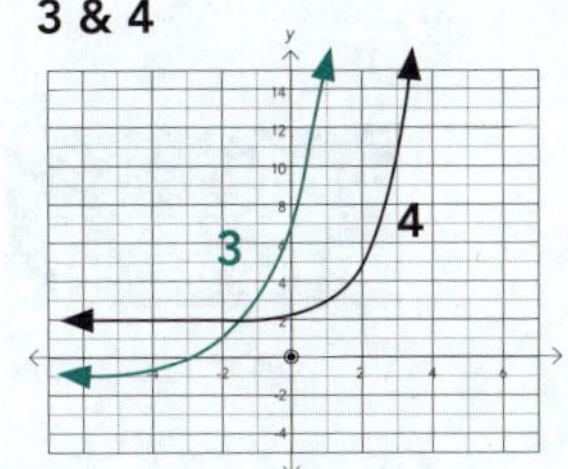

Inverted exponential graphs, $y = -p^{(x \pm b)} \pm c$ (pp. 70–71)

1 & 2

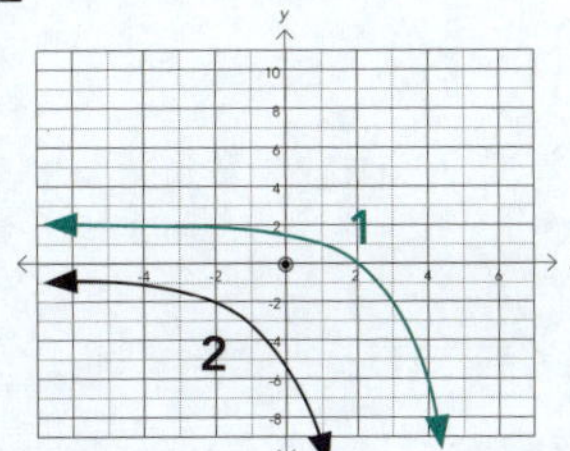

Writing equations for exponential graphs (pp. 72–73)

1 $y = 2^x + 2$

2 $y = 2^{(x + 1)}$

3 $y = 2^{(x + 2)} - 1$

4 $y = 2^{(x - 3)} + 1$

5 $y = 2^{(x - 1)} - 2$

6 $y = 3^x - 1$

Applications and problems (pp. 74–76)

1 a

n	3^n
-1	$\frac{1}{3}$
0	**1**
1	**3**
2	**9**
3	**27**

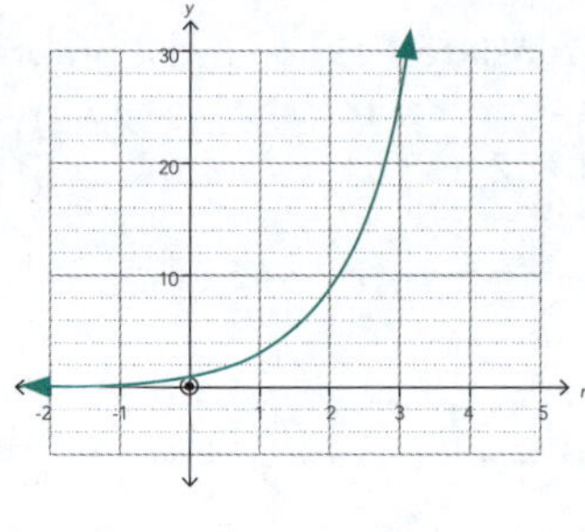

b y-intercept = (0, 1)

c $n \approx 2.6$ or 2.7 or 2.8

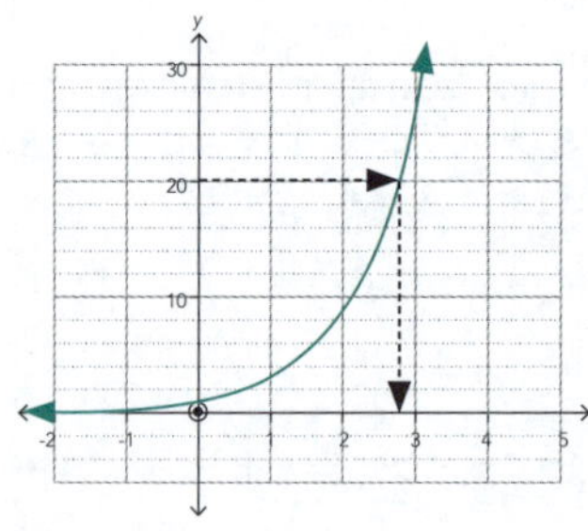

2 Number of grains of rice = $2^{63} = 9.223 \times 10^{18}$ grains. (The total amount of rice won, 18.45×10^{18} grains, would cover India to a depth of about one metre!)

3 a

Day (d)	0	1	2	3	4
Area (mm²) (A)	5	10	**20**	**40**	**80**

b Area on day 5 = 5 x 2 x 2 x 2 x 2 x 2
= 5×2^5
= 160

c $A = 5 \times 2^d$

d

e d = 3.3 or 3.4, so after about 3 days and 8–10 hours.

f Area = 2.5 mm²

g The A-intercept would stay at 5, because that is still the area at the start. The curve would go up much more steeply because the area would grow bigger more rapidly. The asymtote would stay the same.

4 a

q	Prize ($)
1	100
2	200
3	**400**

q	Prize ($)
4	**800**
5	**1600**

b Prize for answering 7 questions correctly
= 100 x 2 x 2 x 2 x 2 x 2 x 2
= 100×2^6
= 6400

c $P = 100 \times 2^{(q-1)}$

d Prize is $51 200

e i $\$100 \times 10^{14} = \$1\,638\,400$

ii $\$200 \times 10^{6} = \$12\,800$

Piecewise functions (pp. 77–80)

1 a

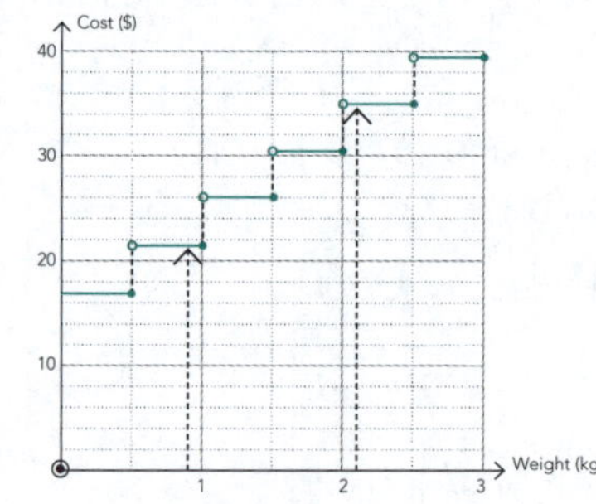

b i Cost = $21.50 ii Cost = $35.00

c Cost = 2.597 c/g

d Cost for a 1499 g parcel = 1.734 c/g
So the 1499 g parcel costs less per gram.

e The y-intercept for post by air is at $17, whereas it is at $12 for post by sea.
Both graphs go up in steps of 500 g.
The steps for post by sea go up by intervals of $4.50 for each 500 g, whereas the post by sea only goes up by intervals of $3.

2 a

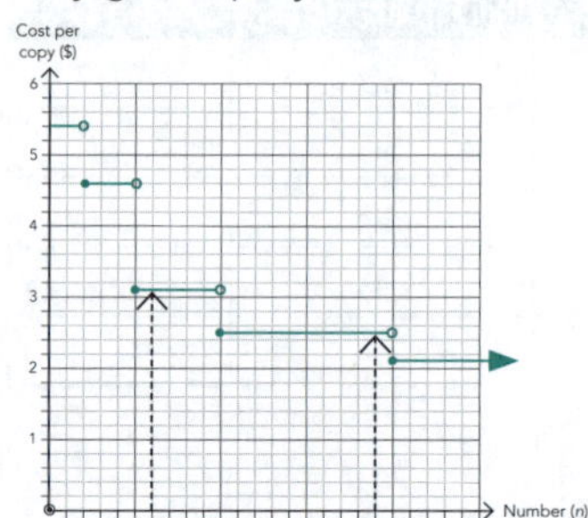

b i Cost = $3.10 ii Cost = $2.50

3 a

Age (years)	Value ($)
new	**38 000**
< 1	**34 000**
< 2	**25 000**
< 3	**18 000**

Age (years)	Value ($)
< 4	**13 000**
< 5	**9000**
< 6	**6000**
< 7	**4000**

b The car is bought for $38 000, but as soon as it is driven from the yard it is worth $34 000. It stays at $34 000 until it becomes one year old, and then its value is $25 000.

 ISBN: 9780170419376

4 **a**

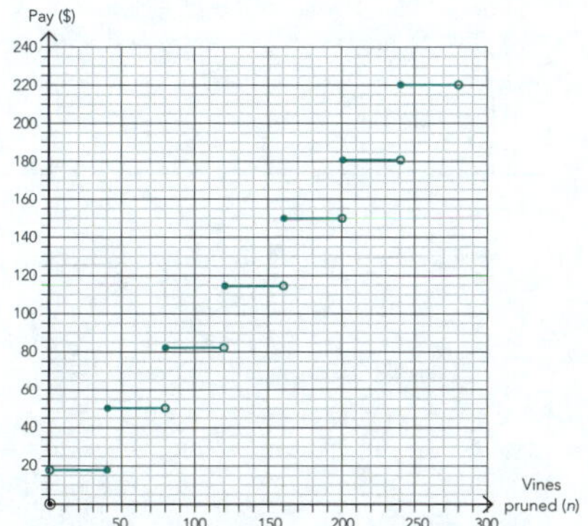

b He was paid \$18 plus \$32 for each complete row.

c If he prunes 161 vines, he earns 93.17 cents per vine. If he prunes 199 vines, he earns 75.38 cents per vine. This happens because he is paid the same amount (\$150) for pruning 161 vines as he is for pruning 199 vines.

d 80 c

e The original graph has a y-intercept at \$18 because this was the minimum amount paid, while the graph for the neighbouring vineyard has a y-intercept at 0, because they pay nothing if no vines are pruned. The first graph goes up in steps because the amount paid for pruning, say, 41 vines is the same as that paid for pruning 80 vines. However, the second graph goes up smoothly because the pruners are paid for every individual vine they prune.

f 40, 80, 120, etc.

Practice questions (pp. 81–86)

Practice question one

a

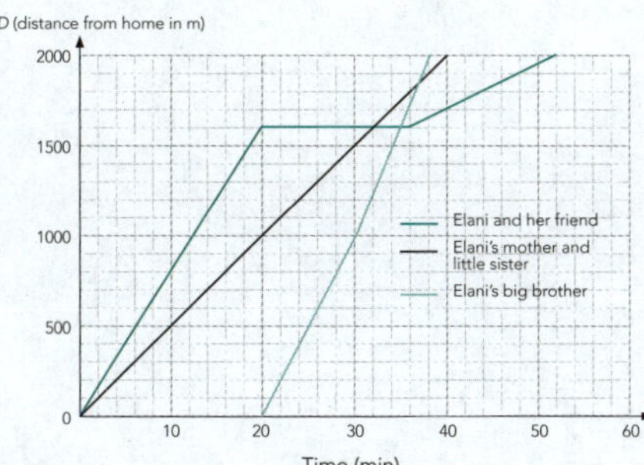

Equations:

Elani: $0 < t \le 20$: $D = 80t$

$20 < t \le 36$: $D = 1600$

$36 < t \le 36$: $D = 25t + 700$

Mother and little sister: $D = 50t$

Big brother: $20 < t \le 30$: $D = 100t - 2000$

$30 < t \le 36$: $D = 125t - 2750$

Arrival at school:

Elani's big brother arrived first, 38 minutes after Elani left home.

Elani's mother and little sister arrived next, 40 minutes after Elani left home.

Elani and her friend arrived last, 52 minutes after Elani left home.

Passings:

Elani's mother and little sister passed Elani 32 minutes after they left home, and while she was waiting at her friend's house, which was 1600 m from home.

Elani's big brother passed Elani 34.8 minutes after she left home, while she was waiting at her friend's house, which was 1600 m from home.

Elani's big brother passed Elani's mother and little sister 36.7 minutes after they left home, when they were 1833 m from home.

b **i** $y = 2^x + 3$

ii $y = -(2^x + 3)$ or $y = -2^x - 3$

Practice question two

a **i**

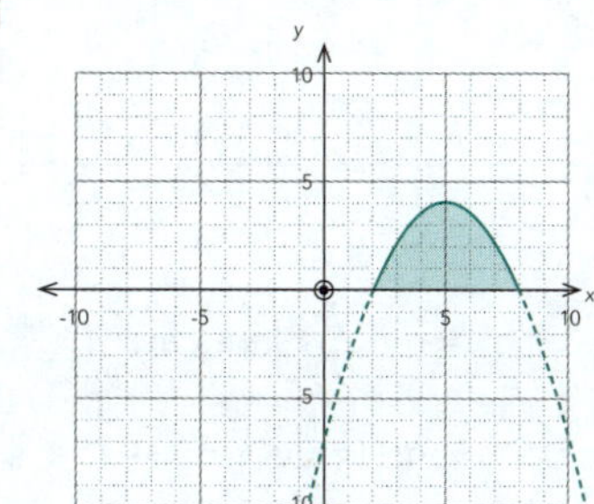

$y = -0.5(x - 2)(x - 8)$

or $y = -0.5x^2 + 5x - 8$

or $y = -0.5(x - 5)^2 + 4.5$

ii Ceiling must be between $x = 3.5$ and $x = 6.5$

$\therefore$ Height = 3.375 m

iii Equation:

$y = -0.5(x - 2 + q)(x - 8 + q) - p$

or $y = -0.5(x + q)^2 + 5(x + q) - 8 - p$

or $y = -0.5(x - 5 + q)^2 + 4.5 - p$

Vertex:

$(5 - q)(4.5 - p)$

b **i**

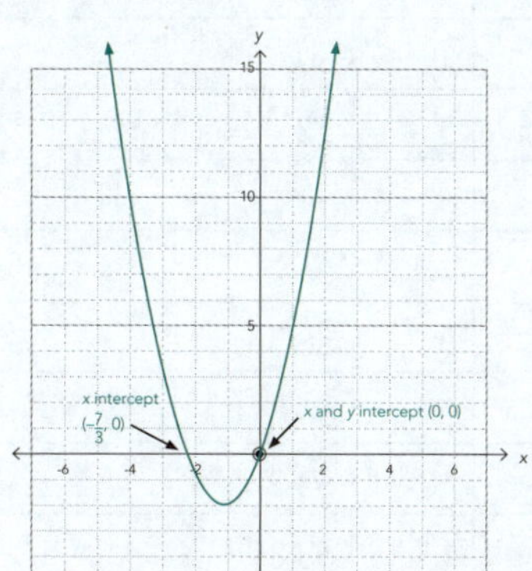

ii
- The graph for B and n would be just points, but the graph for y and x would be a line. This is because button numbers must be discrete, while y and x are plotted as continuous variables.
- The graph for B and n has no values below 1, but the graph for y and x does. This is because there is no pattern number 0 — it would have no buttons.

ISBN: 9780170419376

The graph for B and n cannot possibly take negative values for either variable, but that for y and x can.

Practice question three

a

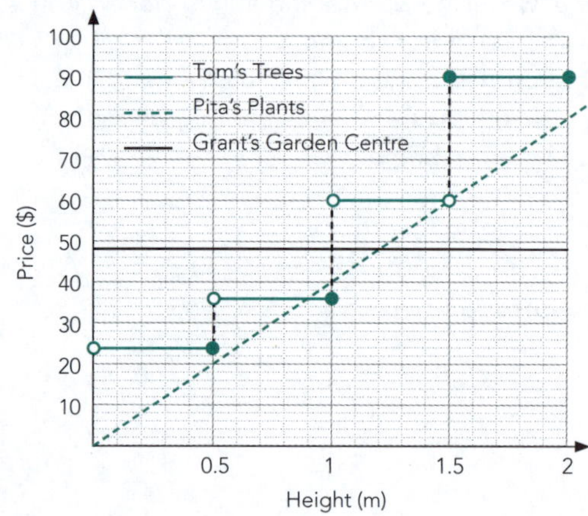

Height less than 0.9 m ⇒ Pita's Plants are cheapest.

Heights between 0.9 m and up to 1 m ⇒ Tom's Trees are cheapest.

Trees of 1 m and less than 1.2 m ⇒ Pita's Plants are cheapest.

Trees of 1.2 m or more ⇒ Grant's Garden Centre is cheapest.

b **i**

Month	(m)	Height (cm) of the kowhai tree at the end of each month (H)
May	1	50
June	2	50
July	3	50
August	4	50
September	5	52
October	6	54.1
November	7	56.2
December	8	58.5
January	9	60.8
February	10	63.2
March	11	65.8
April	12	68.4

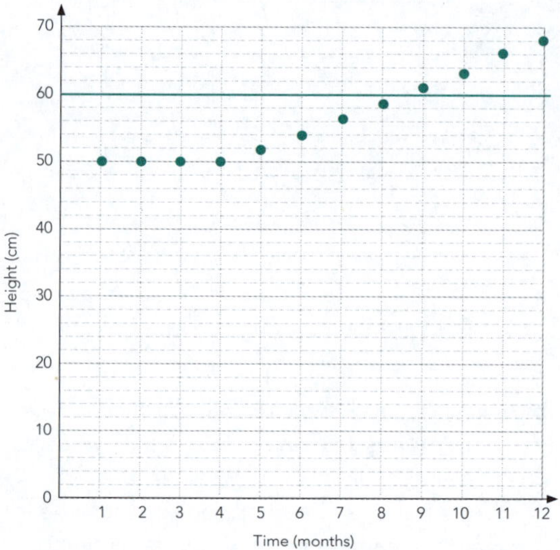

He will need to put in a stake to support the plant at the start of the ninth month, which is January.

ii Let A be the height at planting.

Solve $80 = A(1.04)^{12-4}$

Height = 58.5 cm

ISBN: 9780170419376